THE SUBJECT OF FREEDOM

FORDHAM UNIVERSITY PRESS   NEW YORK 2015

COMMONALITIES

Timothy C. Campbell, series editor

THE SUBJECT OF FREEDOM

Kant, Levinas

GABRIELA BASTERRA

Library of Congress Cataloging-in-Publication Data

Basterra, Gabriela.
    The subject of freedom : Kant, Levinas / Gabriela Basterra. — First edition.
        pages cm. — (Commonalities)
    Includes bibliographical references and index.
    ISBN 978-0-8232-6514-5 (cloth : alk. paper) —
    ISBN 978-0-8232-6515-2 (pbk. : alk. paper)
  1. Autonomy (Psychology)   2. Kant, Immanuel, 1724–1804.
3. Lévinas, Emmanuel.   I. Title.
    BF575.A88B375 2015
    123'.5—dc23

                                                    2014045379

Printed in the United States of America

17 16 15   5 4 3 2 1

First edition

for Jeff Day

CONTENTS

INTRODUCTION:
THE SUBJECT OF FREEDOM

Freedom, writes Kant, manifests itself through the moral law, which "thrusts itself upon us on its own."[1] Freedom, Levinas would write almost two centuries later, is "ineluctably invoked" by a command that "slips in me like a thief."[2] Should we understand freedom, according to these thinkers, as being inseparable from obligation, from a responsibility that in no present has one chosen to assume?[3] And if the law that obligates us does not exactly originate in ourselves, would autonomy consist in believing oneself the author of—and thus becoming responsible for—something one has received? Establishing an implicit dialogue between Kant and Levinas, in this book I propose that approaching freedom and autonomy in their relationship to obligation and responsibility does full justice to Kant's most revolutionary insights into ethics, insights that continue to surprise our thinking today. Conceiving freedom and autonomous subjectivity in this light could revitalize the ongoing task of thinking ethical and political initiative. It could also acquaint us with our capacity for creating objects of knowledge, while alerting us to its risks. As Kant suggests in the *Critique of Pure Reason* (1781/1787), theoretical reason's ability to function smoothly through limitation hinges on the concept of freedom.

But are not Kant and Levinas unexpected interlocutors? Does not Kant emphatically privilege autonomy over heteronomy, whereas for Levinas ethics, which he conceives in terms of heteronomy, is "first philosophy"?[4] Indeed, Levinas explicitly questions the self precisely as Kantian subject, as the all-encompassing, free, and autonomous subject of the law, yet his philosophy is deeply inspired by Kant.[5] An approach to their thinking that sounds out their shared insights will bring into view the auto-heteronomy that renders Kant's concept of autonomy revolutionary, as well as the generative tension in which heteronomy and autonomy are held at the end of *Otherwise than Being*. The conception of the moral law that traverses Kant's practical philosophy bears the trace of alterity. What we call autonomous subject embodies a relationship to the otherness of the law. Only by exploring the relationship the subject incarnates—itself a challenging task, since the two parties in this relationship are incommensurable—may the full potential of autonomy be brought to light.[6] This idea of a subjectivity that bears witness to the *being practical* of pure reason is the one I explore here, seeking inspiration in Levinas.

In this book I consider freedom in the theoretical and practical senses intimated in the title: freedom as an idea and freedom as something other that animates subjectivity.[7] Proposing a close examination of Kant's antinomies of pure reason, I begin by analyzing the possibilities the exceptional concept of freedom opens up for theoretical reason by providing it with a limit.[8] The idea of freedom refers to something unimaginable, something reason locates in an empty space beyond what can be thought. Freedom is a boundary concept that delimits the realm of all other objects we can know, what we call objectivity.[9] Hence Kant's interest to prove in the third antinomy that the idea of freedom is non-contradictory. As an idea lying outside theoretical reason's bounds, freedom introduces a boundary that facilitates the smooth functioning of thought.

But freedom would be inconceivable without presupposing the idea of a subject through which freedom would manifest itself. For there to be freedom, there have to be subjects constituted by freedom, subjects who, motivated by freedom, could introduce its effects in the world. How freedom animates subjectivity is my other focus in this book. In being constituted by freedom, the subject could then be imagined to play the role of limit that enables theoretical thought, but the ability to understand how freedom motivates the human power of desire and constitutes ethical subjects lies beyond theoretical reason's reach.[10] The "human being" presupposed in the *Critique of Pure Reason* will not become a subject in the full sense until freedom can be considered to be actual and constitutive, a challenge Kant takes up in his practical philosophy. A convincing account of how freedom motivates subjectivity therefore becomes indispensable for thinking of the being practical of pure reason, a reason that beyond theorizing must act.[11] As

Kant famously writes in the preface to the *Critique of Practical Reason*, "the concept of freedom . . . forms the *keystone* of the whole edifice of a system of pure reason, even that of speculative reason."[12] But venturing an account of how freedom animates subjectivity is inherently problematic. The difficulty ethical philosophy faces is explaining how something that exceeds knowledge moves subjectivity and manifests itself through the subject's effects in the world. What we here call subjectivity is constituted by an excess that lies beyond the human ability to represent, and thus surpasses the bounds of consciousness and its impulse to represent world and self as objects of thought.[13] As intelligible in the Kantian sense—as a negative being beyond—the ethical demarcates the boundaries of what can be known but also manifests itself practically as an effect and affect in the subject, and therefore in the world. Ultimately, the task concerning the ethical Kant opens up for us is, in Jean-Luc Nancy's words, "thinking 'pure reason' *in terms of its being-practical, and of the duty that constitutes it or enjoins it*."[14]

What, then, is ethical subjectivity? What is its relationship with the excess that allows it to emerge? For both Kant and Levinas subjectivity is constituted by what we may call (for lack of a better word) an event existing outside representation, an element of excess that motivates the itinerary of the subject. At its most challenging and promising, Kant's practical philosophy focuses on how freedom animates subjectivity through the upheaval he calls moral law. The freedom figured in the third antinomy as a power to begin by itself, a beginning that within the limits of the first *Critique* cannot become principle, is now practically envisaged also as a subject's source of ethical motivation. This immanent view of ethics, which Kant develops mainly in the Analytic of the *Critique of Practical Reason* (1788) and in "On the Inherence of the Evil alongside the Good Principle, or, On the Radical Evil in Human Nature" (*Religion*, 1793), is followed in the Dialectic of Practical Reason by a different view of ethics, one that seeks to allay the antinomy into which reason falls when trying to understand its own being practical. In this different conception, the emphasis no longer lies on freedom as a power to begin by itself. Instead of seeking an unconditioned beginning (as do the third antinomy and the Analytic of Practical Reason), the Dialectic posits a goal, the fulfillment of the highest good. Entertaining the possibility to fulfill the highest good would allow reason to encompass the moral itinerary of a human being as a whole. Grasping morality in its totality, however, requires redeeming for practical use two ideas the first *Critique* had proved to be illusory: the postulates of the immortality of the soul and the existence of God. This transcendent version of ethics advanced in the Dialectic of Practical Reason would seem to belie Kant's initial conception of freedom. In problematically seeking to encompass morality as a whole, the version of ethics advanced by the Dialectic may be accountable for the simplified notion of autonomy that has prevailed. Distorted by this dialectic illusion, the very obligation that motivates ethical initiative appears as a constraint on the action of a self-determining autonomous subject.

This prevailing concept of freedom, the freedom of an all-encompassing subject, is the one against which Levinas initially levels his critique: this is the freedom that, according to Levinas, the event of the other interrupts. Turning instead to Kant's revolutionary conceptions of freedom and the law in the Analytic of Practical Reason, Levinas pushes them to their full potential. The break with ontology he attributes to Kant's separation of thinking from knowing rests on the idea of transcendental freedom, "a freedom situated above freedom and prior to knowledge and ignorance."[15] Crucial moments of Levinas's thought may thus be read as a deeply Kantian critique of Kant,[16] a critique energized by the most challenging insights of Kant's practical philosophy, "to which," Levinas writes, "we feel particularly close."[17]

The Subject of Freedom consists of five chapters, two on Kant's *Critique of Pure Reason*, two on his practical works, and one on Levinas's *Otherwise than Being*. The conversation intimated between Kant and Levinas becomes more explicit toward the end of the book. The following pages outline the itinerary I propose.

NEGATION AND OBJECTIVITY

How does reason create objects of knowledge and ideas that imagine a relationship with the objective world? How does reason manage to achieve a sense of completion that would allow it to form the realm of objectivity? Chapter 1 begins by recalling the role Kant attributes to sensibility and the understanding in producing objects of cognition, and to reason in generating ideas of things that cannot be experienced, only thought. It explores reason's attempt to create the idea of the world, an object unavailable to experience, precisely where it fails: in the mathematical antinomy. Seeking inspiration in Monique David-Ménard's excellent study on the power of negation in Kant's first *Critique*, *La Folie dans la raison pure* (*Madness in Pure*

Reason),[18] this chapter offers a close reading of Kant's solution to the mathematical antinomy.

Reason's ability to form wholes depends on its ability to create a synthesis (which is the prime activity of the imagination and the understanding) and on the possibility to produce a closure. In fact, the aspiration to conceive of a complete object is at the heart of any constitutive process, such as the ones to which this book refers: the idea of the world, subjectivity, the social. In Kant's case, the success in attaining a synthesis will depend on the smooth functioning of logical judgments and their ability to posit something. But when the whole reason aims to form is an all-encompassing totality, as it does in the first antinomy by seeking to present a world that would include all phenomena, reason falls in contradiction with itself. This is due to the antinomic rule that traverses reason. As theoretical reason endeavors to present the world to itself, it structures phenomena in a sequence of linked elements, each of them conditioned by a previous one. Since every condition is conditioned, reason's presentation of a series must regress endlessly from each cause to a previous cause. However, in order for the series to become whole reason would have to reach an exceptional phenomenon, an "unconditioned" cause that, escaping the rule of regress, could give the series a closure and allow the imagination to complete the object "world." But the unconditioned, affirms Kant, is not reachable because it is a need of reason and not an existing thing. In sum, the retroactive determination of the regressive series enters in contradiction with the need to find an unconditioned element that, by introducing a limit, would allow the series to become a bounded whole. Thus, when trying to represent the impossible object world, theoretical reason cannot escape this antinomic rule that demands the very systemic completeness it precludes.[19] Reason falters because, being regulative, it takes itself to be constitutive. The mathematical antinomy dissolves because its judgments attribute "objective reality to an idea that serves merely as a rule."[20]

What Kant's solution to the mathematical antinomy reveals is that the principle of absolute totality to which reason aspires is null. Any search for a complete and all-encompassing object—for a world or universe with a beginning in space and time, or for a whole as a stable and self-contained system—is therefore bound to fail. The second dynamic conflict (or fourth antinomy) alerts us, in turn, to the risk reason runs when it conceives of a totality conditioned by a transcendent outside, by a necessary being (such as the idea of God) to which the series of contingent phenomena could be linked. Since this necessary outside could only ground worldly events by being fully unrelated to them, it must remain a mere speculation.

UNCONDITIONED SUBJECTIVITY

It may be possible, however, to imagine a synthesis that does not aim to form an absolute whole. This is the possibility the third antinomy opens up by privileging relationality over completeness, and thereby favoring an ongoing configuration over a stable one. The third antinomy aims to explain how all effects are linked to their causes and derive through synthesis a "nature," a dynamic system of causal linkage. Its thesis includes an exceptional element which, while being present in the series as a condition whose effects may be perceived in the world, does not itself have a cause: it is unconditioned. The name Kant gives this unique element is freedom. Freedom may be envisioned as a cause whose effects reverberate in the series of causally linked phenomena, a cause which is itself uncaused (this is why Kant refers to it as "empirically unconditioned").[21] But freedom exceeds reason's ability to conceptualize. We can only define freedom negatively as an empty space beyond what can be thought.

The unconditioned cause, a relational term, establishes a relationship between two heterogeneous spaces which are otherwise unconnectable. One of them is the phenomenal sequence of things and events in the world linked to each other as cause and effect. The other *space*, what reason thinks of as the intelligible realm of freedom, does not appear (it does not affect our senses), and therefore is not part of experience: it may only be imagined as an empty space beyond phenomena. "Freedom" functions here as a noumenon in the negative legitimate use Kant attributes to this type of idea: one that opens a "range outside the sphere of appearances" which "is (for us) empty," and thus, only in this negative use, functions as a "boundary concept serving to limit the pretension of sensibility."[22] In supplying an uncaused cause that begins its own series of conditions, the causality through freedom inserted by the thesis and then excluded by the antithesis changes the nature of the conflict and has the potential to introduce moments of closure that anchor the series fleetingly and contingently.

But even if one could prove that the possibility of freedom is not a contradictory idea (Kant's goal here), what would enable the unconditioned to play the function of *initiating* cause that potentially bounds the causal chain? What makes the unconditioned conceivable is the singular role Kant assigns the subject. Freedom can be simultaneously outside and inside the causal series, he intimates, because freedom is *in* the subject, even though the subject itself has no access to freedom. A member of natural causality, the subject is also the unwitting *bearer* of freedom, and thus is related to the intelligible. The intelligible is, as we just said, an empty space beyond what can be thought, and is, in this respect, *other* to thought. What constitutes the subject, which Kant had defined so far as a phenomenon of nature (empirical consciousness or inner sense), is therefore its exceptional relationship with that outside. What I propose in Chapter 2 is that as bearer of freedom, the subject may be imagined to play the role of the unconditioned. By unwittingly taking the position of unconditioned cause, the subject would be the element in the series that exceptionally introduces a boundary, a fleeting moment of closure: the subject's intervention allows the series to cohere contingently and retroactively. The contingent synthesis reached here would be, to express it aporetically, a whole in progress, a dynamic system that is reconfigured retroactively time and again. Only in this sense may reason in the third antinomy be considered to achieve a certain sense of completion. "Unconditioned subjectivity" names the relationship and bounding operation that anchors the series time and again. If we understand the third antinomy in this way, what reason accomplishes here is huge: it achieves an immanent synthesis, it bounds the field of objectivity, it rescues reason from self-contradiction, it clears the way for practical reason, no less.

But are we right to place so much weight on Kant's third antinomy? Doesn't the antithesis famously deny freedom, arguing instead that all phenomena originate in natural necessity? ("There is no freedom, but everything in the world occurs solely according to laws of nature.")[23] The anchoring of causally-linked phenomena by an element (the subject) that connects the series with the heterogeneous causality of freedom happens, I will argue, not despite but because of the fact that the antithesis of the third antinomy denies freedom. Although this second judgment excludes freedom ("There is no freedom . . ."), in effect this gesture constructs freedom as the excluded element that enables a certain sense of completion, "everything in the world" ("but everything in the world occurs solely according to laws of nature").[24] If the antithesis had not introduced a boundary by excluding freedom, if it had not thereby opened up an imaginary intelligible space in which to locate the excluded element, freedom, the thesis would not be able to presuppose the outside in which it locates the absent cause of the unconditioned. The thesis, that is, could not imagine the unconditioned as relationship and as boundary. The unconditioned role freedom plays is accordingly determined in the interplay between the asymmetrical operations (one logical, the other one relational) enabled by each judgment: the antithesis creates a boundary and the thesis formulates it as a relationship.

If we read Kant's third antinomy in this way, by elaborating on what his explanation presupposes but does not pursue, it is no longer necessary to attribute the truthfulness of the thesis to an intellectual perspective and that of the antithesis to an empirical one, as Kant famously does. This opens up the possibility of envisaging ethical subjectivity as no longer split between two viewpoints or references, one intelligible and one sensible, from which "the human being" cognizes itself.[25] This subjectivity affected not only by what is given through the senses but also by unconditioned freedom and the moral law—of which, Kant insists, there can be no sensible experience—will make its entry (in the *Critique of Practical Reason*) in Kant's exploration of the unprecedented form of affect he calls "respect" (*Achtung*).

CAUSALITY OF FREEDOM

We may go as far as affirming that as bearer of unconditioned freedom the word "subject" names (from this theoretical perspective) a relationship with that element of excess. But as we envision freedom in the subject as the limit that allows the imagination to create a sense of completion, and thus as a boundary that enables thought, can we simply assume, as we seemingly have so far, that the subject is constituted by freedom? If freedom can manifest itself in the world, it is only insofar as freedom is the excess that constitutes the subject. This excess has to do with the being practical of pure reason, with a pure practical reason that has to act and act itself out.[26] But how freedom constitutes the subject is not easy to explain. First, one would have to prove that what in the first *Critique* was just a possibility, a non-contradictory idea, is in effect actual and constitutive. Proving freedom's existence and its causality in constituting the subject is the challenge Kant's practical philosophy must meet. Here theoretical reason is charged with the formidable task of explaining how practical reason—a reason that does not reason[27]—motivates the power of desire.[28]

If we do not have any direct experience of freedom, if we cannot know it, how can we even venture freedom exists? How can practical philosophy claim that its object, freedom, which theoretical philosophy posited merely as a non-contradictory idea, is actual and constitutive? As one moves from theoretical to practical reason limits shift, but not as radically as one might expect. Although in the *Critique of Practical Reason* we still do not know freedom, freedom manifests itself through the moral law, whose existence, affirms Kant, we know.[29] From this practical perspective, that freedom is actual means it motivates the subject to act. More exactly, freedom manifests itself as a power to obligate that *affects* the faculty of desire through the moral law: we find ourselves and others responding to something unconditionally, without necessarily knowing to what. The existence of freedom is attested to, in sum, by the effect the moral law has on the beings it obligates.[30] But what the moral law is, where it comes from, and how it affects or moves the power of desire, determining the will directly (without the mediation of sensibility), is not easy to discern.

What, then, is the law? We can only answer this question in the negative. The law is unconditioned and does not aim at any particular object. It is not defined by any matter or goal that would arouse the power of desire and thus determine the will heteronomously, through feeling. Heteronomous incentives of the will include empirical inclinations (happiness, pleasure), but also rational aspirations such as perfection or altruism. No matter how highly esteemed, for Kant incentives for action defined by these goals are heteronomous. Since their causality is determined by nature, not by freedom, they are not grounded on the law, which alone secures the autonomy of the will. If once all matter has been excluded from the law only the law's form is left, what comes to play the motivating function of matter? It is the very form of the law, the imperative to act and make universal law, that plays the double function of form and motive,[31] determining the will objectively and motivating it subjectively. Hence Kant's well-known distinction between legality, or following the law by the letter, and morality, or fulfilling the law's spirit. Morality consists not only in acting according to the law, but also because of the law, motivated solely by the law. The spirit refers, in short, to the unprecedented ability of the law's form to motivate. Chapter 3 thus proposes, perhaps counterintuitively, that the law's motivating power (its *spirit*) lies in its letter, in the verbal address the law is.

We could say that the letter and the spirit of the law refer to two modes of effectiveness of the law's form, that is, to two ways in which the law exerts its impact on subjectivity: its power to enjoin through its form of address and its power to motivate. It will be important to understand, therefore, that the law is not something inherent in the subject's nature. The law is, rather, what in the subject exceeds and addresses the subject, what in the subject confronts the subject as something other, as Nancy indicates. The law befalls pure reason as a fact, the *factum rationis*, which confronts reason with the alterity of the law: there is at the core of reason "a facticity other than reason."[32] Being motivated by the law means being affected by it. In the *Critique of Practical Reason*, being free amounts to having the causality of freedom act in and through oneself, that is, being animated by a causality one does not understand. Or to formulate this in terms of Kant's qualification of the law as unconditioned, although the law is its own cause, only the intervention of the subject can give it its power as cause by making of it the element that initiates and motivates its own subjective itinerary.[33]

But how exactly does the subject give the law its power as cause? How does one give oneself the law as the initiating cause of one's itinerary, as the ethical disposition (*Gesinnung*) or supreme ground that leads one to act motivated solely by the law, *because of* the law? Our presentations in search for the first subjective basis of adopting the law as the only motivation would have to regress indefinitely without ever reaching the *initiating* cause, which must be an act of freedom. Yet, reasons Kant in "On the Inherence of the Evil alongside the Good Principle," even if we do not have access to this *originary* cause, we must have chosen it freely. In freely choosing one's disposition one would be, in effect, choosing whether to be free. This choice, however, "did not happen in time," and thus remains inscrutable to the very subject who made it.[34] Through this free act, the subject becomes the author of its own disposition, the one that has chosen to harbor the causality of freedom that constitutes it. By choosing a disposition that has the moral law as the supreme ground of motivation, the subject confers on the unconditioned law the power to be the cause that *initiates* the chain. Here, in "On the Inherence of Evil" (as well as in the *Grounding for the Metaphysics of Morals* and the second *Critique*), the causality at stake is the practical causality of freedom that constitutes the subject. By analogy with the theoretical structure of the third antinomy, reason is able to envisage the subject as beginning its own subjective itinerary, the itinerary of a subjectivity constituted and animated by the causality of freedom. Although the causality of freedom is unconditioned, the subject plays the role of the unconditioned by beginning by itself, that is, by "choosing" the causality of freedom that acts through oneself.[35]

What reason imagines retroactively (tracing back a subjective itinerary toward a first free motivation) as the subject's free choice of its own disposition, a choice not recoverable through consciousness, marks the very emergence of autonomous subjectivity. Facticity is the consciousness that the law is in us. The existence of the unconditioned, which in the cosmological causality explored in the third antinomy was an unknown possibility, finds its practical equivalent in the facticity of the law. If in the third antinomy the unconditioned could be imagined to initiate the cosmological causal chain, facticity in the second *Critique* confirms that the law constitutes the subject and has the ability to motivate freedom's causality in the subject. According to Kant's insight into this originary act of the power of choice, autonomy would consist in authoring what one has received (a law that gives itself, that addresses a freedom). Freely choosing one's good disposition would mean giving oneself what is already in oneself, choosing to be the addressee one already is of the law, choosing to be the one (the freedom) to which the law addresses itself. This law that gives itself to us, that "thrusts itself upon us on its own" as a fact of reason,[36] will be, through the enigma of autonomy, the law we believe we give ourselves. Only in this sense may we say that the subject becomes the unconditioned beginning or "author" of the causality of freedom that animates its subjectivity. Autonomy in this context would consist in putting oneself forward as the origin of what has no origin.

AFFECT OF THE LAW

But the most important question, the truly practical one, still needs to be addressed. How does the causality of freedom affect the subject? What is the subject's relationship with the law? This question concurs with a question we posed above: How can the form of the law play the function of matter and move the power of desire without the help of sensibility? This is, after all, what autonomy is about. Kant addresses these questions with his notion of "respect" (*Achtung*). Faced with the need to acknowledge the presence of affect—how the subject is affected by the unconditioned law—Kant's rational account is overwhelmed by what it cannot theorize but must nevertheless express. Another language unavailable to the *Critique* would be necessary, and yet, the very possibility of venturing a causality through freedom hinges on this account.

The question of the affect of the law, of the subject as *being affected*, concerns the law's otherness and the subject as relationship with it. Kant addresses it in "On the Incentives of Pure Practical Reason," the concluding chapter of the Analytic in the second *Critique*. There he defines the subject's relationship to the law through the notion of respect, a singular feeling that does not originate in sensibility but in practical reason. In explaining respect Kant's causal account would seem to be dislocated. Respect for the law is an affect produced by the law, the impact of the law on the subject, which at the same time furthers the law's ability to motivate. Depicted as both effect and cause, the apparently circular causality of respect as the affect in the subject provoked by its relationship with the law attests to the retroactive and immanent process in which the subject is constituted: the subject emerges in relationship to the law, it is constituted by the affect of the law. It is not the case, then, that the law exists out there, independently from a subject which then adopts it. Rather, the law only exists in the subject (although it is not of the subject) and through the intervention of the subject. In fact, the subject itself embodies the affect of the law. Finding inspiration in Levinas, I propose that it is not only the case that the law leaves its trace in the subject: the subject is itself that trace. This would explain why the causality of respect appears dislocated. The law in the subject and the effect the law produces in the subject are one and the same: a *being affected* by the unconditioned, an "anarchic being affected" (*affection anarchique*)[37]—the subject itself.

Shortly after the affect of respect enters the scene in Kant's text, however, the law is said to provoke a different kind of effect, a fear the subject feels toward a threatening law. The law now adopts a terrifying gaze and voice similar to the shaming voice of conscience, in what appears like a turn away (indeed, a shrinking away) from the unconditioned and formal law the Analytic had described so far. This vision of a humiliating law would seem to contradict the law's ability to act as unconditioned and to animate the subject. Demoting the law to a punishing agency would amount to replacing it with an absolute and threatening other that can function as the legitimizing horizon of one's acts. The version of ethics that would result from this conception of a coercive law would presuppose a transcendent or metaphysical *object* and thus belie the immanence of subjective constitution. Here, in Kant's section on respect, two versions of the law's impact seem to coexist.[38] As the affect that furthers the law's motivating power, the notion of respect provides practical insight into the impact of freedom's causality on the subjectivity it constitutes. As the fear of a threatening law, of a coercive agency that berates the self, respect functions as a heteronomous otherness, a framework that justifies one's pathological choices and contravenes autonomy.

Does this mean that Kant betrays his initial concept of autonomy? After all, being in relationship to a threatening law, wouldn't one act out of fear of being punished, motivated by a desired goal, thus prioritizing heteronomy over autonomy? We should keep in mind, however, that Kant's notion of respect aspires to describe the subject's relationship to the law. Here, for the first time in the second *Critique*, a subjective perspective must have its place. And so in this chapter Kant's account must do justice both to the theoretical distance of his critical stance and to the finite perspective of consciousness from which a subject would perceive and feel its own relationship to the law. Every time Kant refers to this negative effect he is careful to clarify that he is speaking from the limited perspective of consciousness. Hence his insistence that the rational subject affected by inclinations feels humiliated "as the effect of the consciousness of the moral law."[39]

In conceiving of a law that moves the subject to act toward an object or goal, theoretical reason would, in effect, trespass its own limits. In fact, opening up just a few pages below, the Dialectic of Practical Reason (Book II of the second *Critique*) sets out to reveal reason's illusion that it can trespass its bounds by aspiring to reach an unconditioned totality. The illusion explored in the Dialectic marks an explicit departure from the conception of freedom and the law expounded in the Analytic, as Alenka Zupančič points out.[40] The Dialectic also departs from the dynamic sense of closure we find in the third antinomy, where causality may be envisioned as anchored fleetingly and contingently by a subject which, constituted by freedom, plays the role of the unconditioned cause. While the law described in the Analytic had no object, reason in the Dialectic "seeks the unconditioned totality" of its own object (in this different conception, the unconditioned would consist in the whole series, rather than being an exceptional member of the series).[41] The "*object* of pure practical reason" would be, according to this different view, fulfilling the "highest good" toward which a will determined by the law would tend.[42] At this point the way in which reason attempts to form a synthesis, to find a closure, shifts from causality to finality, from seeking an unconditioned beginning to fulfilling an end or horizon. Now reason aims to grasp the morality of a being as a whole.[43] Yet a human life span is too short to fulfill the highest good. Attempting to solve this practical antinomy, the Dialectic must imagine the conditions required for the realization of the highest good: the immortality of the soul (since a good will can only be realized through the soul's infinite progress toward it) and the existence of God (of the external and all-encompassing viewpoint from which the soul's endless progress could be seen as a whole).

Significantly, the attempt on the part of reason to create an unconditioned whole by imagining the conditions in which the highest good would be fulfilled is in consonance with the aspiration of the fourth antinomy. In this second dynamic conflict, thesis and antithesis respectively introduce and exclude a necessary being which, placed fully outside the series of worldly phenomena, could act as their condition. The discrepancy between the two dynamic conflicts (between the third and the fourth antinomy) thus concerns the location of the intelligible—the other—in relation to the causal series, and therefore also the role of the subject. This discrepancy is associated with the two ways of understanding the unconditioned Kant describes in the first *Critique*. In the third antinomy and the Analytic of Practical Reason the unconditioned would also be part of the series, whereas in the fourth antinomy and the Dialectic of Practical Reason the unconditioned would be the series as a totality.[44] I propose to envision the shift from the third to the fourth antinomy as a theoretical anticipation (in the first *Critique*) of a shift from an immanent to a transcendent conception of ethics in the second *Critique*. The fourth antinomy describes a different mode of linkage where the unconditioned element would no longer be the relationship between freedom and the series embodied by the subject, but rather an absolute otherness that lies completely outside the series of worldly events. This different vision of completeness introduced in the fourth antinomy, a vision that prepares the path for the Dialectic of Practical Reason, dispenses with freedom's unconditioned role in forming a contingent whole. Now the support of the series would lie in a completely exterior being from whose *viewpoint* the series would cohere as an unconditioned, all-encompassing, and absolute whole. This metaphysical solution eliminates contingency at the price of dispensing with a subjectivity understood, as I have here, as the relationship between the series and its outside. The path followed by the fourth antinomy and the Dialectic of Practical Reason pushes aside Kant's notion of immanent subjective constitution and advances instead a transcendent account of subject and world.

How are we to understand these two approaches to ethics opened up respectively in the Analytic and the Dialectic of Practical Reason—an immanent view in which the law redoubles as form and motivation, and the transcendent version where the possibility of the law ultimately hinges on redeeming for practical use the postulates of the soul's immortality and the viewpoint of God? Perhaps we could gain insight into this bifurcation by looking at the tension between an immanent and a transcendent vision of the law one can detect in Kant's chapter on respect, where the law's impact on the subject would be perceived alternately as a motivating affect or as a pathological fear of punishment. What this second conception introduces, in effect, is a different other, a dialectic relationship of the subject with it, and ultimately a differential conception of subjective constitution: a conception that results in self-consciousness and identity and leads to the reduced vision of autonomy which, as I noted at the beginning, has prevailed.

Yet, I argue that the two different approaches to ethics do not necessarily signify a shift in Kant's conception. Rather, they should be interpreted in light of the limits of theoretical reason as Kant conceived of it. As he does not tire to insist in his chapter on respect, respect in the negative sense refers to the law's impact on a finite consciousness. Read in this way, Kant's section on respect suggests that the ethical notion of autonomous obligation constitutive of subjectivity must coexist with the finite consciousness and sensibility of the subject it produces, a consciousness from which one's ethical constitution may be perceived, paradoxically, as heteronomy. Kant's practical reason is only conceivable, as Michel Henry would argue, in terms of affect.[45]

AUTONOMY, OR BEING INSPIRED

The affect of ethics configures the core of Levinas's *Otherwise than Being*. This book is written in a language that, while still partly theoretical, is infected by the practicality of its subject.[46] The way in which Levinas's writing evokes the emergence of subjectivity in *Otherwise than Being* invigorates what I consider to be Kant's most powerful insights on freedom, insights that, as I explore them in this book, transpire from the third antinomy, the Analytic of Practical Reason, and "On the Inherence of Evil" (*Religion*). Both philosophers conceive of ethical subjectivity as constituted by the impact of an excess Kant calls freedom and Levinas names the other. This excess in the subject but irreducible to the subject is figured as a command one has received—Kant's moral law, Levinas's order, command, or call—a call that manifests itself only in one's response, when one finds oneself responding without knowing to what. This obligation, therefore, takes the form of a command that is unheard of and unheard (Levinas's term *inouï*). For Kant the law of freedom is a beginning by itself and a form of address. As free beginning, the law can function as the unconditioned element that motivates and drives autonomous subjectivity. The unconditionality of the call is expressed by Levinas in terms of "substitution." As imperative, in turn, the law addresses the subject as would an other, eliciting an unconditioned response in its addressee. Unconditionality and address will come together in Levinas's evocation of subjectivity as an "anarchic being affected" (*affection anarchique*).[47]

I refer to this unconditioned and anarchic excess, to the incommensurable otherness of an obligation both Kant and Levinas evoke as address, with the words "other" or "event" for lack of better terms, because in trying to account for the emergence of ethical subjectivity we really have no knowledge of that of which we are speaking. The term "emergence" is not exact either, because subjectivity does not have a traceable (or untraceable) origin. As Levinas argues in his essay "Humanism and An-archy" (1968), there is a "pre-originary" or "beyond the ultimate" that would never become originary or ultimate. "*Inwardness is the fact that in being the beginning is preceded.*"[48] If subjectivity has no *arché*, can we reconcile Levinas's claim that any origin is preceded with Kant's conception of freedom as a power to begin by itself? In fact, the priority Kant gives to the thesis of the third antinomy, according to Levinas, sums up the tradition of the freedom of the ego that must be critiqued. "The regression to the ultimate or to the original, the principle," he writes, "is already effected by the freedom of the ego, which is beginning itself."[49] Indeed, the freedom of the ego Levinas refers to here has traditionally been taken to justify the very self-positing of the subject that has reached us as Kantian legacy, as Robert Pippin eloquently portrays it.[50] In the first *Critique*, however, Kant insists on the precariousness (if not impossibility) of a subject's self-positing. Although Levinas repeatedly criticizes the unity of transcendental apperception and its synthesizing activity, we must recall that the thinking "I" does not amount to a subjectivity. Rather, the "paradoxical relationship" this "I" has with passive inner sense underscores the inability of the thinking "I" to extend to itself the synthetic activity through which it determines the given. As Kant points out, the spontaneous thinking "I" can only perceive itself in the receptive form of inner sense, as passive.[51]

In this book I argue that Kant's third antinomy opens the potential for a notion of the unconditioned that, far from contradicting Levinas's conception of subjectivity, may in fact help us appreciate the implications of what Levinas calls "substitution." Kant's unconditioned and Levinas's an-archy both refer to the absence of a cause, but the two terms are not equivalent. According to the reading of the third antinomy I propose in Chapter 2, the uncaused cause Kant calls unconditioned, a relational term, ultimately names the relationship and boundary between the series and its outside and can therefore be envisioned as a provisional beginning of sorts. The theoretical notion of unconditionality will prove both challenging and crucial at the moment of explaining the autonomy of the practical subject. For Levinas, in turn, anarchy is a "diachrony without synthesis"[52] that refracts any notion of origin. Anarchic subjectivity is a relationship with "illeity," with an irreducible other that signifies outside all modalities and alternatives of being. The ethical excess that affects subjectivity anarchically disturbs the ontological order of being and discourse, and thus also the ability of *Otherwise than Being* to conceptualize that disturbance through philosophical language. In Chapter 5 I read *Otherwise than Being* as a book that takes up the challenge of expressing ethical disturbance by performing its own being disturbed as a text. If Kant's second *Critique* theorizes the constitution of the subject by freedom in causal terms, Levinas refers to subjectivity as "signification" and performs textually its emergence as "substitution." In both cases, as unconditioned and as substitution, subjectivity contingently embodies the relationship between two incommensurate realms. If in the third antinomy the effects of freedom reverberate in the series through the unconditioned role of the subject, in *Otherwise than Being* it is through the subject's substitution for the other that the trace of illeity—ethical signification—has an impact on the world.

But what allows us to theorize Levinasian subjectivity in this way, let alone establish a structural parallel with the Kantian unconditioned? Given that *Otherwise than Being* is concerned with a proximity of the self to the other that verges on obsession, given that this text is disturbed by an ethical affect that configures it to the core, what would allow it to adopt the distance necessary for theorizing? And then, from this distance, how are we to avert the risk of mistaking substitution for an act of an already constituted subject, despite Levinas's insistence that "substitution is not an act"?[53] These questions bring us back to the notion of autonomy. Autonomy, for Levinas, is the possibility of finding in oneself a law one has received, believing oneself its author, and speaking it in one's own voice. Autonomy thus consists in taking oneself for the origin of what has no origin, in standing for a beginning that is always preceded. Autonomy manifests itself to reason, not to ethical experience, and can therefore only appear in *Otherwise than Being* at the point in which Levinas evokes the entry of the third party. What the third makes appear is an other who is another subject related to others. The third introduces the distancing from oneself that enables consciousness, self-consciousness, and representation. This distancing allows Levinas's text and its reader to theorize, to envision "*essence* as synchrony" and justice as "the intelligibility of a system."[54] In the midst of the diachronic and anarchic relationship Levinas calls subjectivity, contingent moments of synchrony—and thus fleeting "*essence*" effects—can arise.

From this theoretical perspective, the ethical subject that emerges by substituting itself for the excess-other that constitutes it can be envisaged as anchoring signification. In both roles, as unconditioned (Kant) and as substitution (Levinas), subjectivity emerges as the anchoring of the diachronic that allows causality and signification to cohere contingently. When read side by side with subjectivity as substitution, the link between Kant's theoretical and practical approaches to freedom gains momentum. The ethical subject that emerges by substituting itself for the excess-other that constitutes it (as *Otherwise than Being* evokes and performs it) embodies the relationship between two incommensurate spaces, the relationship Kant calls unconditioned cause. If the bounding effected by the unconditioned in Kant allows objectivity to emerge, the objectivity that arises from substitution is the articulation of social justice and of political community. "*Essence* as synchrony: *togetherness-in-a-place*."[55] The community contingently cohering here, "togetherness-in-a-place," is the "dwelling of others,"[56] "what is incumbent on me from all sides."[57] What emerges with subjectivity as substitution is a social space-in-progress fleetingly anchored by each subject's relatedness to the alterity of freedom on which autonomy rests.

1

NEGATION AND OBJECTIVITY:
METHODOLOGICAL PRELUDE

How does theoretical reason create objects of knowledge and ideas that imagine a relationship with the objective world? In the *Critique of Pure Reason* Kant attributes this role to the synthetic activity of the imagination and the understanding. Reason, in turn, produces ideas of things that cannot be experienced, only thought. This chapter explores reason's attempt to create the idea of the world, an object unavailable to experience, precisely where it fails, in the mathematical antinomy. Through a critical reading of the first antinomy and of the productivity of negation inspired in Monique David-Ménard's *La folie dans la raison pure* (*Madness in Pure Reason*),[1] it examines reason's failure to form all-encompassing, self-contained totalities. There is only one type of negative idea, noumenon in the negative sense, to which Kant accords a legitimate use. By opening an empty space beyond experience, negative noumena bound the realm of objectivity and provide thinking with a sense of completion. Since the most productive instance of this type of boundary concept is arguably the idea of freedom, the analysis of noumenon in the negative sense I offer at the end of this chapter contextualizes the achievements I attribute to the third antinomy in the next chapter. I begin this reading of the first antinomy by introducing briefly Kant's notion of synthesis of the imagination and the understanding, and the synthetic illusion that makes reason fall into antinomies.

Kant starts the *Critique of Pure Reason* by calling attention to the two mental faculties involved in the process of cognition, sensibility and the understanding, which produce intuitions and concepts.[2] Sensibility, our receptive faculty, is passive, whereas the understanding is the active faculty of thought that brings forth the spontaneity of cognition through conceptualization and rules.[3] Synthesis is the operation through which the understanding creates objects of knowledge out of a manifold of appearances or apparitions (*Erscheinungen*). Kant's use of this term does not presuppose there is a positive and authentic essence lurking behind deceptive appearances.[4] Rather, *Erscheinungen*, perhaps more accurately translated as "apparitions," refers to what appears to our senses (the still indeterminate object of empirical intuitions), information about the world that we receive as sensations provoked by empirical things and events. "Intuition . . . takes place only insofar as the object is given to us; but that, in turn, is possible only . . . by the mind's being affected in a certain manner."[5] The human subject as empirical being would be a *being affected*. Space and time are, for Kant, the pure forms of intuition, the only forms sensibility presents a priori through which we, empirical subjects, present the objects that appear to us in an immediate way, without the mediating activity of the imagination.[6] Categories or concepts, on the other hand, are a priori forms of human understanding.[7] Space and time (the forms of intuition), on the one hand, and the synthetic activity of the understanding through categories, on the other, constitute the conditions of apparition that allow the understanding to determine the given, what can be cognized.

Synthesis requires a mediation between sensibility and the understanding, and that mediator is the imagination. The task of the imagination consists in combining the multiplicity of sensible intuitions in a spatial and temporal sequence Kant calls figurative synthesis. In the 1781 edition of the *Critique of Pure Reason*, where Kant describes synthesis as threefold, he envisions figurative synthesis as encompassing two steps, synthesis of apprehension in sensibility (according to which we present the manifold in space and time) and synthesis of reproduction in the imagination (by means of which the imagination reproduces the preceding and following elements and combines them as a succession in space and time); in the 1787 edition, figurative synthesis only refers to the imagination's activity of reproduction.[8] The imagination synthesizes, but in order for cognition to take place, the understanding must refer the imagination's syntheses to the unity of a concept or category.[9] In effect, the understanding *represents* what presents itself in intuition (it relates sequences of apparitions to a concept) and in so doing produces objects of knowledge.[10] Objects of knowledge are thus formed in synthesis. Synthesis contains in a representation (a concept or form of an object: synthesis of recognition) a multiplicity that appears or presents itself not only in space and time (synthesis of apprehension), but also as a sequence formed by a diversity of preceding and following spaces and times (synthesis of reproduction). Only thus does the complete synthetic act, the synthesis of recognition, occur.

What exactly does it mean, though, that concepts are a priori forms of human understanding? This is where the thinking subject comes into play. In order for the unity of the object to take place through categorial conditions, that unity must come together "in one consciousness."[11] The conceptual unity of consciousness the understanding achieves in the synthesis of recognition is produced in what Kant calls transcendental apperception. Transcendental apperception is an a priori condition (a condition preceding all experience) that makes experience itself possible.[12] The "I" of transcendental apperception, the "transcendental unity of self-consciousness," is something one adds to the presentation of the manifold so that intuitions are "*my* presentations" by belonging to one self-consciousness. It is important to understand that this unity of apperception Kant calls self-consciousness, the "I" that accompanies all my presentations, does not refer to a substantial being, but rather to a function of thought.[13] Through this function of thought the empirical consciousness, which is "intrinsically sporadic and without any reference to the subject's identity," gains a sense of identity.[14] The sense of identity of the empirical subject, that is, the sense of continuity of its experience, is assured precisely by the synthesis of recognition realized by the understanding.[15] The synthetic activity of the understanding and apperceptive self-consciousness are, therefore, correlative—they necessitate each other. Yet, paradoxically, the very apperceptive self-consciousness that secures the sense of identity of an empirical subject cannot produce itself as an object of cognition.

Hence, "this intelligence" Kant calls the thinking "I" is confronted with "something paradoxical," the question of why the transcendental unity of the "I think," itself the spontaneous condition of all thought, should be subjected to the "limiting condition" of receptive inner sense.[16] For "how can the I who thinks be distinct from the I that intuits itself, and yet be the same as it by being the same subject?" How can "I, as intelligence and *thinking* subject, cognize *myself* as an object that is *thought*, . . . not as I am to the understanding, but as I appear to myself?"[17] The "I think" is the form of determination that corresponds to the unity of synthesis of the understanding, but when it comes to inner sense, to one's experience of oneself, the "I think" cannot determine anything. "Inner sense," in other words, denominates the appearing of the thinking "I" to itself not under the forms of the understanding (categories, concepts) through which it would be determined as an object of cognition, but rather as a passive receptivity that cannot be synthesized.[18] Thus the notion of subjectivity outlined in the first *Critique* consists in the "paradoxical" coexistence of two heterogeneous and irreducible forms: the spontaneous or active form of thought (the "I think" as synthetic act of the understanding) and the empirical and receptive form of inner sense, time.[19] Hence the paradox of inner sense: although we are active, "we intuit ourselves through it only as we are inwardly affected by ourselves," as passive.[20] The "limiting condition"[21] of thinking, the limit that enables thought, is inherent in thinking.[22]

As the imagination and the understanding collaborate in producing empirical objects and events through synthesis, their activity stays within the bounds of empirical cognition (it meets the conditions of apparition). But beyond producing phenomena—that is, objects out of what affects our sensibility, objects of experience we can cognize—we also create ideas of what cannot be experienced, only thought.[23] Here is where the critical problem arises, where reason itself runs into trouble. Reason falters when it aims to create ideas to which no object of experience corresponds. If the understanding gave unity to the manifold of intuition by referring it to a concept, thus producing objects of experience, reason aims to reach the unity of all acts of the understanding, by arranging "all acts of the understanding, in regard to every object, in an *absolute whole*."[24] What reason seeks to do is to refer all syntheses of the understanding (and thus all resulting phenomena) to transcendental objects that can never appear to sensibility, "pure concepts of reason" or transcendental ideas that can be neither experienced nor cognized.[25] Reason's ideas would thus include the "absolute totality in the synthesis of conditions."[26] The aspiration of reason, the principle that drives its totalizing impulse, is the following: "*if the conditioned is given, then the entire sum of conditions and hence the absolutely unconditioned* (through which alone the conditioned was possible), *is also given*."[27]

The problem is that in order to form a totality that includes every condition—every appearance and every phenomenon (that is, every object, event, or state)—one must venture beyond experience in search for an unconditioned element that would provide the closure necessary to complete the synthesis, to form a synthetic whole.[28] But, as it turns out, the unconditioned is a need of reason, not an empirical reality. Since finding an unconditioned element is impossible in experience, transcendental ideas refer to objects we can think (we can imagine), but on whose existence we cannot pronounce: these objects can never be thought of as *being*.[29] Unlike the use of understanding, which in the first *Critique* is constitutive (it constitutes objects of cognition), the aspiration of reason, to form a regression that aims to run up to an unconditioned element, is simply regulative: it refers to a principle of totality which in the case of the mathematical antinomy will turn out to be null.

Taking up the three categories of relation (substance, causality, and community),[30] reason aims to form three transcendental ideas, "the absolute (unconditioned) unity of the thinking subject" (the soul), "the absolute unity of the series of conditions of appearance" (the world), and "the absolute unity of the condition of all objects of thought as such" (God).[31] In the Transcendental Dialectic Kant critiques these three ideas as illusory, as based on fallacious thinking, and devotes its three sections (the "Paralogisms," the "Antinomy," and the "Ideal of Pure Reason") to proving how the rational sciences of psychology, cosmology, and theology rest on dialectic inferences: paralogisms (that attribute to the thinking subject a substantial and simple soul that is identical to itself), antinomies (where reason falls in contradiction with itself), and transcendent ideas (that assume an ideal to which no object of experience corresponds).[32] Of these three types of illusory ideas, the antinomy is noteworthy because unlike paralogisms and ideal—which are produced "by a merely one-sided illusion"—the antinomy is antithetical. The attempt to think of the world in its totality gives way, in other words, to a thesis affirming something, the unconditioned condition of all phenomena, which an antithesis then denies.[33] This discord of reason gives rise to a "conflict of laws" (antinomy): reason falls in contradiction with itself. "The Antinomy of Pure Reason," the largest section of the Dialectic, aims to expose any error hidden in the assumptions of reason and reveal how reason falls prey to illusions—and thus how its failure is produced—so as to save reason from dogmatism and skepticism, and forestall "the death of sound philosophy."[34] Since what is ultimately at risk in the Antinomy is the integrity of reason, Kant's goal in this section is to secure the possibility of philosophical thinking, to restore the smooth functioning of thought. I now turn to

reason's failure to form the idea of the world as a "given whole of all categories" in the first antinomy.

INCONCEIVABLE WORLD

The aspiration in the first mathematical conflict to form a complete "world"
out of a multitude of phenomena, an absolute whole that presupposes no
further premises outside itself, gives way to two conflicting propositions: "The
world has a beginning in time and is also enclosed within bounds as regards
space" (thesis) and "The world has no beginning and no bounds in space,
but is infinite as regards both time and space" (antithesis).[35] At first view,
the confrontation between thesis and antithesis Kant calls antinomy manifests itself in discourse as a contradictory opposition between A and non-
A. For two arguments presented side by side to form a contradictory
opposition, two conditions must be met: first, one judgment has to deny the
other without leaving any remainder behind, that is, without saying any more
than is needed for the contradiction, and second, if one of the propositions
is false, the other one must be true.[36] Here, however, beyond denying the
other each judgment goes on to posit something else toward the other extreme.[37] Since their opposition does not exhaust all possibilities—since it
leaves a remainder behind—each argument is able to prove the falsity of the
other but fails to establish its own truth. Instead of choosing between two
false alternatives, Kant proves that the dilemma is false. "Since, after all, they
can so nicely refute each other—they are disputing about nothing, and . . .
a certain transcendental illusion has painted for them an actuality where
none is to be found."[38] Kant sets out to reveal how this transcendental illusion is formed by showing that what initially presented itself as an analytic
or contradictory opposition is in effect a dialectic or contrary conflict.

Is the world finite or infinite? The dilemma posed by the thesis and the
antithesis taken together presents itself as the disjunction "the world is
either infinite or finite."[39] One is thus forced to choose between two mutually
excluding statements without being allowed to consider any further alternatives. Kant illustrates this illusory binary logic with an empirical example:
"Any body either smells good or smells not good."[40] In this example a body
is insufficiently characterized, since smell (whether good or bad), a contingent condition of bodies, still remains in the counterargument. But is a

body necessarily always characterized by having either good smell or bad smell? In not exhausting all possibilities, in leaving out bodies that do not have any smell, this seemingly unsolvable conflict turns out to be logically imperfect. Why should a body have either good or bad smell? And likewise, why should the world be either infinite or finite? Is the opposition between infinite and finite indeed contradictory, does it exhaust all possibilities? The mathematical antinomy suffers from a similar logical imperfection, because the disjunction it presents about a world described as either finite or infinite does not exhaust all possibilities. In qualifying the world still in terms of its magnitude, just as the thesis does, the counterproposition leaves out a remainder, the possibility that the world may have no magnitude at all (neither finite nor infinite), that the world does not exist.[41] In disputing about the world's magnitude (finite or infinite), both judgments take the world to be an existing thing whose totality one may characterize as if it were an object of experience, rather than an idea of reason. Refusing to submit to a forced choice between an infinite or a finite world, Kant proves the inadmissibility of the premise on which the judgments are based, the world's existence. Since in illegitimately qualifying the world in its totality as an object of experience both arguments turn out to be false, the antinomic conflict in which they were entwined dissolves.

Let us take a closer look at this antinomy's logical failure. At first view, thesis and antithesis appear to form a contradictory opposition, with the negation bearing on the copula: "the world has a beginning," "the world has no beginning." However, closer scrutiny reveals a distinction neglected by the grammar of negation but visually displayed by the typographical disposition of thesis and antithesis side by side, as David-Ménard observes. In effect, the two arguments do not form a contradiction, but rather a dialectic opposition. An antinomy turns out to be not a contradiction (*Widerspruch*) at all, as we were initially led to assume, but rather "a conflict of reason with itself [*Widerstreit*]."[42] Once this becomes clear, all one needs to do is show how the antinomy does not meet the requirements that would make it a contradiction. Again, in a contradictory opposition one judgment should merely contradict the other without saying any more than is required for the contradiction: if one of the judgments is false, the other must be true.[43] To return to the example of bodily smell, a contradictory proposition would read "any body either is good-smelling or is not good-smelling (*vel suaveolens vel non suaveolens*)," thereby including bodies that do not smell at all.[44]

In the case of the world's magnitude, writes Kant, "if I say that, as regards space, either the world is infinite or it is not infinite (*non est infinitus*), then if the first proposition is false, its contradictory opposite, that the world is not infinite, must be true."[45] In limiting the negation to what the contradiction requires by simply stating that the world is not infinite, "I would only annul an infinite world, without positing another world, viz., the finite one."[46] Here the second judgment prevents the conflict from being locked into a binary structure ("either infinite or finite"). In stating that the world "is not infinite (*non est infinitus*),"[47] in simply denying an infinite world without posing a finite one, this second judgment opens up a space for other alternatives it does not specify.[48]

The problem with the antinomy is that beyond simply declaring that the world is not infinite as a contradictory judgment would, it goes on to affirm (in the thesis) that the world is finite, and in so doing it "says something more than is required for contradiction."[49] Here the negation bears on the predicate ("the world is either infinite or finite"), leaving the copula intact ("the world is").[50] The antinomic conflict assumes the world actually *is*, because the attempt to determine the magnitude of the world (whether infinite or finite) presupposes, in other words, the existence of the world. "If one regards the two propositions, that the world is infinite in magnitude and that the world is finite in magnitude, as opposed to each other contradictorily," writes Kant, "then one assumes that the world (the entire series of appearances) is a thing in itself. For [in either proposition] the world remains, whether I annul in the series of its appearances the infinite or the finite regression."[51] So long as the world is considered to exist the conflict is a contradictory one, and one is obliged to choose one of the two alternatives.[52] But since the opposition does not exhaust all possibilities and leaves a remainder behind, the conflict turns out to be dialectic and both statements false.

> But if I said that the world is either infinite or finite (noninfinite), then both of these propositions can be false. For I then regard the world as in itself determined in terms of magnitude, because in the counterproposition I do not merely annul the infinity, and with it perhaps the entire separate existence of the world; rather, I add a determination to the world taken as a thing that is actual in itself, and this may likewise be false, viz., if the world were *not* given *as a thing in itself at all* and hence also not in terms of its magnitude—neither as infinite nor as finite.[53]

In affirming that "the world is either infinite or finite," the opposition ex-cludes other alternatives: i.e., the possibility that the world may be simply not infinite, or, what is more important, the possibility that the world may not be at all, that the object world may simply not exist. The first falsity in this contrary conflict (i.e., assuming that the world is either infinite or finite, thus excluding a merely non-infinite world) leads to a second one, namely, defining the world by its magnitude as if it were an actual thing, thus assuming that the world is, that it exists in itself, as a mere look at the syntax of each opposition demonstrates. In a contradictory opposition, the disjunction bearing on the copula[54]—"*Either the world is* infinite *or it is not* infinite (*non est infinitus*)"[55]—could be read as "either the world is . . . or is not . . . ." In a dialectic conflict, in turn, the disjunction in the predicate— "*the world is either* infinite or finite (non-infinite)"—affirms "the world is . . . ." Here the world remains independently from whether one annuls the finite or infinite regression of reason's presentation of appearances.[56] If we were able to confirm that the world exists, then both judgments would form a contradictory opposition: they could be mutually exclusive and we would be urged to choose between the world's infinitude or finitude.[57] "But if I remove this presupposition—or [i.e.] this transcendental illusion—and deny that the world is a thing in itself, then the contradictory conflict of the two assertions is transformed into a merely dialectical one."[58] Against the illusion that the world is a thing in itself, then, Kant affirms that the world is not, that it "does not exist in itself at all."[59] Given that the conflict was based on an unacceptable assumption, the existence of the world, both as-sertions of the mathematical conflict are revealed to be false: each of them drops out for illegitimately assuming the existence of the world, and the antinomy dissolves.[60]

REASON'S ANTINOMIC RULE

One cannot affirm the world exists, in sum, because what we call world is nothing but a series of presentations. The world does not exist "indepen-dently of the regressive series of my presentations,"[61] as Kant does not tire to insist. However, even though at the end of this passage Kant affirms that "the world is to be met with only in the empirical regression of the series of appearances, but not at all by itself,"[62] he devotes the next section to proving that, in fact, neither the regressive series of my presentations can ever reach the idea of the world.[63] Indeed, the "regressive series of my presentations" can never be completed because its first element, the unconditioned, is not accessible to us. What is ultimately at stake in the antinomic judgments is affirming or denying the existence of an unconditioned, of a limit that will halt regress. That limit that would bound our finite experience and allow us to conceive of an empty beyond, is, however, not possible in the mathematical antinomy where all elements are "homogeneous," subject to the rule of regress. Without the unconditioned, an idea and need of reason but not a reality in the world, reason cannot complete the series and fulfill its illusion that the world exists as a whole. In this sense, the world cannot exist.[64]

So the world cannot exist in a double sense: first, in what concerns its reality, the world as a total object that includes all phenomena cannot be an object of experience, and thus cannot be cognized. Second, in what concerns reason's aspiration to conceive of the world as an "absolute totality in the synthesis of conditions,"[65] the idea of the world fails to cohere as such because reason is unable to complete the series of conditions without an unconditioned element that stops regress and gives the series a closure. If the world as an object of experience is an impossibility, so is the idea of the world.

The way out of the skeptical impasse provoked by the antinomy lies in proving that experience cannot pass judgment about the world's existence. When one claims the world exists, as those who qualify it by its magnitude assume, one takes the world to be an object of experience, an object sensibility can reach. Yet this is impossible, as the antinomic rule of reason teaches us. On the one hand, the conditions of experience stipulate that every conditioned presupposes an endless series of conditions that are linked to each other in a spatial and temporal succession: there is no outside element that could allow us to represent a beginning, no external position from which to conceive the world as totality.[66] On the other, the idea of the world as an all-inclusive whole can only be grasped as a simultaneity, and simultaneity precludes the very successive regression of conditions in the series. "If, therefore, this series is always conditioned, then it is never given wholly; and hence the world is not an unconditioned whole, and thus also does not exist as such a whole . . . ."[67] The rule of successive regression clashes with the simultaneity of completion. Since one cannot grasp a successive regression as a simultaneous totality, the world turns out to be a self-defeating concept, as Joan Copjec points out.[68] The only way to undo the antinomy is to prove that the world cannot be an object of experience, and therefore its existence can neither be affirmed nor denied.[69]

A way of dealing with the incompatible requirements of diachronic regression and the synchronicity of completion that reduce the world to a self-defeating concept is to insist, as Kant does in the following section ("Pure Reason's Regulative Principle Regarding the Cosmological Ideas"),[70] that these requirements do not characterize sensible phenomena but are instead rules of reason. One can begin to understand the antinomy in which reason is entangled by keeping in mind, first, that regress is a rule of reason, not an object of experience or a predicate of things in themselves, and, second, that the principle of absolute totality is null. The rule of regression results from reason's aspiration to encompass the series of phenomena ascending from the conditioned through its nearest and then more remote conditions "upward" to the unconditioned. Spatio-temporal experience, however, only has access to the conditioned and perhaps a few of its conditions, but cannot reach the unconditioned. Only ideas are able to "continu[e] empirical synthesis up of the unconditioned (which is never found in experience but only in the idea)."[71] That is, in fact, what transcendental ideas are, "nothing but categories expanded up to the unconditioned."[72] In its search for totality, the imagination assumes the possibility of an unconditioned that will limit the series by giving it an initiating cause. However, since the appearances theoretical reason organizes are its own presentations, the unconditioned element that would begin the series turns out to be a speculation, a limit reason presupposes but cannot reach. Again, reason's aspiration to form a totality—to achieve a complete synthesis of phenomena—clashes with the rule of regress.

Just like the rule of regress, which is not a constitutive cosmological principle, the principle of totality that clashes with it is an aspiration of reason and not an actual thing: "This absolutely completed synthesis is again only an idea; for we cannot know, at least not in advance whether such a synthesis is indeed possible with appearances."[73] What we envision as the cosmological principle of totality—a principle that would seem to describe nature—is, in effect, not a constitutive, but rather a *regulative* principle of reason.[74] This *rule* of completeness aims not at what is given in itself, at the object or nature, but rather at what we are to do with the regression, that is, at the *concept* of the object: it "cannot tell us *what the object is*, but only *how the empirical regression is to be performed* in order for us to arrive at the complete concept of the object."[75] The mathematical conflict was due to the illusion of absolute totality, an idea only applicable to the empirical objects known by the understanding, but not to reason's presentations, which are always subject to the rule of regress.[76] Since "the cosmological principle of reason is, in fact, a rule that commands us to perform, in the series of conditions of given appearances, a regression that is never permitted to stop at anything absolutely unconditioned,"[77] the problem that dissolves the mathematical antinomy lies in "our attributing . . . objective reality to an idea that serves merely as a rule."[78]

This proves that the world is an impossible concept, a concept that defeats itself.[79] The revelation that totality is just an illusory idea, that forming a whole out of a seemingly endless regression is impossible, undoes the antinomic impasse. Should one conclude, as Kant does regarding the world conceived as a self-contained totality, that such a whole is an impossibility, an illusion produced by attributing objective reality to what is only a rule of reason, that is, by taking something regulative as constitutive? The risk reason runs when it enjoins itself to conceive of the world as an existing totality—that is, as a large-scale and all-inclusive object of knowledge—is taking as constitutive what is only its own rule. Kant's double solution to the mathematical antinomy paves the way from the sterility of dialectic conflict to the positing power of indefinite judgment.

BREAKING DIALECTIC IMPASSE

Once his reader understands that the mathematical impasse lies in "our attributing (by transcendental subreption) objective reality to an idea that serves merely as a rule,"[80] Kant can go ahead and propose two solutions to the problem of the world's magnitude, one negative and one affirmative, aiming at restoring the integrity of theoretical reason. The first, negative solution reiterates the first half of the antithesis, "the world has no first beginning as regards time and no outermost boundary as regards space,"[81] simply denying the finitude declared by the thesis while stopping short of affirming, as does the second part of the antithesis, that the world—that is, the empirical regression in the series of the world's appearances—is infinite. Every conditioned is conditioned, there is no member of the series that escapes the rule of regress. Were one to affirm the world has a first beginning in time and an outermost boundary in space, the other side of that boundary would have to be empty—the world could only be bounded by empty time and empty space.[82] Since the world consists of appearances, we should be able to experience such temporary and spatial void as another object of experience, but according to Kant it is impossible to have an experience empty of content, and so the world must remain empirically unbound, without boundary. Experience does not have access to any limit of phenomena, to an unconditioned phenomenon, and so there can be no limits one can experience in the sensible world.[83] Again, the idea of world cannot become a whole.[84]

But that there is no limit to phenomena does not mean, on the other hand, the world is unlimited, limitless, as Copjec clarifies.[85] The problem with the mathematical antinomic conflict is that the antithesis does something more than simply negate the thesis. Hence Kant's second, affirmative solution: "The regression in the series of the world's appearances, as a determination of the world's magnitude, proceeds *in indefinitum*."[86] Rather than being infinite, the regression through which we present the world's appearances proceeds *indefinitely*, because the possibility of a first cause remains unknown and unreachable (just like when tracing the ascending line of a family, a tracing that proceeds indefinitely, one does not presuppose that the series is infinite, that there is no unconditioned). Nevertheless, that the regression proceeds indefinitely rather than infinitely, that not all phenomena can be known, does not imply there is at least a phenomenon that escapes the rule of regress.[87] This reaffirms the fact that the world is a self-defeating idea, since the indefinite extension of the regressive series of our presentations can never form the whole or totality required by the concept "world."[88]

Kant's affirmative solution thus accomplishes two things. It first insists that the world is a series of appearances, and that all reason can refer to is our presentation of the world (our empirical regression) rather than the world in itself (on whose existence we cannot pronounce), thereby repeating in affirmative terms what the first solution stated negatively (namely, the impossibility to represent a totality). Then, breaking with the impasse created by dialectic oppositions (the world is either finite or infinite, the world can be divided in either finite or infinite parts, as the second antinomy pretends), this second solution reformulates the mathematic conflict in the direction of an indefinite judgment: the world is not finite (but it is not infinite either), it is *indeterminate*. To be more precise, after the negative solution had proved the thesis (the world is finite) to be untrue, the positive solution avoids saying more than is necessary for the contradiction and annuls the conflict by revealing its dialectic form. Reformulated this way, in avoiding saying too much and in not leaving a dialectic remainder behind, this judgment is able to produce a limit: it leaves the subject out of the sphere of the predicate and places it in a space which, according to Kant, is not strictly speaking a sphere, but rather "the bordering of a sphere on the indefinite or bounding itself."[89] Although the production of that bounding effect could already be ascribed to the negative solution, the affirmative one underscores the indeterminacy of what lies beyond the boundary. What the affirmative solution does is replace the impossible premise of an existing world (of finite or infinite magnitude) with the indeterminate magnitude or length of the regression (our presentations have to go back to an indefinite length). It replaces the illegitimate assumption of a thing-in-itself (the world), in other words, with a rule of reason (how far one's thought would have to go back in its attempt to reach the unconditioned). What was initially presented as cosmological magnitude may now be understood as the indefinite expansion of reason's regression in the risky attempt to encompass large-scale and all-inclusive objects such as the "world." The reformulated conflict—the world is not finite (but is not infinite either), it is indeterminate—transfers the antinomic character from the world to the self-contradictory idea of the world: the world is a concept that annihilates itself.

What Kant accomplishes with the solution to the mathematical antinomy, in sum, is revealing the falsity of a binary logic (of the dialectic logic at play in "the world is either finite or infinite") in which each judgment denies the other but cannot prove its own truth. From this dialectic opposition, which consists of two determinate but contrary judgments, Kant's solution moves to two judgments that do not exist in the same space: one judgment says the world is not finite, the other states it is indeterminate. This is the logic Kant attributes to indefinite judgment. In reiterating the first part of the antithesis, Kant denies the existence of any limit to phenomena. In turn, the indefinite toward which the second part of the solution points may have the ability to introduce a limit, and in so doing posit something there where there seemed to be nothing.

ILLEGITIMATE POSITING

Let us now assume we have learned the lesson from the logical failure of the mathematical antinomy. If the world existed, if it were a thing-in-itself, the arguments about it would be contradictorily opposed. But since its existence cannot be affirmed, conflicting judgments concerning the world as appearance are revealed to be in dialectic opposition, and the antinomy dissolves.[90] What are the consequences, though, of forgoing the presupposition that the world exists? If the world cannot be an object of experience, if as Kant's solution teaches us its existence can neither be affirmed nor denied, then how is objectivity formed? Kant's distinction between antinomy and contradiction merits further attention, since it offers valuable insight into other forms of negation that succeed in creating objects of knowledge there where the antinomic conflict failed.

As we know, what Kant calls antinomy is a conflict defined by its difference from contradiction, whose appearance it initially takes. Therefore, the act of revealing the vice hidden in antinomic conflicts would seem to depend on the ability to establish a clear distinction between conflict and contradiction.[91] At first, Kant's explanation "seems to oppose the logical perfection of contradiction, which does not leave any remainder behind, to the imperfection of conflict, which in putting in relationship subject and predicate leaves out one of the conditions of the link between them" (bodies do not necessarily have either good or bad smell, a world is not necessarily described in terms of magnitude—whether finite or infinite—because it is not an actual thing).[92] It may therefore come as a surprise to realize that in fact he does not privilege contradictory opposition over dialectic conflict. If it is true that contradiction is not favored over conflict, then why would the distinction between them gain the momentum it does in this text? The reason why contradiction is present in this analysis at all is that by initially taking the appearance of contradiction the two antinomic propositions force reason into a skeptical impasse: one has to choose, but the choice turns out to be impossible because none of the two arguments can prove its own truth.[93] The fact that the two judgments seem to form a contradictory opposition should be taken as a symptom of reason's conflict with itself.

This does not imply, however, that contradictory judgments should be espoused as a fruitful or desirable way of gauging reason's productivity. The difference between antinomy and contradiction concerns formal logic. An antinomy is a conflict whereas a contradiction is the annulation of one judgment by the other. In those instances of conflict in which logical negation has the ability to posit something, to produce objectivating judgments, this purely logical distinction is linked to a transcendental one. This is, however, not the case with contradiction. Even though a contradiction does not formally drop for falsely presupposing the existence of the world, contradiction has no bearing on the existence of the world. For all the logical rigor of its power to suppress, contradiction lacks the transcendental power to posit anything, to create any knowledge of appearances, because, as David-Ménard puts it, it cannot have "any effect on the logical subjects concerned in the propositions in which it intervenes."[94] Contradictions or analytical oppositions are simply formal and therefore sterile when charged with the task of positing an object to be cognized. Dialectic oppositions, by contrast, have a certain positing power, argues David-Ménard. Even if in the antinomy they drop because each element reveals the falsity of the other without establishing its own truth, their negation "brings into play (in an untimely manner) the existence of the subject (the world) about which the propositions are confronted in an antinomic fashion."[95]

As David-Ménard proposes, in leaving a remainder behind, dialectic oppositions acquire positing power:

> . . . in the counterproposition I do not merely annul the infinity, and with it perhaps the entire separate existence of the world; rather, I add a determination to the world taken as a thing that is actual in itself, and this may likewise be false, viz., if the world were *not* given *as a thing in itself at all* and hence also not in terms of its magnitude—neither as infinite nor as finite. . . . Thus of two dialectically opposed judgments both can be false, because one judgment not merely contradicts the other but says something more than is required for contradiction.[96]

Precisely in saying "something more than is required for contradiction,"[97] in leaving a remainder behind, the conflict about the world excludes that remainder from the jurisdiction of its judgments.[98] The excess produced by dialectic negation is, as David-Ménard indicates, "nothing else than the transcendental, that is, the logical in a redefined sense that can apprehend an existence instead of being simply formal."[99] While the empirical example of smell left out a contingent condition of bodies, what the dialectic opposition leaves out is no less than the existence of its logical subject, the world.[100] Even though the dialectic conflict mistakenly presupposes the world has magnitude, it brings into play the world's existence, albeit illegitimately: "I add a determination to the world taken as a thing that is actual in itself, and this may likewise be false."[101] Nevertheless, the existence of their subject remains beyond the reach of both judgments because existence is something reason can neither confirm nor deny. What antinomic negation leaves outside its jurisdiction is the very existence of the world.[102]

We should not forget, however, that if the antinomic conflict leaves existence outside itself, it is precisely because it had illegitimately brought in existence in the first place. Hence, in mistakenly qualifying the world as an actual thing, dialectic opposition introduces the modality of existence *chaotically*, suggests David-Ménard.[103] Significantly, she notes, there is in this section (section 7 of "The Antinomy of Pure Reason," titled "Critical Decision of the Cosmological Dispute that Reason Has with Itself") a relative degree of inconsistency that may be detected from its very first statement. "The entire antinomy of pure reason rests on this dialectical argument: If the conditioned is given, then the entire series of all its conditions is also given; now objects of the senses are given to us as conditioned; consequently, etc."[104] Kant's text envisions the world at one time as a purely logical category ("if the conditioned is given, then the entire series of all its conditions is also given") and at the next as an empirical one ("objects of the senses are given to us as conditioned"). This oscillation in approaching the category of existence first through a rule of reason, then as an empirical category, is replicated by a certain instability in the sense of the term "conflict," which shifts several times in only two pages.[105] "Conflict" initially denominates the "relationship of reason with itself in the antinomy," which nevertheless takes up the appearance of a contradiction. Once the conflictual character of the opposition is revealed, "conflict" names a non-contradictory opposition that presupposes through negation the existence of its subject, the world—precisely what the antinomy turns out to be. This first logical distinction between conflict and contradiction, one defined by the sphere—copula or predicate—on which negation exerts its impact, is soon reformulated as the difference between dialectic opposition and analytic opposition, a pair that initially coincides with the logical pair conflict and contradiction.[106] Despite this initial coincidence between dialectic opposition and conflict, on one side, and analytic opposition and contradiction, on the other, Kant leaves aside this merely logical distinction by indicating that a contradiction concerning the notion of the world may be considered to be either analytic or dialectic.[107]

Kant's reader may initially be inclined to conclude that the stakes in differentiating a dialectic opposition from an analytical one are high, since on this distinction would seem to depend the deconstruction of the antinomy. However, as I anticipated above, he does not accord any privilege to analytic opposition. In fact, this passage ultimately suspends any substantial difference between dialectic and analytic opposition by making this distinction depend on the context, either metaphysical or critical, in which it appears:[108]

> If one regards the two propositions, that the world is infinite in magnitude and that the world is finite in magnitude, as opposed to each other contradictorily, then one assumes that the world (the entire series of appearances) is a thing in itself. For [in either proposition] the world remains, whether I annul in the series of its appearances the infinite or the finite regression. But if I remove this presupposition—or this transcendental illusion—and deny that the world is a thing in itself, then the contradictory conflict of the two assertions is transformed into a merely dialectical one.[109]

Whether one envisions the antinomy as an analytic or as a dialectic opposition depends on whether one adopts a metaphysical perspective or undertakes a critical or transcendental examination of rational propositions, as Kant himself does in his unraveling of the mathematical antinomy.[110] By exposing the failure of dialectic opposition and the inability of analytic opposition to posit anything, the antinomy dispels the illusion that our finite experience can ever produce the large-scale object of knowledge world. Even though the antinomy fails (it turns out to be a dispute "about *nothing*"),[111] the failure of reason clears the space for the understanding to introduce the constraints that make it possible to cognize *something*. The understanding can constitute objects of cognition precisely through the forms of negation that effectively introduce a boundary: real opposition in epistemology and indefinite judgment in logic.[112]

THE POWER OF NEGATION

The antinomy's failure to reach the all-inclusive object of knowledge "world" results from taking a thing-in-itself, a thing that can only be thought, for something that can be experienced and known. David-Ménard proposes we should understand this failure of dialectic conflict as the negative side of the success of indefinite judgment in logic and real opposition or real conflict (a negation determining a reality) in epistemology. I follow David-Ménard's argument closely, going back to the production of objects by the understanding and to logic, so as to prepare the transition from the failure of the mathematical antinomy to the contingent bounding I will attribute to the transcendental idea of freedom in the next chapter. Unlike dialectic conflict, real opposition succeeds in enabling the understanding to determine the existence of smaller objects of experience. The connection between dialectic conflict in logic (*dialektischer Widerstreit*) and real conflict in epistemology (*realer Widerstreit*) is signaled in Kant's *Critique* by his use of the relatively infrequent term *Widerstreit* to refer to both, as David-Ménard observes.[113] The relationship between dialectic and real conflict is, however, an inverse one. Antinomic conflict, which illicitly makes its propositions pass for knowledge about the world, functions as the negative proof of what real conflict accomplishes: its determining negation characterizes empirical objects the understanding can cognize.[114] Therefore, taking into account the proximity of dialectic conflict to real conflict (in epistemology) and to indefinite judgment (in logic) may prove fruitful, especially given that such proximity happens by contrast. Unlike the rigorous exclusion realized by indefinite judgment, dialectic exclusion is surreptitious, as has become clear in Kant's explanation of the mathematical antinomy. As compared to the constitutive function of real conflict, dialectic conflict leaves behind itself a remainder that approaches epistemological constitution only in negative terms. In disputing about the finitude or infinitude of the world, reason in the antinomy disputes about forms (space and time) only applicable to appearances. When the task at hand is exploring how the understanding determines existing objects through negation, disputing about appearances—which amount to nothing when existence is at stake—leads to a dead end.

For it is through the power of negation that the understanding determines the existence of objects (*das Dasein der Gegenstände*).[115] This claim, which underlies the entire first *Critique*, dates from a paradoxical discovery Kant made in his 1763 essay "Attempt to Introduce the Concept of Negative Magnitudes into Philosophy." What allows the understanding to determine a reality and constitute objects of knowledge (beyond simply positing the concept of an object that transcends the limits of our experience) is a real opposition between two equal forces whose consequences cancel each other. Kant's paradoxical discovery is that this determination of an existence never appears so clearly as when its conceptual instrument is a negative magnitude. Kant refers to this suspension of movement produced as a consequence of the antagonism between two opposing forces as *nihil privativum*, a nothingness of privation that must be differentiated from *nihil negativum*, the nothingness of an empty notion that can never be filled with experienced content, such as that of the antinomic object world.[116] Real opposition functions, in other words, as a positive counterpoint to the illegitimate assumption of the world's existence that makes the dialectic conflict fail, and of which the antinomy offers negative proof.[117] The two effects that cancel each other in real opposition—a moment in the determination of a reality—take place in the physical world, something Gottfried Wilhelm von Leibniz and Baron Christian von Wolff did not fail to see. What Kant critiques is that they fail to recognize the crucial consequences of real opposition for philosophical thought: negation loses its metaphysical pretension and reality is determined as phenomenal, both in physics and in morality.[118] We recall that the antinomy appeared as an analytical opposition (that is, as the opposition of two contradictory predicates of a subject, the world, considered as an existing thing in itself) from a metaphysical perspective. Its dialectic nature is unveiled from the critical perspective Kant takes, a perspective that reveals the world's existence to be an illusion. Although regarding real conflict, in turn, the mutual neutralization of two forces in mechanics is a phenomenon independent from any critique of reason, real opposition receives its rational status precisely from its inverse relation to analytical opposition (which proves sterile) and dialectic opposition (which fails).[119] Kant devotes so much attention to them because in offering negative proof of the success of real opposition they confer on it rational status. But there is another reason why dialectic and analytic opposition deserve the attention I am according them here with David-Ménard by following her reading closely. The better we can recognize the unproductive exclusion they generate, the better we can differentiate them from the rigorous and productive exclusion performed by indefinite judgment.

In order, however, for real conflict to take place, the two forces that neutralize each other and produce a reality must share a common ground, as do, for instance, the positive and negative poles in a magnetic field. Despite its productivity and the occasion it gives the understanding to determine existence, epistemological negation in real opposition cannot produce all kinds of objects, only those objects in which the two parties in relationship share a common ground. Real opposition cannot describe, for example, the relationships that constitute ethical subjectivity, or the social antagonisms that articulate society. Restricted to opposing poles that share a common ground, real opposition, though epistemological, can have no bearing on the real antagonism created between two opposing social forces that belong in different spaces. It cannot express, either, the conflict between two dimensions that do not share a common ground such as Kant's phenomenal and intelligible realms. Therefore, at the moment of explaining the relationship pure reason establishes between the empirical and the noumenal, between nature and freedom, we need to turn to the fruitful form of logical negation called indefinite judgment. In contrast with the sterility of dialectic and analytic oppositions, indefinite judgment has the transcendental power to open up a space for other objects, as Kant affirms in the *Logic*.[120] What form does that positing power in indefinite judgment take?

Indefinite judgment must be distinguished from other forms of logical negation, but also from any simply affirmative or negative statement. In an affirmative judgment, writes Kant in the *Logic*, "the subject is thought of under the sphere of a predicate; it, in a negative, is placed without the sphere; and, in an indefinite, put within the sphere of a conception, which lies without the sphere of another conception."[121] Unlike affirmative propositions whose copula affirms a predicate ("the soul *is* mortal," to take Kant's example) or negative propositions whose copula denies it ("the soul is *not* mortal"), the copula of indefinite judgments affirms a negative predicate: "the soul is *non*-mortal" (or the soul is not-mortal). Or, as Kant puts it, "in negative judgments the negation always affects the copula; in indefinite, not the copula, but the predicate is affected by it."[122] In affirming a negative predicate, indefinite judgment can determine the boundaries between subject and predicate more rigorously than negative judgment.[123] If we say, for example, "the universe as a totality (the thing in itself) is non-phenomenal, not an object of experience," we are not simply denying its phenomenality as the expression "it is not phenomenal" would. By simply denying the phenomenality of the thing in itself, we would be limiting all phenomena to particularities, thus making a positive claim on something on which we cannot pronounce. In affirming "the world is non-phenomenal," in turn, indefinite judgment does not simply deny something, since in so doing it would be making a positive claim. Rather, it excludes the world from the realm of appearances without pronouncing about its existence. What indefinite judgment does, in sum, is introduce a boundary and inscribe its subject (here, the world) in an unspecified void beyond that boundary.

In affirming a negative predicate, indefinite judgment simply restricts the jurisdiction of its subject and makes explicit its limitation. In Kant's own words, "The indefinite judgment shows not only that a subject is not contained under the sphere of a predicate, but that it lies without its sphere somewhere in the indefinite sphere; this judgment therefore represents the sphere of the predicate as limited."[124] Indefinite judgment excludes the subject from the sphere of the predicate; it transfers it to a sphere outside the predicate, which, as Kant clarifies, "is not a sphere at all, but the bordering of a sphere on the indefinite or bounding itself."[125] It is precisely by introducing a limit that indefinite judgment acquires transcendental power. "Though the exclusion is a negation," adds Kant, "the limitation of a conception is a positive operation. Hence are bounds positive conceptions of limited objects."[126] In inscribing objects that cannot be experienced in an unspecified void beyond, those objects are posited conceptually. The function of exclusion effected by indefinite judgment creates the conceptual world of objects for the understanding. In this sense, David-Ménard is right to consider indefinite judgment to be, "in the logical-formal sphere, the space of manifestation of the transcendental."[127] The logically rigorous limitation this type of judgment performs opens up an empty space beyond in which to locate noumena.

BOUNDARY CONCEPTS

Kant explains the notion of noumenon at the end of the Analytic of Pure Reason. In 1787 he adds a crucial remark in order to differentiate from the positive and illegitimate meaning of "noumenon" a negative and legitimate sense. In the positive sense a noumenon is "an object of nonsensible intuition." In the negative meaning, noumenon is, in turn, "a thing insofar as it is not an object of sensible intuition."[128] A superficial look at the grammar should not deceive us: the former is a negative judgment, whereas the latter works in the direction of indefinite judgment.[129] This distinction constitutes one of the most significant instances of what separates the illegitimate productivity of negative judgment and the legitimate transcendental power of indefinite judgment. In excluding noumena from the reach of sensible intuition and thus opening up for them an empty space beyond the empirical, indefinite judgments perform a bounding negation.

Let us first consider noumenon in the positive sense. The definition of noumenon as "an object of nonsensible intuition" assumes the existence of a special form of intuition that "is not ours" and into which we have no insight, since the only form of intuition we know is sensible.[130] Although the goal of this negative judgment is to differentiate noumenon from phenomenon, its subject, noumenon, is still qualified, just like a phenomenon, as an object of intuition, even if nonsensible. We are not acquainted, however, with any form of intuition which is not empirical, as Kant does not tire to insist. In conceiving of noumenon as object of nonsensible intuition, this judgment attaches to noumenon a predicate that still qualifies it in terms of intuition: something sensible (intuition) still defines the link between subject and predicate, as well as between noumenon and phenomenon. In so doing (rather than in simply affirming a negative predicate), the negation leaves a remainder behind. In qualifying the link between the subject and the predicate it puts in relationship in terms of intuition, this negative judgment illicitly presupposes that the subject, noumenon, has a positive status.

The positive use of noumenal objects by theoretical reason consists in assuming they are objective. This illicit objectification of noumena is done by applying to them the forms of intuition (space and time) and categories of the understanding, as does the mathematical antinomy. Noumenal ideas are illegitimately presupposed, furthermore, when reason extends its presentation of appearances in a regressive series of such a length that it must seek a thing-in-itself beyond experience in which to anchor the chain. This second positive use also assumes the unconditioned is available to experience (as the thesis of the mathematical antinomy does), rather than simply a need of reason. As I noted earlier, Kant strikes down these two uses in the solution of the mathematical antinomy. As soon as the judgments envisioning the world in terms of magnitude or divisibility are revealed to be in dialectic opposition, the antinomy drops. Kant's reformulation of the conflict first denies there is an unconditioned element where the regression of reason's presentations might stop, and then affirms that reason's presentations would have to regress to an indeterminate (rather than infinite) length.

What, then, is the negative sense in which noumenon can be legitimately used? "If, by abstracting from our way of intuiting a thing, we mean by noumenon a thing *insofar as it is not an object of our sensible intuition*, then this is a noumenon in the *negative* meaning of the term."[131] A noumenon is a "being of the understanding" of which sensible intuition lacks any reference. It is an object we can think but not experience. But unlike the positive and illicit use traditional metaphysics makes of these notions, noumenal things may be signified negatively as something to which our concepts of understanding do not extend.[132] The concept of noumenon is therefore a problematic one.

> And inasmuch as the understanding warns sensibility not to claim to deal with things in themselves but solely with appearances, it does think an object in itself [*Gegenstand an sich selbst*]. But the understanding thinks it only as transcendental object [*nur als transzendentales Objekt*]. This object is the cause of appearance (hence is not itself appearance) and can be thought neither as magnitude nor as reality nor as substance, etc. (because these concepts always require sensible forms wherein they determine an object [*Gegenstand*]).[133]

Noumenon is an "object in itself" on whose existence we cannot pronounce. We can only signify this type of object negatively, through sequences of negative phrases: "not itself an appearance," a noumenal object "can be thought neither as magnitude nor as reality nor as substance . . . . Hence concerning this object we are completely ignorant as to whether it is to be found in us—or, for that matter, outside us . . . ."[134] The positive status of the thing, as it was intimated by the positive definition of noumenon, is here suspended.

> If we want to call this object noumenon, because the presentation of it is not sensible, then we are free to do so. But since we cannot apply to it any of our concepts of understanding, the presentation yet remains empty for us, and does not serve for anything but to mark the bounds of our sensible cognition and to leave us with room that we can fill neither through possible experience nor through pure understanding.[135]

As a problematic concept that does not posit anything, noumenon nevertheless functions in a productive way. With it "the understanding limits sensibility, but without therefore expanding its own realm."[136] By means of this limitation the understanding opens the possibility that there may be "room" for "more and different objects" to which the validity of sensible cognition does not reach, objects we can neither determine nor deny which the understanding must locate in a space outside the reach of sensible cognition.[137]

> We can say, viz., that because sensible intuition does not deal with all things without distinction, there remains room for more and different objects, and that therefore such objects cannot be absolutely denied; but that in the absence of a determinate concept [of such objects] (since no category is suitable for this) they also cannot be asserted as objects for our understanding.[138]

The fact that sensible intuition "does not deal with all things"[139] allows the understanding to prepare "room" for those potentially remaining "things"[140] (noumena), a "range outside the sphere of appearances"[141] that serves to bound the realm of things sensible intuition does "deal with." What matters here is not the problematic "different objects," but rather the "room" or space we open for them.

We are already acquainted with the productivity of introducing a boundary, an operation we encountered in the form of negation realized by indefinite judgment. In fact, Kant's own definition of a noumenon is itself, we should note, an indefinite judgment: "a thing insofar as it is not an object of our sensible intuition." Noumena are objects of indefinite judgment and they operate as such, as is made evident by Kant's 1787 explanation of what the understanding achieves through them.[142] Significantly, this explanation resonates with the definition of indefinite judgment he offers in the *Logic* (1800):

> Yet, in the end, we can have no insight at all into the possibility of such noumena, and the range outside the sphere of appearances is (for us) empty. I.e., we have an understanding that problematically extends further than this sphere . . . . The concept of noumenon is, therefore, only a *boundary concept* serving to limit the pretension of sensibility, and hence is only of negative use. But it is nonetheless not arbitrarily invented; rather, it coheres with the limitation of sensibility, yet without being able to posit anything positive outside sensibility's range.[143]

We should think of noumena as "boundary concepts" that "limit the pretension of sensibility." A noumenon functions as a limit that bounds the sensible sphere by opening a space beyond it, "the range outside the sphere of appearances" which "is (for us) empty." Regarding this void place beyond, and contrary to what one may assume, the emptiness of the space in which the understanding locates noumena does not necessarily qualify the noumenon itself. What emptiness qualifies, as David-Ménard observes, is the *relationship* of the concept of a noumenal object to sensible intuition.[144] It is true that a noumenon can only be signified negatively and problematically as a concept devoid of an intuited object. But precisely because we cannot affirm anything of its object, we cannot qualify it at all, not even in terms of its nothingness, for "we cannot think of any way in which such objects might be given; and the problematic thought which yet leaves open a place for them serves only, like an empty space, to limit the empirical principles, but without containing or displaying any other object of cognition outside the sphere of these principles."[145] That a noumenon can only be signified negatively means that the understanding can only envision it problematically, in the form of an empty place beyond.[146]

It would be inaccurate to affirm, then, that a noumenon is an absolute nothing because we cannot attach any predicate to it; "the only possible determination of it," writes David-Ménard, "is the empty place that thought attributes to it, and which only makes sense in relation to a limit."[147] This empty space is (to quote, again, Kant's *Logic*) a "bordering of a sphere on the indefinite or bounding itself."[148] Thus does the sphere of sensibility emerge positively as a full place on account of the exclusion and therefore the limitation produced by noumenal negativity ("not an object of our sensible intuition"). This indefinite negation extends, in other words, to the two terms separated by the limit: on the one hand it makes of noumenon an excluded and thus negative being that the understanding places in an empty place beyond, "but without therefore expanding its own realm." On the other, the indefinite negation limits and bounds the phenomenal field, giving it empirical reality. "Though the exclusion is negation, the limitation of a conception is a positive operation. Hence are bounds positive conceptions of limited objects."[149] By means of limitation, the sphere of empirical objects and of principles of the understanding acquires positive consistency and coheres as such. This is why Kant insists that the concept of noumenon "is not arbitrarily invented; rather, it coheres with the limitation of sensibility, yet without being able to posit anything positive outside sensibility's range."[150]

Above I pointed out that the problem in the mathematical antinomy lies in our theoretical aspiration to conceive the world as an all-inclusive whole. One could envision, however, a way out of the aspiration to absolute completeness by way of exploring the transcendental power of exclusion as suggested by logic: the transcendental power of logical conflict when examined in terms of indefinite judgment, as Kant's second, affirmative solution to the mathematical antinomy suggests.

The antinomy teaches us what kind of wholes we may not aspire to form: neither total objects unavailable to experience and determined by categories that are only applicable to experience (such as magnitude in the first antinomy or divisibility in the second); nor a self-contained unconditioned totality produced by linking the contingent (what would constitute that totality) with the necessary (a guarantee that lies completely outside, which in addition to being heterogeneous to the elements within the whole it constitutes is unrelated to them) (fourth antinomy). The whole we may aspire to form would be what in the next chapter, on the third antinomy, I will describe aporetically as a contingent whole in progress.

2

UNCONDITIONED SUBJECTIVITY

Pure trace of a "wandering cause," inscribed in me.
—EMMANUEL LEVINAS, *OTHERWISE THAN BEING, OR BEYOND ESSENCE*

Solely the concept of freedom permits us to find the unconditioned and intelligible for the conditioned and sensible without needing to go outside ourselves.
—IMMANUEL KANT, *CRITIQUE OF PRACTICAL REASON*

Kant's introduction of freedom in the third antinomy of pure reason is momentous.[1] In this antinomy reason famously rehearses the tension between freedom and determinism, between spontaneity and receptivity, and thus the paradox whereby the thinking I of transcendental apperception must present itself as a passive empirical consciousness subjected to natural causality. If we compare this first dynamic conflict with the mathematical failure to form the idea of the world, here reason succeeds in forming a synthesis of causal linkage. And unlike the fourth antinomy, whose synthesis presupposes the transcendent idea of a necessary being unrelated to the empirical world, the third antinomy manages to form a dynamic system immanently, without having to presuppose a transcendent outside. Even if we did not take into account the obstacle Kant's explanation of this antinomy removes for reason's practical use by proving freedom is a non-contradictory idea, what theoretical reason accomplishes here without trespassing its bounds is immense.

But Kant's solution to the third antinomy has usually been considered to trespass reason's bounds. After all, should the transcendental idea of freedom not follow the same critical fate as the ideas of the soul, the world, and God, and be declared illusory? Indeed, the synthesis achieved here could be deemed to be transcendent rather than immanent, and it traditionally has. Kant's explicit solution relegates the idea of freedom to a subject's intelligible mode of thinking, while attributing the sole existence of natural causality to sensible experience as manifested to the subject's empirical consciousness or inner sense. By attributing thesis and antithesis to two different standpoints, one intelligible, the other empirical, Kant claims to have annulled the antithetical conflict and thereby achieved his stated goal: proving that the coexistence of natural causality with a causality through freedom is at least a non-contradictory idea. But the insights into causality afforded by Kant's explanation of the third antinomy reach beyond the goals his explicit solution aims to meet. Revealing the possibilities Kant's thinking opens up here, as I propose to do in this chapter, will require following the impulse of his argument closely, pursuing what it presupposes and accomplishes beyond what it claims to achieve.

What different conditions does thinking meet in this first dynamic conflict for reason even to entertain any possibility of success? Appreciating reason's ability to form a synthesis here depends on acknowledging the role in Kant's argument of a subject that does not simply coincide with the I of transcendental apperception (spontaneity) and the empirical consciousness or inner sense (receptivity) to which he refers elsewhere in the first *Critique*.[2] This subject should not be envisioned as a standpoint—whether intelligible or empirical, as Kant's explicit solution would have it—but rather as the site of the relationship between the series and its outside. For the sake of conciseness we may call it unconditioned subjectivity, clarifying from the outset that subjectivity in this sense names a structural position that plays an exceptional role in the series, rather than a substantial being or event. This operation we just called unconditioned subjectivity has the potential to introduce in the series fleeting moments of anchoring, and thus contingent effects of closure that open up new and fruitful ways of understanding synthesis. The immanent synthesis of causality forming here would crystalize as a dynamic system which is not stable or self-contained, but rather contingent and in progress.

The third antinomy's potential to form this dynamic system is underscored (and not undermined) by the lessons on reason's ability to form wholes the other antinomies afford us. From the mathematical failure we learn that reason's aspiration to form the idea of a world that includes all phenomena—or of any all-encompassing and self-contained totality—invariably fails. The fourth antinomy alerts us, in turn, to the different risk reason runs when it conceives of all phenomena as a totality enabled by a transcendent outside: it poses a necessary being (such as the idea of God) that may be imagined as the necessary ground of all contingent events in the world. Since this necessary being, an "*ens extramundanum*,"[3] would be thought as lying completely outside, unrelated to the worldly events reason expects it to anchor, it remains a mere speculation.[4]

It may be possible, however, to imagine a synthesis not aiming to produce an absolute whole (unconditioned, necessary, or self-contained). This is the possibility the third antinomy opens up by privileging relationality over absolute completeness, by favoring an ongoing configuration over a stable one. The third antinomy seeks to explain how all effects are linked to their causes and derive through synthesis a "nature," a dynamic system of causally-linked events. Its thesis includes an exceptional element, a condition whose effects may be perceived in the empirical world, but which itself does not have a cause: it is unconditioned. The name Kant gives this unique element is freedom. By adding freedom to natural necessity the third antinomy introduces an unconditioned or empirically uncaused cause.[5] Its thesis—"The causality according to laws of nature is not the only causality, from which the appearances of the world can thus one and all be derived. In order to explain these appearances, it is necessary to assume also a causality through freedom"[6]—is, according to Kant, only apparently contradicted by the antithesis: "There is no freedom, but everything in the world occurs solely according to laws of nature."[7] Freedom may be envisioned as a cause whose effects reverberate in the series of causally linked phenomena, an exceptionally uncaused cause Kant refers to as the "sensibly unconditioned condition of appearances."[8] By introducing this unconditioned cause, reason in the third antinomy supplements natural necessity with a different causality one may imagine to originate outside the phenomenal series.[9]

As our exploration proceeds we will need to keep in mind that the term "unconditioned" names a structural position that plays a special role in the series, rather than a substantial or essential event. We may understand the term "unconditioned cause" as a relational concept. The unconditioned lies at once inside and outside the series: it is a member of the series whose cause, if by analogy one were to imagine one, would lie outside.[10] In lying at once inside and outside, at the boundary, the unconditioned establishes a relationship between two heterogeneous and otherwise unconnectable spaces. One of them, the phenomenal series, consists in sequences of worldly things and events linked to each other as cause and effect. These sequences result from the imagination's figurative synthesis of apparitions in time. The other *space*, what reason thinks of as the intelligible realm of freedom, does not appear (it does not affect our senses), and therefore does not belong in the temporality of experience. Theoretical reason may only imagine it as an empty *space* beyond phenomena. "Freedom" functions here as a noumenon in the negative legitimate use Kant attributes to this type of idea: one that opens a "range outside the sphere of appearances" which "is (for us) empty."[11] Only in this negative use may noumenon function legitimately as a "*boundary concept* serving to limit the pretension of sensibility."[12] The unconditioned thus relates the sensible series with its outside,[13] an empty *space* that matters primarily insofar as it introduces a boundary. In supplying an uncaused cause that begins its own series of conditions, the causality through freedom inserted by the thesis has the potential temporarily to anchor the series by introducing fleeting moments of closure. As the unconditioned fleetingly anchors the series, it allows causality to crystalize as a system, as a contingent whole or, better, a *whole in progress*. As will soon become clear, the boundary introduced by freedom does not function like an external guarantee that allows reason to reach a total and stable object. Rather, in punctuating the series with fleeting moments of closure, it enables an unending interplay between stability and instability.

But even if one could prove freedom is not a contradictory idea (Kant's goal here), what would enable the unconditioned to play the function of *initiating* cause that provisionally bounds the causal chain? What makes the unconditioned conceivable is the singular role Kant assigns the subject. Freedom can be simultaneously inside and outside the causal series, he intimates, because freedom is *in* the subject. Even though the subject itself has no access to freedom, it can introduce the effects of freedom in the world. A member of natural causality, the subject is also related to the intelligible as the unwitting *bearer* of freedom. The intelligible, for Kant, is, as we just said, an empty space beyond what can be thought. More simply put, the intelligible is *other to thought*. What constitutes the subject, which Kant had defined so far as a phenomenon of nature (empirical consciousness or inner sense), is therefore its exceptional relationship with the other to thought, with that outside.

In this chapter I propose that the role of the unconditioned is played by none other than the subject. The subject's intervention in the series should be understood in this theoretical context as a structural operation rather than as any willed action of a human agent. We may say that as bearer of freedom (if a causality through freedom were to exist) the subject plays the role of the unconditioned. The subject may be imagined to take the position of the unconditioned or initiating cause. By unwittingly taking the place of the unconditioned, the subject would be the element in the series that exceptionally introduces a boundary, a fleeting moment of closure: the subject allows the series to cohere (to become whole) contingently and retroactively. Only in this precarious way may reason in the third antinomy be considered to achieve a sense of completion. Unconditioned subjectivity would name the boundary and relationship that anchor the phenomenal series time and again.

DYNAMICALLY UNCONDITIONED

In the mathematical antinomy, we recall, reason fails to form the idea of a self-contained world—a world that would include all phenomena—qualified in terms of magnitude and divisibility. In the first place, the world is not an objective reality existing out there that experience could reach, but rather a series of appearances that does not exist "independently of the regressive series of my presentations."[14] What we call world turns out to be just the way we imagine a world we cannot cognize. But in fact, not even the imagination can make the idea of a world cohere. Even if we were fully aware that the opposing judgments about the world's finite or infinite magnitude and divisibility do not refer to a thing in itself (the object "world") but rather to reason's presentations, the world still cannot cohere as an idea. The illicit assumptions of its thesis and antithesis make the first antinomy drop not only because the totality we call world does not exist (theoretical reason cannot pronounce on its existence because the world cannot become an object of experience). Reason, furthermore, caught in the contradictory requirement to refer a seemingly endless regression of (successive) apparitions to the (simultaneous) unity of an object, cannot even form the idea of the world. Thus, according to Kant's second solution to the first antinomy, the world is not finite (but is not infinite either), it is indeterminate. Refusing to pronounce on the existence or non-existence of an objective world, Kant's affirmative solution reminds us instead that reason is regulative, not constitutive. In trying to form the idea of the world reason's presentations would have to regress indefinitely in search for an unconditioned condition reason presupposes but cannot reach.[15]

This mathematical failure could lead us to surmise that the dynamic antinomy's aspiration to explain how all effects are linked to their causes is bound to fail too. This time, however, Kant suggests that the two propositions in conflict may be true from different perspectives. Now, he writes, "in the dynamical antinomy, perhaps there occurs a presupposition that can coexist with reason's pretension" and "the conflict can be *settled* to the satisfaction of both parties."[16] What the explanation of the dynamic antinomy sets out to prove is precisely this, that here reason succeeds in forming a synthesis of causal linkage "from which the appearances of the world can thus one and all be derived."[17] But what allows Kant to argue that the dynamic antinomy succeeds in forming a synthesis the mathematical antinomy had failed to achieve? Can reason indeed manage to form a synthesis of causal linkage? Part of the answer lies in the different nature of a mathematical and a dynamic whole. The mathematical antinomy aims to find an existing substantial universe that encompasses the total sum of phenomena, to which reason applies the empirical categories of magnitude and divisibility as if that whole were something one could experience. The third antinomy, in turn, seeks to link events to their causes. Since a synthesis of causal linkage would require an unconditioned cause, here the category of causality, which applies only to phenomena, is allowed a transcendental use that extends to an empty space opening up beyond experience.[18] The fourth antinomy, finally, aspires to refer the contingent existence of substance (that is, phenomenal existence) back to necessary existence. Reason's concern here is therefore not "unconditioned causality," but rather "the unconditioned existence of substance itself,"[19] a unity to which it can only tend by analogy with the unity through a concept the understanding imposes on experience. Thus, in its attempt to link contingent substance to a necessary being, reason frames a concept of the latter "through pure concepts of things as such," and, in so doing, ventures "the first step outside the world of sense."[20]

In consonance with the different kind of whole they seek to form, then, the mathematical and dynamic ways of understanding the configuration of the series are asymmetrical. Unlike the mathematical antinomies, the dynamic ones are allowed to conceive of an outside. If in the mathematical antinomy reason was limited to series of homogeneous and subordinated presentations, "the dynamical series of sensible conditions . . . does also admit of a heterogeneous condition that is not part of the series but, *as merely intelligible*, lies outside the series."[21] A dynamic conflict is thus characterized by the heterogeneity of one of its elements. From a logical viewpoint, what confers on the dynamic synthesis the potential to succeed is the fact that all conditioned elements and their condition are no longer members of the same space. At least one element, the unconditioned, belongs in a different realm (if we may call it so), because its condition (if by analogy we were to imagine it) lies outside the series, and so absolves itself from the rule of regress. "Outside" is how Kant refers to the heterogeneous space in which reason in the third antinomy would locate what it imagines as the missing cause of the unconditioned, freedom's causality.[22] But how that "outside" functions in relationship to the series varies from the third antinomy to the fourth. The theses of both dynamic antinomies, we said, introduce an unconditioned element that is heterogeneous to the series, "other." But in the fourth antinomy, which seeks to link the contingent with the necessary,[23]

> this way of laying an unconditioned existence at the basis of appearances would thus differ from the empirically unconditioned causality (freedom) treated in the previous item. For in the case of freedom the thing itself, as cause (*substantia phaenomenon*), belonged nonetheless in the series of conditions, and only its *causality* was thought as intelligible. Here, on the other hand, the necessary being would have to be thought as entirely outside the series of the world of sense (as *ens extramundanum*) and as merely intelligible; for only thereby can one prevent that this being itself is subjected to the law of the contingency and dependence of all appearances.[24]

Although the fourth antinomy also introduces the possibility of an outside element, the unconditioned here is fully heterogeneous, unrelated to the series, completely outside.[25] The problem with the fourth antinomy is that "as soon as we posit the unconditioned . . . outside all possible experience, the ideas become *transcendent*."[26] Precisely because the fourth antinomy aspires "to look for an intelligible object with which this contingency will cease,"[27] the "necessary being" added by its thesis and negated by its antithesis is "merely a thought entity,"[28] a speculation with no bearing on the world.

The third antinomy, in turn, introduces an unconditioned or uncaused cause (what a perspective that ignores retroaction would imagine as a *first* cause) as an exceptional member of the series. The first judgment makes the intelligible conceivable without necessarily qualifying it as unrelated or as absolutely exterior to the phenomenal world (as the solution of the fourth antinomy will). It does so by supplementing the sensible series with an unconditioned element—a free cause, a beginning by itself[29]—whose cause is intelligible. This exceptionally unconditioned element establishes a relationship between the series and its outside. Though the *initiating* condition (the unconditioned) and its series of effects are still sensible, empirical, the causality that would produce that initial condition (if one were to assign to it a "preceding" causality) can only be imagined as absent from the chain (as missing), as "outside." What reason locates outside here, in other words, is not the unconditioned condition itself (an initiating or free cause, an act of freedom), but rather what it imagines as its absent, intelligible cause.[30] "But such an intelligible cause is not, as regards its causality, determined by appearances . . . . Hence this cause, along with its causality, is outside the series of empirical conditions, whereas its effects are encountered within the series."[31] We do not have access to freedom's intelligible causality, only to its effects as they manifest themselves in the sensible world. The unconditioned that initiates the series is therefore the "sensibly unconditioned condition of appearances,"[32] a condition reason envisions as lacking a previous cause (and thus as having an intelligible cause) that establishes a relationship with the series' outside.[33] Unlike the fourth antinomy, which introduces a transcendent necessary being, the third antinomy is the antinomy of immanence.

Because the unconditioned is related both to the series of appearances and to the intelligible that lies outside, the third antinomy offers unprecedented insight into causality, as we will soon see. Indeed, this dynamic conflict provides a meeting place for the two uses of pure reason, theoretical and practical, while staying within the bounds of theoretical thought. The unconditioned as it is imagined in the third antinomy has dramatic theoretical and practical consequences. Theoretically, the presence of the unconditioned in the series allows reason to arrange discrete phenomena in a synthesis of causal linkage. As I propose in this chapter, however, this dynamic synthesis does not constitute a stable whole. Instead, it performs a contingent completion which is provisionally enabled by an element of the chain that plays the role of the unconditioned.

Does this mean that the dynamic antinomy succeeds in explaining the linkage of *all* events to their causes? As happened in mathematical conflicts here "regression is never given in absolute *entirety*."[34] Nevertheless, the supplementation of natural causality with a causality through freedom incites us to imagine some kind of impact on the diachronic series. By initiating its own effects, freedom provides the series with a boundary through which it can achieve a certain sense of completion.[35] But how can the unconditioned give the series a closure and allow the dynamic antinomy to form a whole, however contingently?[36] If, as Kant argues in his explanation of the mathematical antinomy, there is no outside position from which one could actually conceive of a universe,[37] or (in today's terms) no metalanguage, then how can the third antinomy anchor the series in something that exceeds it, an unconditioned cause that establishes a relationship with an element of excess?

THE SUBJECT BEGINS THE SERIES BUT NOTHING BEGINS IN THE SUBJECT

The heterogeneity allowed in the third antinomy opens up a new outlook on reason's conflict with itself by supplementing natural necessity with the transcendental idea of freedom. Freedom is "the power to begin a state *on one's own*. . . . Freedom, in this meaning of the term, is a pure transcendental idea."[38] In order to complement natural causality and its rule of regress, "reason creates for itself the idea of a spontaneity that can, on its own, start to act—without, i.e., needing to be preceded by another cause by means of which it is determined to action in turn, according to the law of causal connection."[39]

Kant begins the section titled "Solution of the Cosmological Idea of Totality in the Derivation of World Events from Their Causes" raising questions on the transcendental idea of freedom. Is freedom "even possible at all"? Can it "coexist with the universality of the natural law of causality"? Must every effect in the world "arise *either* from nature *or* from freedom" and if so, how can thesis and antithesis be reconciled? The answer to these questions lies in the unconditioned with which the thoroughly conditioned can be linked. "As so connected, this thoroughly conditioned can satisfy the *understanding*, on the one hand, and *reason*, on the other."[40] The simultaneous satisfaction of the understanding and of reason has important consequences at the moment of creating the realm of objectivity, given that this realm, as produced by the understanding, can only be bounded in relationship to reason and its aspiration to reach beyond. Significantly, reason's impulse to trespass its own bounds creates a boundary that puts in relationship what lies on both sides, the bounded realm of objects the understanding can cognize, and the empty space beyond where reason would locate noumenon in the negative sense.[41] Kant's explicit solution to the third antinomy (and the most easily remembered one), however, is to affirm that both nature and freedom "can, with one and the same event but in different reference, take place simultaneously."[42] The same effect could be considered to originate in freedom in intelligible reference and to result from natural necessity in sensible reference. Perhaps anticipating the considerable critical resistance his double-reference theory would meet, Kant himself acknowledges this distinction "must appear extremely subtle and obscure," but, he claims, "it will become clear in its application."[43] Even if one could prove that freedom is not contradictory as an idea, as this solution claims,[44] what would enable this uncaused cause potentially to anchor the causal chain and allow it to cohere as a whole? Kant refers to the relationship between nature and freedom in terms of coexistence ("coexist," "*both*," "take place simultaneously"), but where and how would that coexistence take place?

Freedom and nature coexist in what we call the subject.[45] The term subjectivity names the interaction between the two. The possibility of anchoring the regressive series of causal linkage thus becomes manifest in Kant's text when the subject enters the scene: "This subject . . . begins its effects in the world of sense *on its own*."[46] What allows the third antinomy to prove that the idea of freedom at least does not enter in contradiction with theoretical reason is the unique position it attributes to the subject in relation to the series. The subject is here depicted as an element of the empirical series which, playing the exceptional role of the unconditioned, introduces a causality through freedom: "In our power of choice [lies] a causality for producing, independently of those natural causes and even against their force and influence, something that in the time order is determined according to empirical laws—and hence a causality whereby we can begin a series of events *entirely on our own*."[47] "We" and "our power of choice" (*Willkür*) refer to the subject. If freedom was "the power to begin a state *on one's own*,"[48] that same power is attributed to the subject, because freedom may be imagined to be *in* the subject, even though the subject (when conceived practically, as I will in the next chapters) will have no understanding of it.

This "power to begin" in the subject is what Kant calls practical reason: "If reason can have causality in regard to appearances, then it is a power *through* which the sensible condition of an empirical series of effects first begins."[49] Here Kant introduces the *being practical* of pure reason I will examine in the next chapter, the fact that beyond speculating pure reason is enjoined to act. Practical reason is *in* the subject, it is what in the subject exceeds the subject's ability to reason.[50] Therefore, the causality of practical reason, which is that of freedom, is not sensible or empirical. The subject, which Kant envisages as traversed by practical reason, is also a part of the empirical series of causally linked phenomena. Subjectivity in the third antinomy would be, again, the *space* where nature and freedom coexist. Thus, when Kant speaks about the subject beginning "its effects in the world of sense *on its own*," he refers to the free causality that would act through the subject if both freedom and a subjectivity constituted by it could be proved to exist. Practical reason would then be the "permanent condition" of the subject's voluntary actions, even while the understanding envisions those same actions as having been predetermined *before* their occurrence by a chain of natural events.[51] As the "unconditioned condition of any voluntary action,"[52] reason is present in all actions of a particular subject in all time conditions, but is not itself "in time."[53] "*Determinative* but not *determinable*,"[54] practical reason is the unconditioned element that "begins the series" but does not exist in time, and so does not manifest itself in the series except *in* and through the subject.

What the power of practical reason in the subject would produce is the "sensible condition" which "first begins" a series of events.[55] The impact of practical reason on the series, in other words, is imagined as the operation we call unconditioned, the initiating condition for which no previous cause can account.

For the condition that lies in reason is not sensible and hence does not itself begin. Accordingly, there takes place here what in all empirical series we were unable to find: viz., that the *condition* of a successive series of events can itself be empirically unconditioned. For here the condition is *outside* the series of appearances (viz., in the intelligible) and hence is subjected to no sensible condition and no time determination by a preceding cause.[56]

In this paragraph Kant equates the impact practical reason exerts on the series, the possibility to begin by oneself, with the role of the unconditioned. The unconditioned may be considered to be an initiating member of a series because what theoretical reason would imagine by analogy to be its cause lies outside. Because theoretical reason imagines the intelligible condition of the series to lie outside, we may say that two heterogeneous spaces, that of the empirical series and what reason imagines as an empty space beyond (the space of negative noumenon), meet in the unconditioned cause. The unconditioned embodies, therefore, the relationship and the boundary between the two. It is through the idea of this unconditioned cause that theoretical reason can conceive of the impact of freedom on the causal chain. The boundary and bounding operation we call "unconditioned," however, would be inoperative—it would be, in fact, inconceivable—if theoretical reason did not attribute the role of the unconditioned to a subject through which practical reason operates.

As soon as Kant claims that the subject "begins its effects in the world of sense *on its own*," however, he adds an important qualification: "without the action's beginning *in the subject* itself."

> Of this subject we would say quite correctly that it begins its effects in the world of sense *on its own*, without the action's beginning *in the subject* itself. And this would be valid without any consequent need for the effects in the world of sense to begin on their own.[57]

Nothing begins in the subject, because from the understanding's empirical perspective, the only one the understanding can really take, actions—even those that originate in freedom—appear in the series as a result of natural causes. And so Kant's text can triumphantly go on to affirm: "And thus freedom and nature, each in the complete meaning of its term, would be found in the same actions—according as these are compared with their intelligible or with their sensible cause—simultaneously and without any conflict."[58] The subject begins its own effects in the world, but nothing begins in the subject itself because every event can only be perceived as a result of natural causality.[59] When one reads the entire paragraph, and when in the following section Kant refers to practical reason in nearly the same terms,[60] one can confirm this is what Kant primarily means.

But the problem is far from solved, because the main difficulty to be addressed is not the way the subject's actions, some of which may be motivated by freedom, appear in the natural causal chain. Even perhaps more challenging is the task of explaining how the subject is related to that element of excess, indeed how the subject is the bearer of freedom—how it is that freedom, were it to exist, acts through the subject. What I propose, therefore, is that we sustain our attention beyond the relationship that explicitly occupies Kant here, the coexistence between nature and freedom in the series, to consider also the other relationship that the impulse of Kant's thinking, if followed beyond its explicit reasoning, invites us to entertain: the relationship we call unconditioned. The question for us, then, the question we need to address, is how the subject that plays the role of the unconditioned is related to freedom. Beyond Kant's explanation of the subject's relationship with the series, and beyond his explicit solution on the subject's two references (empirical and intelligible), we need to interrogate the subject's relatedness to the intelligible, to the series' outside. Freedom, as the *Critique of Practical Reason* will depict it, is a causality acting in the subject that the subject itself does not understand.

I would like to invite us, therefore, to hear in Kant's statement the echo of this other relationship that is presupposed but can be explained neither by theoretical reason nor from the perspective of practical thought, as I will argue in Chapter 3: the subject's relationship to the otherness freedom is.[61] We may thus repeat Kant's words with this other relationship in mind: The subject begins its effects in the chain but nothing begins in the subject itself because the subject is not the other (is not freedom), only the location of the other or, more exactly, a relationship to the other. Action begins in the subject if we understand this to mean that freedom initiates its own effects in the chain through the subject. It is through the subject, through its practical reason (if they could be considered to exist) that unconditioned freedom reverberates in the chain. The subject's relatedness to freedom and to the sensible series of which it is part would allow it to play the role of the unconditioned, and thus render the effects of freedom present in the world. By virtue of the mediation of the subject—by virtue, more exactly, of the mediation we call "subject"—freedom's causality, were it to exist, would be able to manifest its effects in the world.

Since action begins in the subject because freedom's "power to begin a state *on one's own*" operates through the subject,[62] the subject *retroactively* becomes the cause through its own effects: "the subject is indeed the cause."[63] In unwittingly taking the place of the unconditioned, the subject would be the element in the series that exceptionally introduces a boundary, a fleeting moment of closure: the subject allows the series to cohere (to become whole) contingently and retroactively. By presupposing the unwitting intervention of the subject, reason may imagine the causal series as being reconfigured retroactively: the idea of an unconditioned cause emerges from its empirical effects. Reason's presentations would go from recent effects backward, in search for an event that would become—that would be instituted as—their cause.

The regressive character of reason's synthesis of causality that allows us to conceive the cause as emerging from its effect defines, in fact, Kant's conception of reason's presentations, and is at the center of Kant's introductory remarks at the beginning of the Antinomy chapter.[64] In imagining the causal series, reason, with its demand for the totality of conditions, is not concerned with consequences resulting from conditions, which matter only insofar as they "presuppose" their conditions. Reason, affirms Kant, is only concerned with regressive synthesis, the synthesis of the series of conditions ascending from a given apparition (what we may take as the present time in which an appearance is given) up to the unconditioned. In the case of the third antinomy, the regressive synthesis Kant describes here functions retroactively, that is, by seeking for a cause "backward" from its effects.[65] Kant arrives at the four antinomic world-ideas by taking the four categorial headings (quantity, quality, relation, modality)[66] and isolating in each of them "only those categories in which the synthesis makes up a *series*—a series, moreover, of conditions for a conditioned that are subordinated to (not coordinated with) one another."[67] Time and space (quantity), which are at the basis of the first antinomy, also constitute, as the a priori forms of intuition, the formal condition of all series. Concerning time, in order to advance from the present moment in a series toward the unconditioned, reason would have to cover "the entire elapsed time" or "by-gone time" from the "given instant." It would have to do so looking back, retroactively, since only "through the going-by of the preceding time . . . does this [given] instant arise in the first place."[68] When it comes to space, however, regions of space are not subordinated to one another, but rather coordinated as an aggregate of simultaneous parts. But since all intuition happens also in time, we do apprehend space as a sequence of diverse parts, that is, as a succession that "occurs in time and contains a series."[69] "And in this series of aggregated spaces (e.g., the feet in a rod), from a given space onward, the further spaces that are added in thought are always the *condition of the boundary* of the previous spaces."[70] Kant's description of space as an aggregate succession of bounded elements that occurs (that is, that we apprehend) in time allows us to envision the series as a regressive sequence that the unconditioned would anchor temporarily. In addition to being inflected (like all series) by time and space, the third antinomy emerges from the only category of relation that gives rise to a series, causality.

The fact that the function we call "cause" comes into being retroactively means it is not accurate to envision causality as something originating in the past that evolves in a forward movement toward the present and future. If we adopt the illusion that causal sequence exists in nature, then we may be tempted to assume that a cause must precede its effects. Yet, when we think of causality as a category (as Kant insists we should), that is, as a rule through which the understanding relates the sensible manifold to the concept of an object,[71] we realize that present events do not simply evolve from an initial cause to which reason's regressive presentations aim. Since here, in the antinomy, we are not dealing only with the ability on the part of the understanding to form objects of cognition, but also with reason's aspiration to form ideas that exceed experience, it is important to clarify what the position of the unconditioned is in the chain. The fact is that in the third antinomy causality does not necessarily start *ex nihilo* or without a previous cause, as my remarks on the unconditioned element may appear to have presumed so far. What in reason's presentation of causal sequence could be considered the most "recent" descending cause is not simply the result of preceding causes. If we think of the causal series in terms of time, we may say an event becomes cause after a lapse of time, the time it takes for the cause's effects to appear as echoes of an unreachable *event*, the unconditioned *cause*.[72] Since reason seeks the unconditioned retroactively, the notion of cause emerges from its effects. The cause is created when its effects make us look back in search of a cause to which to attribute them.

The retroactive determination of causality requires us to qualify the notion of initiating cause. Should the retroactive functioning of causality lead us to conclude that the element taking the place of the (initiating) cause would not necessarily be the first one? Wouldn't it rather appear as the most recent element in the series, or at least as the "given instant" from which reason would begin looking back? We can, in fact, make both claims. The element becoming the cause would be the most recent one if we focus on the effects from which the cause arises, that is, if we adopt the perspective from which what appears as an effect in the present determines the past—that is, our presentation of the past. Here the term "recent" refers to the "given instant" from which reason would begin presenting a particular causal chain retroactively. Once the effects of a cause produce the cause—that is, once the cause results from its effects—the cause may be imagined, in turn, as the element that initiates a series of events.[73]

The subject, itself a member of the empirical series, takes the place of the unconditioned, and in so doing it plays the role of the cause. As the subject takes the position of the cause, thus enabling the anchoring of the regressive series, a contingent and retroactive effect of synthesis may be imagined to come about: a fleeting sense of closure is produced time and again. Since the series of causal linkage is determined retroactively, from the future and the present toward the past (if we choose to describe retroaction in temporal terms), every new anchoring operation has the potential to reconfigure the entire chain. Now we can understand better how extraordinary Kant's claim on the coexistence of nature and freedom is. Even events apparently linked by laws of nature could be retroactively attributed to subjective interventions, to acts of freedom that, playing the role of new initiating causes in the midst of causal sequence, temporarily anchor the chain.[74] Envisioning the series of causal linkage as a system which is permanently reconfigured also allows us to gain insight into the apparent circular causality we find in Kant's claim that "reason begins the series in such a way that nothing begins in reason itself."[75] It is as if the system of causal linkage "reacted" to the incorporation of a new foreign element, an act of freedom, by reorganizing itself. The contingent synthesis formed here would be, to express it aporetically, a whole in progress, a dynamic system that is reconfigured retroactively time and again. If we understand the third antinomy in this way, what reason accomplishes here is huge: it rescues itself from self-contradiction, it achieves an immanent synthesis, it bounds the field of objectivity, it clears the way for practical reason, no less.

The third antinomy proves, in sum, that the ability to form a whole depends on conceiving of that whole as contingent: the fact that the series is always being rearranged prevents it from reaching any lasting stability. In fact, the very possibility of completion rests on fully grasping its contingent character. What theoretical reason thus accomplishes by introducing freedom in the third antinomy while managing to stay within its own bounds is immense: it achieves a synthesis of phenomena and it secures the possibility of an intelligible space, and with it of a boundary that enables the smooth functioning of thought (what matters here is less the space beyond than the boundary it introduces). Yet, since the illusion of completion depends on the subject's unwitting intervention, the functioning of thought will henceforth be marked by the contingency, precariousness, and dynamism brought on in the unceasing reconfiguration of the causal chain.

SUBJECTIVITY AS RELATIONSHIP

But are we right to place so much weight on Kant's third antinomy? Doesn't the antithesis of the third antinomy famously deny freedom, arguing instead that all phenomena originate in natural necessity? ("There is no freedom, but everything in the world occurs solely according to laws of nature.")[76] The anchoring of causally-linked phenomena by an element (the subject) that connects the series with a heterogeneous causality, that of freedom, happens not despite but because of the fact that the antithesis of the third antinomy denies freedom. Although this second judgment excludes freedom ("There is no freedom . . ."), in effect this gesture constructs freedom as the excluded element that enables a certain sense of completion, "everything in the world" ("but everything in the world occurs solely according to laws of nature").[77] The antithesis tends toward a different conception of the unconditioned. So far, I have focused on the unconditioned as conceived by the thesis, where "the absolutely unconditioned is only a part of the series, a part to which the remaining members of the series are subordinated."[78] But one can also think of the unconditioned "as consisting merely in the whole series, in which therefore all members would without exception be conditioned and only their whole would be absolutely unconditioned."[79] Kant warns us, however, that "this absolute whole of such a series is only an idea—or, rather, a problematic concept whose possibility must be examined."[80] In fact, the impulse toward completion in the antithesis, its "everything in the world," does not seek to reach the type of totality that was declared to be null in the mathematical antinomy. As the antithesis in the third antinomy stipulates that the causality of all elements in the series is conditioned without exception, "it promises us thoroughgoing and law-governed unity of experience," "an experience having thoroughgoing coherence," writes Kant in the Proof of the Antithesis.[81] What is produced here is indeed not an unconditioned totality but rather a bounding of the field of objectivity, of the realm of objects the understanding can cognize.

In effect, the negation of freedom in the antithesis logically creates a "boundary concept" understood as the negative, legitimate use Kant attributes to "noumenon." As I pointed out in my study of noumenon in Chapter 1, we should think of noumena in the negative sense as "boundary concepts" that "limit the pretension of sensibility." A noumenon functions as a limit that bounds the sensible sphere by opening a space beyond it, "the range outside the sphere of appearances" which "is (for us) empty."[82] Noumenon is something excluded from experience, from sensibility, and thus a negative being the understanding places in an empty place beyond, "but without therefore expanding its own realm." This exclusion (which has the form of an indefinite negation),[83] bounds the phenomenal field, making it a full space in the positive sense, the realm of objects the understanding can cognize. Through the bounding performed by negative noumenon the field of objectivity is produced. Noumenon, therefore, "is not arbitrarily invented; rather, it coheres with the limitation of sensibility, yet without being able to posit anything positive outside sensibility's range."[84] More than a simple limit, then, the unconditioned in the third antinomy is a boundary putting in relationship what lies at each side. Because the two sides the boundary separates constitute heterogeneous spaces, the relationship established between them is not dialectic, as I argue in Chapter 4.

If the antithesis had not introduced a boundary by excluding freedom, if it had not thereby opened up an imaginary intelligible space in which to locate the excluded element, freedom, the thesis would not be able to presuppose the outside in which it locates the absent cause of the unconditioned.[85] Without this antithetical gesture, then, the thesis could not imagine the unconditioned as relationship and as boundary. The unconditioned role freedom plays is accordingly determined in the interplay of thesis and anti-thesis, rather than in the thesis alone, as is generally assumed. Could we venture, therefore, that in the third antinomy two conceptions of unconditionality interact?[86] The interaction at stake here is that between two structural operations, synchronic operation of substitution presupposed by the thesis (where the subject, as bearer of freedom, plays the function of the unconditioned) and a logical exclusion in the form of indefinite judgment performed by the antithesis. But the operations enabled by each judgment are not symmetrical. In fact, a solution to the third antinomy would not be conceivable without the different kind of contribution each judgment makes. The contribution of the antithesis is logical and that of the thesis is relational: the antithesis creates a boundary and the thesis formulates it as a relationship. We may go as far as affirming that as bearer of unconditioned freedom the term "subject" names (from this theoretical perspective) a relationship with that element of excess.

But as we envisage the subject as the relationship between the series and the empty space that lies outside of sensibility, can we simply assume, as we seemingly have so far, that the subject is constituted by freedom? If freedom can manifest itself in the world, it is only insofar as freedom is the excess that constitutes the subject. Only by embodying this relationship may the subject be envisioned as playing the role of the unconditioned cause of events. But conceiving of freedom as actual and explaining how it constitutes ethical subjects whose acts introduce its effects in the world lies beyond the reach of theoretical reason. One would have to prove that what in the first *Critique* was just a possibility, a non-contradictory idea, is in effect actual and constitutive. Proving freedom exists and that its causality constitutes the subject is the challenge Kant's practical philosophy must meet.[87] Thus in the second *Critique*, theoretical reason is charged with the formidable task of explaining how practical reason—a reason that does not reason[88]—motivates the power of desire.

3

CAUSALITY OF FREEDOM

One would never have committed the daring deed of introducing freedom into science had not the moral law, and with it practical reason, come in and thrust this concept upon us.

—IMMANUEL KANT, *CRITIQUE OF PRACTICAL REASON*

The category in reason's idea of freedom . . . is the category of *causality*.

—IMMANUEL KANT, *CRITIQUE OF PRACTICAL REASON*

Only if we are scrupulous to live in accordance with maxims of freedom as if they were laws of nature.

—IMMANUEL KANT, *GROUNDING FOR THE METAPHYSICS OF MORALS*

The third antinomy could not introduce the possibility of freedom without the mediation of a subject that embodies it. As bearer of freedom, the subject establishes a relationship between the phenomenal causal series and the intelligible, whose causality exceeds thought. Because it holds together a co-presence, both spatial and temporal, of the two realms, the subject can be envisaged as playing the role of the unconditioned cause or boundary that anchors the cosmological causal series. In lying at once inside and outside, at the boundary, the unconditioned is the *site* of an encounter between two heterogeneous and otherwise unconnectable spaces, as I argued in Chapter 2. By being constituted by freedom, then, the unconditioned position we call "subject" acts as the meeting place and boundary that delimits the realm of objects the understanding can cognize.

Kant's theoretical account of freedom in the *Critique of Pure Reason* there-fore necessitates the "human being" or the "subject" that would embody it,[1] a subject theoretical reason can only presuppose. In order to function in the series as the bearer of freedom, the subject would have to be itself consti-tuted by freedom. The subject can play the role of the unconditioned cause only insofar as freedom is the excess that constitutes subjectivity. But the ability to explain how the causality of freedom motivates the human power of desire and constitutes ethical subjects whose acts introduce effects of free-dom in the world[2] lies beyond the reach of theoretical reason. The "human being" presupposed in the first *Critique* will not become a subject in the full sense until freedom can be proved to be actual and constitutive, a challenge Kant takes up in his practical philosophy. A convincing account of how free-dom constitutes the subject becomes therefore indispensable for the produc-tion of objects of knowledge that drives theoretical thought. Venturing such an account, however, is inherently problematic, even if one could assume, as Kant's practical works do, that freedom exists. The challenge practical philosophy faces is that of explaining how something exceeding knowledge constitutes subjectivity and manifests itself as an effect on the subject, and through it on the world. Constituted by an excess that lies beyond the hu-man ability to represent, what we here call subjectivity thus surpasses the bounds of self-consciousness and its impulse to represent world and self as objects of thought. As noumenal or intelligible—as a negative being beyond— the ethical demarcates the boundaries of what can be known, but it also man-ifests itself practically as an effect and affect in the subject, and therefore in the world.

What then is this subjectivity constituted by freedom? What is the sta-tus of the excess that allows it to emerge? Is it just a need of the imagina-tion, a function of thought? And even though this constitutive excess is not knowable, can we perceive its effects in the world? Can what withdraws from language signal itself in it?[3] When we say that the subject embodies the re-lationship between the series and its outside, we are still speaking in terms of theoretical reason. As we approach subjectivity in practical terms—by ask-ing, for example, what moves the power of desire—it is crucial to note that the term "subject," which in the previous chapter I described as an excep-tional position or role, as the boundary or relationship between two hetero-geneous spaces, now also extends to the "human being" reason envisions as playing that role. This practical subject does not embody the position of the unconditioned voluntarily, as a result of a conscious decision, and is not necessarily aware of the impact the free causality acting through it has on the chain. In fact, as I pointed out above, freedom is an element of excess that constitutes the subject. What animates the subject's ethical motivation is a causality the subject itself does not understand. What then is subjectivity? How is it constituted? In order to address these questions Kant's critical project must adopt the perspective of practical philosophy. In this chapter and the next I propose, in fact, that in exploring how the causality of freedom constitutes the subject, practical philosophy can provide the very subject theoretical philosophy envisions as the mediation or relationship that allows cosmological causal linkage to cohere. Practical philosophy focuses on the ways in which the causality of freedom affects the power of desire and motivates the ethical subjects it constitutes.

As one moves from theoretical to practical reason limits shift, but not as radically as one might expect. The methodology of Kant's main ethical works—*Grounding for the Metaphysics of Morals*, *Critique of Practical Reason*, *Religion within the Bounds of Bare Reason*, and *Metaphysics of Morals*—is still theoretical. What changes are the object of the critique and the direction of its inquiry. If the first *Critique* focused on reason's relationship to empirical objects, the second *Critique* studies reason's relationship to the will, moving from the principles of unconditioned causality, to concepts that determine the will, to the sensible subject of that will.[4] As it initiates its inquiry into the causality through freedom that determines the will, the second *Critique* can begin by affirming that freedom exists and that it constitutes subjectivity. But beyond this affirmation, practical philosophy cannot gain any further insight into freedom.

Although from a practical perspective we still do not know freedom, freedom—whose actuality practical philosophy nevertheless needs to assert—manifests itself through the moral law, of whose existence, affirms Kant, we know.[5] Freedom envisioned practically through the moral law now secures what for speculative reason was a "problematic concept of freedom" and provides it "with *objective reality* that, although only practical, is yet indubitable."[6] That freedom is actual means that it motivates the subject to act. More exactly, freedom manifests itself as a power to obligate that affects the faculty of desire through the moral law: we find ourselves and others responding to something unconditionally, without necessarily knowing to what. Or as Kant also formulates it, we are addressed by an imperative we find in ourselves. When dealing with practical reason, the *Critique* explores the moral law of freedom through the impact it has on the subject, or, more exactly, *as* the impact that constitutes the subject. The actuality of freedom is attested to, in sum, by the effect the moral law has on the beings it obligates.[7] But what the moral law is, where it comes from, and how it moves the power of desire, determining the will directly (without the mediation of sensibility), is not easy to discern.

What, then, is the law? What does it command? Autonomy, according to Kant, consists in giving oneself the law and freely obeying it. He nevertheless describes this necessary law as unconditioned and empty or incomprehensible (*unbegreiflich*).[8] The law is unconditioned because it is not the effect of a previous cause. What, then, is the true origin of the law? Kant insists it happens as a fact of reason (*factum rationis*) and thus comes from something which is in the subject but is not of the subject. But the law does not offer any precise indication as to how to act. One cannot find in the law a prescription for a concrete course of action, because its power is not associated with any object but rather with its ability to motivate. That the law is empty or incomprehensible means, furthermore, that the law is excluded from the sphere of cognizable or representable objects. The law does not enjoin us to fulfill a particular order, but rather to take the law itself as one's sole motivation. The law's power to drive a subject's itinerary, in other words, is not prescriptive (it does not command a particular course of action one should refrain from or fulfill) but affective.

If the law exceeds the limits of theoretical reason and its ability to synthesize and comprehend, how can we, autonomous subjects, give ourselves a law we have not consciously created? How can we give ourselves a law we do not understand? What is the status of our freedom with regard to a law which is incomprehensible? Or to put it otherwise, where does the law come from, the subject or elsewhere? Unless the law comes from an elsewhere (from something other) whose trace—the law itself—is in the subject. In the *Opus Postumum*, Kant writes: "in man there dwells an active principle . . . accompanying him not as soul . . . but as spirit [*Gemüt*], one that . . . commands him irresistibly according to the law of moral practical reason."[9] What Kant means here, as Jean-Luc Nancy indicates in "The *Kategorein* of Excess," is that "the imperative does not exist in the psychic substance known to us only phenomenally (and so never really as *substance*), but only in this *Gemüt* whose main sense is to be the unity of transcendental constitution."[10] The imperative is not inherent in the subject's nature. Rather, the law is that which in the subject exceeds the subject and addresses the subject. This excess has to do with the being practical of pure reason, with a pure practical reason that has to act and act itself out.[11]

What in the subject is not reducible to the subject is what I, in my study of the unconditioned in the third antinomy in the previous chapter, proposed to call provisionally *other* to thought. We begin our exploration of practical reason and the emergence of the ethical subject—of the subject as impact—by examining the relationship between freedom and the moral law through which freedom manifests itself.

DOUBLING OF FORM

The fact that in the third antinomy theoretical reason attributes the position of the unconditioned to the subject does not mean the subject plays that role intentionally. When the subject perceives himself as free, writes Kant in the *Grounding for the Metaphysics of Morals*, "when he transfers himself to the standpoint of a member of the intelligible world," he does not participate in the intelligible realm actively or by choice. Rather, the subject is "involuntarily forced [to it] by the idea of freedom."[12] That the subject's self-perception as free should be associated with being "involuntarily forced" is surprising, to say the least. This involuntary *being forced* does not originate in any natural determination, because the idea of freedom is the idea "of being independent of determination by causes of the world of sense."[13] Or as Kant formulates it in the second *Critique*, practical reason "determines the [subject's] will directly,"[14] without the collaboration of any sensible motives, which are psychological or "pathological." If freedom is independent from the constraints of natural causality, yet it has the power to "involuntarily force" the subject, what does freedom mean? Would conceiving of freedom in this way not amount to replacing natural determinism with another form of coercive determinism that could turn out to be worse?

Perhaps surprisingly, the idea of practical freedom Kant advances still involves choosing an action one wills. Practical freedom differs from the common psychological understanding of freedom in the fact that the action one wills consists in one's duty. The second *Critique* thus associates one's duty with a mode of acting one desires or, more exactly, with the unprecedented form of desire through which the will determines itself. Even though in instances of psychological freedom (which Kant differentiates from practical freedom) one's will may be driven by the desire of perfection, prosperity, or doing good in the world, this form of freedom, argues Kant, is ultimately impelled by personal advancement, even when the actions deriving from it promote the advancement of others. In the case of practical freedom, however, the will is not motivated by any object, that is, by any particular goal one intends to achieve; a free will is, rather, determined by one's duty.[15] Counterintuitively, then, freedom manifests itself as a power to obligate. One could, in fact, equate freedom with duty, something Kant does in effect when he defines morality as acting out of duty and because of duty, which amounts to acting out of freedom and only because of freedom. According to Kant's conception, if freedom exists at all, in it duty, desire, and will must coincide. What then, we must ask, is the nature of this cause able to motivate the power of desire independently from natural forces? And why would human beings, whose desire is naturally shaped by presentations of the agreeable, come to desire their own duty in the first place?

In the *Critique of Pure Reason* Kant introduced transcendental freedom in terms of causality. A causality through freedom coexisting with natural causality allows reason in the third antinomy to achieve a synthesis of causal linkage. The second *Critique* envisions practical freedom also in terms of causality,[16] but this time referring to the causality of freedom in the subject, that is, to the fact that freedom determines the subject's will and itinerary. Practical reason, writes Kant, "deals with determining bases [*Bestimmungsgründe*] of the will." The will (*Wille*) is a "power either to produce objects corresponding to one's presentations, or, at any rate, to determine itself to bring about these objects . . . , i.e., determine its causality."[17] But how does the will determine itself as cause of the objects it produces? Is practical reason alone sufficient to determine the will? It would seem the will would require, in turn, an empirically conditioned determining basis to be moved, but is this necessarily so? To this question Kant answers that practical reason alone is sufficient to determine the will, and at this point he alludes to the concept of a causality through freedom, a concept that the first *Critique* justified by proving it was not contradictory, even if it could not be exhibited empirically. The *Critique of Practical Reason* must thus fulfill two interrelated tasks: establishing that freedom exists (and therefore that freedom determines the human will immanently)[18] while preventing theoretical reason (which is "empirically conditioned") from presuming it has the ability to determine a free will.[19] Accordingly, we need to give up the illusion that from the phenomenal perspective of consciousness we can gain access to the determining basis of the will, let alone consciously decide to determine our own will. Being free means, in short, having the causality of freedom act in and through oneself, that is, being animated by a causality one does not understand.[20] Awareness of one's freedom would consist in experiencing oneself as inhabited by something one cannot comprehend, by a causality or an otherness that delimits (by exceeding it) the boundary of what the understanding can conceptualize.

But if, as Kant affirms, we do not have any direct experience of freedom, then how do we know of its existence? The actuality of freedom manifests itself through the moral law. We become aware of freedom's causality through the presence of the law. Although we have no direct access to freedom, we know it exists because it is the condition of the moral law, "which we do know."[21] Trying to deflect potential criticism that might accuse him of evoking an inconsistent causality "if I now call freedom the condition of the moral law and afterwards, in the treatise, maintain that the moral law is the condition under which we can first of all *become aware* [*bewußt*] of freedom," Kant clarifies that although freedom is the *ratio essendi* of the law, the law is the *ratio cognoscendi* of freedom.[22] (The law is also the *ratio cognoscendi* of evil, as we shall soon see.) In short, we can infer the existence of freedom retroactively, from our experience of the moral law: "if the moral law were not *previously* thought distinctly in our reason, we would never consider ourselves entitled to *assume* such a thing as freedom."[23] Here causality would appear circular only from the limited viewpoint of our power of speculation (our ability to "become aware" or conscious [*bewußt*]), which, as Kant says in the next paragraph, "is not so well off."[24] At stake in this causal ordering is the imagination's passage from one unconditioned ground (the law) to its condition of possibility (freedom). Since, however, "it is utterly impossible to unite the principle of causal relations in the world with freedom; for that would be an effect without a cause,"[25] in the *Opus Postumum* Kant clarifies that the notion of freedom is not the basis on which the concept of duty is founded, but rather the other way around. "The concept of duty contains the ground of the possibility of the concept of freedom, which is postulated through the categorical imperative."[26] Hence, "the property of a rational being, to possess freedom of the will in general . . . , cannot be directly proved as a causal principle, but only indirectly, through its consequences; insofar,

that is, as it contains the ground of the possibility of the categorical imperative."[27] It is not accurate, therefore, to think of the relation between freedom and the law in terms of cause and effect. Rather, freedom "contains"
the grounds of the law, and the ground of the possibility of freedom is contained by the law. The law is not, in sum, founded by freedom. Assuming
the law is founded by freedom would presuppose in freedom the power to
invent the law. Rather, the law addresses itself to a freedom,[28] as I will soon
propose with Nancy. "But if there were no freedom, then the moral law *could
not be encountered* in us at all [*würde das moralische Gesetz in uns gar nicht
anzutreffen sein*]."[29] The law is associated with the condition of possibility
of a reason which is practical, with a pure reason that must act.[30] Does this
allow us to assume, though, that while freedom cannot be experienced the
law manifests itself phenomenally? If so, how is the moral law *"encountered
in us"* and how do we encounter it?

What is the law? The law does not enjoin us to fulfill a particular object
or goal. It is not defined by its matter, that is, by prescribing or proposing
objects to the will.[31] "Any matter of practical rules rests always on subjective conditions,"[32] and thus determines the will through sensibility. If the
law were defined by its matter, it would influence the power of desire empirically by presenting it with objects that would produce feelings of agree-
ableness or disagreeableness. But since the law determines the will *objectively*,
all sensible incentives are excluded from the law. Initially freedom is conceived in a negative sense as freedom *from* natural causality, from sensibility. After excluding all matter, only the law's universal form is left.[33] "Now
if from a law all the matter, i.e., every object of the will, is separated (as determining basis), nothing remains of the law but the mere form of a universal legislation."[34]

> After the exclusion of all matter, i.e., cognition of objects, from pure
> reason which thinks this ideal, nothing remains over for me except such
> reason's form, viz., the practical law of the universal validity of maxims;
> and in conformity with this law I think of reason in its relation to a pure
> intelligible world as a possible efficient cause, i.e., as a cause determin-
> ing the will.[35]

When, in Chapter 2, I studied the third antinomy, I argued that the unconditioned role freedom plays depends on the interaction between the
asymmetrical operations (one logical, the other one relational) enabled

by the antithesis and the thesis: the antithesis creates a boundary and the thesis formulates it as a relationship. If the antithesis had not introduced a boundary by excluding freedom, if it had not thereby opened up an imaginary intelligible space in which to locate the excluded element, the thesis would not be able to presuppose the outside in which it locates the absent cause of the unconditioned. The exclusion performed by the antithesis of the third antinomy is therefore indispensable for the thesis to imagine the unconditioned as boundary and as relationship. According to the *Grounding for the Metaphysics of Morals* and to the second *Critique*, in turn, practical reason excludes from itself all sensible motives, that is, anything that may point to a natural cause. In the paragraph just quoted, the function of "a cause determining the will" is said to be played by "reason *in its relation* to a pure intelligible world."[36] We already clarified that the intelligible does not name any positive fullness, but rather an empty space beyond, a space exceeding experience in which reason locates freedom, which functions as a noumenon in the negative, legitimate sense Kant gives to this type of idea.[37]

This restrictive action clears the way for practical reason to function as an efficient cause, as that which determines the will directly, motivating the subject to act *because* of the law. Only through this exclusion can the law's legislative character associated with freedom in the positive sense, with freedom *to*, emerge. If after excluding any sensible motivation all that is left of the law is just pure form, yet the law determines the will directly, what in the law comes to play the motivating function that matter plays in sensible incentives? Given that the form of the law is the only motivation, the only incentive, it is the objective form of the law itself that plays the motivating function of matter. Form determines the will not only objectively but also subjectively by having an effect on the power of desire without the help of any sensible incentive. That a free will is "determined *by the mere form of law*"[38] means that the very universal and empty form of the law makes itself an object of desire of the will, the very object a free will wants to reach without presupposing any feeling.[39] In order to affect the power of desire the form of law must, in short, play the double function of form and motive.[40] Beyond determining the will objectively, the form of the law must also determine it subjectively, by becoming its "efficient cause." Being free in this sense entails pushing aside any grounds external to the law—all *pathological* incentives—and having the law itself function as one's only motivation, as the only "efficient cause" of the course of action one wills.

This double functioning of the law's form as universal legislation and as motive defines moral action. Or as Kant also formulates it, the form of the law has the ability to move the will to act not only *according to* the law (by determining it objectively) but also *because of* the law, subjectively motivated only by the law's pure form. An action that fulfills the letter of the law without being motivated by the law itself—without containing the law's *spirit*—would be *legal* but not *moral*. Legality, according to Kant, is still guided by natural necessity, because in this case one's motivations are psychological and depend on sensibly desired objects or what Kant calls pathological motives (not being punished, being considered good by other people, reaching perfection, etc.). In the theoretical context of the third antinomy, an act according to the letter would have its place in the phenomenal series of events caused by nature, and its motive would be psychological freedom. In addition to fulfilling the letter of the law (legality), then, a subject must fulfill the law's spirit (morality) by taking the law as its sole incentive. Here the word "spirit" names the law's ability to motivate the will, that is, to determine the will directly. In Kant's terms, the subject would be constituted both legally (as someone who acts according to duty) and morally (as someone acting according to duty and only because of duty). As compared to legality (following the law *by the letter*) morality is moved by a causality through freedom. Morality means that practical reason prevails over any "pathological" competing motivation and has the law as its only incentive: duty becomes the only motivation of the will.

Kant's readers may already be attuned to our lack of penetration into morality. Our lack of insight into legality, however, may come as a surprise. The fact is that in practice it is not possible to distinguish a legal action from one which is also moral, according to Kant. Although in the first essay of *Religion within the Bounds of Bare Reason* (1793), titled "On the Inherence of the Evil alongside the Good Principle, or, On the Radical Evil in Human Nature," Kant insists on the necessary distinction between a person of good morals (*bene moratus*, a person acting legally) and a morally good person (*moraliter bonus*, a person acting morally), he also clarifies that there is no difference "as regards the agreement of their actions with the law, except that the actions of the former precisely do not always have . . . the law as the sole and supreme incentive, whereas those of the latter *always* do."[41] The difference between legality and morality lies in the cause or source of motivation, but whether a course of action is only legal or also moral is not discernible in its effects. Even in those cases in which the law is one's only source of motivation, one cannot gain awareness of this fact. In the *Religion* Kant defines evil as acting only in a legal way. As we know, legality does not fulfill the requirement of "freedom *from*" sensibility because one's will is driven by sensible motives instead of by the law itself. The inscrutability of one's source of motivation even to oneself implies, significantly, that from the perspective of their own consciousness those subjects that follow the law would perceive themselves as merely legal. Even if they believe themselves to act in a disinterested manner and motivated only by the law, they could never ascertain they are moral.

Perhaps the fact that the subject lacks access to what ultimately drives its decisions will prove less surprising than it initially appears if we keep in mind that morality depends on the letter of the law, since in it the form of the law comes to play the motivating function of matter. Even though the moral dimension of the subject exceeds its ability to act legally, the element of excess that defines morality depends fully on legality. It is all very well to think that in morality taking the law itself as the only incentive ("only because of duty") adds a purely moral motivation to a decision "according to duty." From the perspective of the moral subject (from the perspective of consciousness), however, legality and morality would coexist. Legality would be a result of the reduced "perspective" of self-consciousness, which, as Kant remarks, is limited by experience, phenomenal. What the perspective of self-consciousness would reduce, in other words, is the fact that the law is not only letter but also spirit: however motivated by sensibility one may perceive oneself, one may well be driven by the law.

THE LAW'S LETTER

We should note, perhaps counterintuitively, that the law's motivating power (its *spirit*) lies in its letter, in the verbal address the law is. Kant's insistence on differentiating between the letter and the spirit of the law should not obscure the fact that both terms refer to the same thing. We could say that the letter and the spirit of the law refer to two modes of effectiveness of the law's form, that is, to two ways in which the law exerts its impact on subjectivity: its power to enjoin through its form of address and its power to motivate. The spirit would express the letter's motivational force,[42] and so the acting because of the law or motivated by the law Kant calls morality concerns the law's ability to affect the subject. The distinction between letter and spirit of the law refers, in sum, to two ways in which the form of the law exerts its influence on subjectivity: address and motivation. We may also trace Kant's conception of the law's letter as form and of spirit as form's ability to motivate in the two negative qualifications of the law that recur in his text: "incomprehensible" or "empty" and "unconditioned." We will need to keep in mind, however, that the incomprehensibility of the law does not refer to an inaccessible substantial content, but rather to the fact that the law interpellates its addressee, that it adopts the discursive form of address.

Kant's emphasis on the fact that acting legally is not sufficient to be moral would seem to imply that following the law by the letter is a task one may attain, that acting legally would merely require discipline and the desire to do well (itself a psychological motivation). Perhaps because it is difficult to understand how in moral action the law motivates the will directly, indeed how (universal) objective form can function as a subjective incentive, the fact that the law determines the will objectively is often taken for granted. But how legality functions in practice, how it is that the law acts as an objective determining basis, is far from evident. Although one may initially consider the letter of the law to be more readily understandable than its spirit, this purported transparency of the letter should not be taken at face value. In the first place, the law's letter does not offer any explicit content that would prescribe a particular course of action. Breaking with a venerable ethical tradition that had the idea of the good as its horizon (an idea often identified with God), Kant reverses the direction in which ethical motivation should be understood by affirming that there is no longer any substantial concept of the good to which the law would aim,[43] no *telos* ordered by an *arché*. Since the law is not defined by any matter or object, since we can no longer create ethical laws in relation to the idea of the good, we must determine what is good starting from the law.[44]

This is baffling, to say the least. For all its critical scrutiny of legality and its insufficiency, Kant's text does not offer a systematic account of the law's letter that would guide particular courses of action, beyond a few practical instances of ethical dilemma.[45] What Kant's thinking advances, instead, is a difficult proposition that has formidable implications. The law, he writes, appears to us, finite human beings, in the form of an imperative. The letter or form of the law is a categorical imperative, which prescribes the need to incorporate to one's maxim the principle of universality: the law's "mere practical form . . . consists in the suitability of maxims for universal legislation."[46] Initially, in the *Grounding for the Metaphysics of Morals*, Kant advances four formulations of the categorical imperative.[47] The first and best known one, "Act only according to that maxim whereby you can at the same time will that it should become a universal law,"[48] is often interpreted reductively as a test of universality, a test that may help determine which courses of action should be ruled out but still does not offer any precise indication of how to act. Reducing the law's letter to a test of universality may produce unintended effects due to the test's alleged efficiency as much as to its inefficiency.[49] Even more important, as long as one considers the categorical imperative to be a test of universality, a formula against which to measure the morality of particular acts, it cannot constitute a satisfactory answer to the question of how the law functions as an objective determining ground. Although Kant does indeed insist that when all matter is excluded all is left is the law's form, the form of universal legislation, identifying the law with an imperative that could work as a test for the suitability of concrete actions (an imperative that would not be categorical after all; it would be hypothetical) fails to take into account the full implications of the universality of the law.

How then are we to understand Kant's claim that the law's form is the empty form of universal legislation, that it is not associated with an object (since all objects are sensibly determined) but rather determines the will objectively? Given that the law's letter seems to exist beyond the limits of knowledge or to exceed representation, one must avoid the temptation to assume that obedience of "the law according to the letter" presupposes there is some kind of inaccessible content lurking behind the law. Attributing to the law an inaccessible but substantial content, imagining the law as an unreachable content (that is, still in terms of content) denotes a desire for an essential content that would provide a horizon that supports one's acts. It is therefore crucial to keep in mind that the letter of the law does not refer to any content but rather to *form*.[50] The revolutionary character of the law's form, of the law's letter, is ignored by those interpretations that understand Kant's ethics as a theory of agency rather than as a study of motivation.[51] When one approaches Kant's practical philosophy aiming to derive a theory of agency from it, one runs the risk of reducing the letter either to some unreachable substantial content or to an empty test. The impossibility to give the law a stable content does not come, therefore, from the fact that it is either too "universal" (and therefore may be used to justify the unjustifiable)[52] or not universal enough (and hence unable to account for the endless array of particular situations to which that content would apply). The problem reason encounters when confronted with the law's letter is not associated with any deficiency of particularity or of universality, but rather with the fact that universalization is a task, the very task the categorical imperative enjoins. This task, the task of universality, calls for the intervention of the one—the subject—the imperative addresses and enjoins: "Act . . ."

ALTERITY OF THE LAW

In the *Critique of Practical Reason* only one formulation of the categorical imperative prevails: "So act that the maxim of your will could always hold at the same time as a principle of a universal legislation [*Gesetzgebung*]."[53] Why does Kant give the law of freedom an imperative form? What conditions must reason meet in the second *Critique* that the form of the law is formulated as an injunction? What does "Act . . ." mean?[54] These questions invite us to explore three aspects of the law related to origin: facticity, unconditionality, and address.[55] Let us begin by proposing a few reflections on practical reason and the "fact" (*Faktum*) that happens to pure reason—the *factum rationis*, that is, through which the being practical of pure reason befalls reason.[56]

The pure reason at stake in Kant's practical philosophy is no longer a reason that reasons, rationalizes action, or provides a rule against which particular acts must be measured. Here thinking must deal with a pure reason whose being practical means being enjoined by duty, a pure reason that has to act.[57] The acting of pure practical reason would coincide, as Nancy remarks with brilliant simplicity, with reason's *acting itself out*, with reason's acting out what it is.[58] Reason's being practical is not something reason itself would reveal, but rather something that befalls reason as a fact, as the fact of reason (*factum rationis*), of which neither reason nor the subject is the origin.[59]

The consciousness of this basic law may be called a fact of reason [*Faktum*], because one cannot reason it out from antecedent data of

reason—e.g., from the consciousness of freedom (for this is not anteced-
ently given to us)—and because, rather, it thrusts itself upon us on its own
as a synthetic a priori proposition not based on any intuition, whether
pure or empirical.[60]

The fact of reason does not emerge from reason, but rather happens *to* reason, and only in this sense is pure reason (a reason that here does not reason)[61] practical by itself.[62] The law, as I said above, is not inherent in the
subject's nature. The law is, rather, what in the subject exceeds and addresses
the subject, what in the subject confronts the subject as something other.
This excess is possible because the being practical of reason does not exactly depend on pure reason itself, but rather happens to it as a fact, as a
factum rationis that, again, does not originate in reason, but "thrusts itself"
upon it.

The fact of reason confronts reason with the alterity of the law. This alterity, writes Nancy, is not the alterity of "any assignable other, whether a
great Other or a little other" (it is not something suprasensible, or a predis-
cursive or a dialectical other), "even though it determines the being-other
of any other."[63] This alterity will also determine, as we shall see in Chapters 4 and 5, the subject's relationship to the being-other of any other. The
alterity of the law is that of the fact of reason, "the fact that there is a factu-
ality or a facticity of the injunction in reason to reason, a facticity other than
reason in reason," at the core of reason.[64] This otherness, this *outside* or *elsewhere* at the core of reason, belongs in the structure of address of the injunction, an injunction that falls on reason as a fact. The law is thus excessive,
it is incommensurable with the subject that receives it. It is, again, what in
the subject is incommensurate to the subject.

The law appears to us, finite subjects, in the form of an imperative, according to Kant. The imperative enjoins rational beings to act, that is, to initiate a causality by oneself while being oneself without origin. The
unconditioned law prescribes unconditionality. What the imperative ultimately enjoins rational beings to do is to act so that universality can be attained. Universalization is a task, a duty that consists in beginning a causality
by oneself: "Act" so that freedom can begin something by itself. "Act" so that
you can initiate a series, even though nothing initiates in you. In terms of
the first *Critique*, freedom is "the power to begin a state *on one's own*,"[65] and
"this subject . . . begins its effects in the world of sense *on its own*, without

the action's beginning *in the subject* itself."⁶⁶ This "power to begin" in the subject is what we call practical reason: "if reason can have causality in regard to appearances, then it is a power *through* which the sensible condition of an empirical series of effects first begins."⁶⁷ It is as if the categorical imperative enjoined the subject to act, in short, so that the causality of practical reason is realized and freedom's presence in the world is actualized. We may say that in the categorical imperative come together the theoretical activity of pure reason and the being practical of pure reason. What the imperative prescribes, as Nancy indicates, is *"acting legally,* in the *legislative* sense. It prescribes that the maxim of action be the founding act of a law, of the law."⁶⁸ The law is not a law already formed; it is the imperative to form the law. The imperative prescribes to make law,⁶⁹ that is, to act. The acting at stake here is not, therefore, a specified modality of action that would constitute a *telos* germinating in an *arché,* but rather a beginning by itself, "an initiative or an initial move without any end."⁷⁰ The imperative enjoins the practical rationality in each subject, then, to become a beginning. In enjoining reason to act freely in this originary sense, the imperative links reason to what exceeds it.⁷¹

The imperative linking reason with that excess, the *factum rationis* confronting reason with the alterity of the law, takes the verbal form of an address. The imperative is a mode of enunciation, a saying that interpellates the subject, as if the subject were addressed by something other. Although the imperative addresses the subject (the subject's pure reason), the addressee here is not exactly the subject, but rather that which in the subject exceeds the subject (freedom). The fact that the law gives itself does not mean, as is often believed, that freedom gives itself the law. "The categorical imperative, which founds the incomprehensible system of human freedom, does not begin from freedom but ends and completes with it," writes Kant in *Opus Postumum.*⁷² The law is not founded by freedom,⁷³ but rather addresses itself to a freedom.⁷⁴ It is not the case, therefore, that what makes a freedom free is its obedience of its own law, of a law that would be inherent in freedom's nature. Freedom consists, rather, in beginning by itself.⁷⁵ Freedom is unconditioned, and hence inaugural. It consists, as Kant explains in the third antinomy, in "the power to begin a state *on one's own.*"⁷⁶ Distinguishing between practical laws and categorical imperatives in the *Metaphysics of Morals,* Kant writes: "The ground of possibility of categorical imperatives lies in the fact that they refer to no other determination of choice (by which a purpose could be ascribed to it) than simply to the freedom of choice."[77] The imperative addresses itself to a freedom, the addressee of the injunction is freedom. As addressee, writes Nancy,

> this freedom, which is not the self-position of the Subject, is not the free-dom of choice of the individual subject. It concerns what, in the individ-ual, is not the individual. And what is not of the individual—and neither of the "collective" as such—, is the possibility of being "addressed" by the other, from the alterity of the other (and not of being ratified by [*homo-logué sur*] the sameness of the other); it is the possibility of being inter-pellated or, even, according to the Greek sense of the term, of being *categorized* by the other. *Kategorein* is to accuse, to speak the accusative truth [*la vérité accusatrice*] of someone, and so to affirm, impute, and at-tribute. *The imperative categorizes its addressee*: it affirms the freedom of the addressee, imputes evil to it, and destines or abandons it to the law. In this triple way, the imperative categorizes in excess of every cat-egory, of every proper mode, essence or nature, of man [*l'impératif caté-gorise dans l'excès de toute catégorie, de tout mode propre, essence ou nature, de l'homme*].[78]

We may, in sum, think of the law and its relationship to freedom in two in-separable senses: law as address, as imperative, and law as unconditioned, as free beginning. The law as unconditioned, as freedom, entails a begin-ning by itself. The law as address, as accusative address, will be evoked by Levinas as its addressee's unconditioned response in the accusative: "me voici." Thinking the law as imperative or address and as unconditioned be-ginning, as freedom, should dissuade us from understanding freedom as a subject's self-legislating or self-positing action. And yet, freedom envisioned as a subject's self-legislation will be the form one's *consciousness* of being autonomous takes.[79]

A FREE CHOICE NOT MADE IN TIME

So far my study of the causality of freedom, law, and subject has explored the law's form and form's ability to motivate by examining, as Kant does, a practical object through a theoretical mode of reasoning. Echoing the third antinomy and also referring to it directly,[80] the *Critique of Practical Reason* gestures toward the theoretical sense of freedom as a spontaneity able to initiate the causal series through the mediation of the subject. The terms "initiate" and "motivate" both refer to an unconditioned beginning. "Initiate" concerns the power of cognition and refers to the impact of the causality of freedom on the cosmological series of causal linkage. In this theoretical sense freedom contingently anchors and reconfigures the causal series by manifesting its effects through the unconditioned functioning of an exceptional member, the subject. "Motivate" concerns, in turn, the causality of freedom in the subject and refers to freedom's constitutive power to affect the subject's desire and become the sole motivating force of the subject's itinerary. Both theoretical and practical operating modes of the unconditioned, initiation and motivation, come together in the first "piece" of the *Religion within the Bounds of Bare Reason*, "On the Inherence of Evil." In this essay Kant sets out to explain how freedom's ability to constitute a free subjectivity must manifest itself as a subject's initial having chosen freedom rather than evil as its ultimate constitutive ground. The choice at stake here is not one between a good and an evil act, but rather between a free disposition (unconditioned freedom) and an evil one (radical evil). If human beings were not disposed toward evil, the law would not take the form of an address. The fact that there is an imperative law, a law that addresses itself to a freedom, implies the possibility of an evil disposition. Just as the law is the *ratio cognoscendi* of freedom, it is also the *ratio cognoscendi* of evil,[81] and in this respect evil is as incomprehensible as freedom.[82]

How can we explain the presence of evil in the world? Is evil innate or can we attribute it to a free choice for which a subject could be held responsible? Is one, in other words, free to choose not to be free? The notion of evil is fundamental to autonomy, because the possibility of being autonomous is premised on having chosen the law as one's only moral ground and source of motivation. As Kant analyzes the structure of morality in this essay, he poses once again the question of morality's unknowable grounds.[83] Radical evil, he argues, does not concern the matter of maxims, but rather their form, that is, the way in which a subject incorporates incentives (*Triebfedern*) into its maxims. The law motivates the moral itinerary of a subject at two levels, that of the maxim's structure (where an incentive [*Triebfeder*] can exert its motivational power only when the subject incorporates it into its maxim) and that of the subject's disposition or ultimate ground of adoption of maxims (*Gesinnung*). In what concerns the form of maxims, "the freedom of the power of choice has the quite peculiar characteristic [*Beschaffenheit*] that it cannot be determined to an action by any incentive *except insofar as the human being has admitted [aufnehmen] the incentive into his maxim.*[84] An incentive is "consistent with the absolute spontaneity of the power of choice (i.e., with freedom)" only by being admitted into a maxim—and thus adopted as a universal rule "according to which he wills to conduct himself"—by a subject.[85] "However," continues Kant, "in the judgment of reason the moral law is on its own an incentive, and whoever makes it his maxim is *morally* good."[86] An act is free, in other words, only when a subject incorporates the moral law in its maxim as the only incentive. An action is evil even if it is lawful, on the other hand, when the power of choice is not determined by the moral law, but rather by the sensible incentives one has admitted into one's maxim and privileged over the law. For instance, suggests Kant, a person may stop lying so as not to be inconvenienced by the need to be consistent with one's lies, become moderate for the sake of health, be caring with others in order to gain their favor. Since these actions were ultimately driven by the impulse of self-love, they are still evil.[87]

Radical evil names, in sum, the prevalence of the law of self-love over the moral law as a subject's motivating ground. Thus, "whether the human being is good or evil must lie not in the distinction of the incentives that he admits into his maxim (not in the maxim's matter), but in their *subordination* (in the maxim's form): *which of the two he makes the condition of the other.* Consequently the human being (even the best) is evil only because he reverses the moral order of the incentives in admitting them into his maxims."[88] Since a maxim's form consists in the proper subordination of the incentives one admits into it, radical evil ultimately depends on the causal ordering of the motivating grounds that lead to each particular action. If a human being's incentives follow the "moral order," so that self-love is subordinated to the moral law as the supreme condition of a maxim, and therefore as the sole source of motivation, then that human being is good. Evil consists, in turn, in reversing that order and subordinating the moral law, which is the only moral incentive, to the incentives of self-love.[89] "This evil is radical because it corrupts the basis of all maxims."[90] Here the word "radical" refers literally to the root or ultimate ground of adoption of maxims,[91] and the terms "basis," "subordination," and "reversal" of incentives refer to the modes of causal linkage of motivating grounds. "Evil," writes Nancy, "is the corruption of the ground of the maxim and a maxim thus corrupted is a maxim that is no longer law making [*qui ne fait plus loi*]. Evil is not a contrary law; it is the disposition contrary to the law, the il-legislative disposition."[92] The lawful acts of those who have an evil disposition would be driven by self-love, and although becoming proficient in them could lead to a certain virtue, without the law as their motivation those acts would never be moral; they would not make law.

Whether one incorporates the moral law to one's maxim as the sole incentive or subordinates it to incentives associated with self-love depends on whether the supreme ground of adoption of one's maxims is good or evil. This ground of grounds in the subject, the cause of the subject's adoption of good or evil maxims, is what Kant calls one's disposition, orientation, or attitude (*Gesinnung*). A person with a good disposition has the law as the sole motivation for action and thus his or her incentives follow the "moral order," whereas a person with an evil disposition reverses the moral order by allowing sensible incentives to prevail over the law. If we envision freedom's ability to motivate a subject's itinerary in terms of causality, as Kant does, a subject's disposition (*Gesinnung*) would play the function of the unconditioned element in that subject's own ethical constitution. According to the function they play in a subject's disposition, freedom is unconditioned and evil is radical. But how is one's free disposition accorded this unconditioned role?

If, as Kant argues, the will (*Wille*) is indeed the power to determine itself as the cause of objects (or effects),[93] it would seem the concept "will" implies a decision or choice through which the subject of that will becomes a cause. And here is where a subject's choice comes into play. A subject's disposition or "subjective principle of maxims"[94] (*Gesinnung*) is acquired "through a free power of choice (*Willkür*), for otherwise it could not be imputed."[95] In freely choosing one's disposition one would be, in effect, choosing whether to be free. Evil may be thus defined as the refusal to be free, a refusal for which one can be held responsible because it is itself a free choice. But here Kant also claims that even when one has incorporated the moral law to one's maxim and has made it prevail over all sensible motives, that is, even when one acts following the moral inclination that one's disposition or orientation inspires, one really does not know what one's own disposition is. Kant vehemently insists that one's disposition is chosen because otherwise responsibility could not be imputed. In effect, however, one is not aware of having chosen one's disposition, because that choice, he writes, did not happen "in time" (*in der Zeit*). Since our *Gesinnung* "has not been procured over time" and thus cannot be derived "from any first act of the power of choice in time [*Zeit-Actus der Willkür*]"[96] (its adoption is not a "time-act of the power of choice"), we cannot gain conscious access to it: our free choice of disposition is "inscrutable [*unerforschlich*] to us."[97] In effect, we cannot even be certain whether we chose to have a "*good or evil heart*,"[98] "although inquiring about it is unavoidable."[99]

Kant expresses the fact that the free choice of one's disposition exceeds the consciousness of its author by excluding it from temporality.

> To have the one or the other attitude [*Gesinnung*] as an innate characteristic [*Beschaffenheit*] by nature also does not mean here that it has in no way been procured [*erworben*] by the human being who harbors it, i.e., that he is not the originator; rather, it means only that it has not been procured over time (that one or the other he *has always been, from his youth*). The attitude, i.e., the first subjective basis for the adoption of maxims, can only be one, and it applies universally to the entire use of freedom. But the attitude itself must also have been adopted through a free power of choice [*Willkür*], for otherwise it could not be imputed.[100]

Because "we cannot derive this attitude, or rather its supreme basis, from any first act of the power of choice in time we call it a characteristic of the power of choice belonging to it by nature (even though in fact it has its basis in freedom)."[101] Although with these words Kant confirms reason's inability to access the unconditioned cause of a subject's morality, the effectivity of that unconditioned cause (the "first act of the power of choice," which "has its basis in freedom") must be assumed. Since we have no awareness of that originary choice, we say that the good or evil character of a human being is innate. The term "innate" does not evoke a literal temporality or causality that would point to birth as the cause of one's choice of character, but rather what we may be tempted to imagine as a different and inscrutable temporality coexisting with time.[102] As Kant puts it, "the good or the evil in the human being (as the subjective first basis for the adoption of this or that maxim with regard to the moral law)" is not a fact that can be experienced. Therefore, it "is called innate merely in the sense that it is laid at the basis (in earliest youth, back to the point of birth) prior to any use of freedom that is given in experience, and thus is conceived as present in the human being simultaneously with birth—though not exactly as having birth as its cause."[103] At stake here, therefore, is not a distinction between temporalities, but rather a distinction in the way of understanding origin. *Gesinnung* as the origin or initiating cause from which all effects would descend should be understood in terms of reason and not in terms of time.[104]

The free choice of one's disposition is not a conscious decision. If it were, it would belie the causality of freedom (where the initial choice is unconditioned) and contradict the facticity of the law (where one's being addressed by the imperative is not the result of a decision but an unconditioned fact). A free act cannot depend on a conscious decision, since consciousness is phenomenal, driven by sensibility, and therefore the power of choice would tend toward an object or goal. A free act emerges from the causality of freedom that animates the subject, a causality of which the subject can have no knowledge. Hence, all theoretical reason can do is conceive the inscrutability of our own disposition and of our free choice of it in rational causal terms.[105] As reason traces each maxim back to what motivated its choice, the regression from each ground to the previous one would continue indefinitely in the impossible aspiration to reach the ultimate ground of our actions.[106] Its having been freely chosen would act as an unconditioned cause. Although our disposition is chosen freely, although the subject authors that choice, reason's presentation of the causality of freedom in the subject can only conceptualize it as an unreachable cause. "Now, the subjective basis or the cause of this adoption cannot again be cognized (although inquiring about it is unavoidable), because otherwise one would in turn have to adduce a maxim into which this attitude [*Gesinnung*] had been adopted, and this maxim must likewise have its basis in turn."[107] The choice of the initial disposition is a free act: it has been "procured by the human being who harbors it," he is its "originator" because it must "have been adopted through a free power of choice."[108] This initial choice by the subject is presented by reason as the unconditioned element heterogeneous to the regressive series of grounds that Kant locates out of time, in an intelligible and thus empty space beyond; hence its inscrutability.

Within freedom's causality in the subject, the choice of *Gesinnung* would constitute the unconditioned element in the causal series. In this respect, Kant's essay "On the Inherence of Evil" echoes the structure of the third antinomy. Here it is not a matter of attaining a cosmological synthesis of causal linkage, but rather of imagining how the subject becomes itself the cause of its own causality and itinerary. Conceiving a subject's disposition as acquired through its own power of choice allows reason to attribute to the subject the role of initiating the causality through freedom that animates it. If in the third antinomy the object of reason had to be limited by experience, and so the idea of freedom could only be presented as non-contradictory, in this essay (whose ultimate concern is practical reason) Kant can affirm that "this adoption (of moral maxims) is free," that it has an "ultimate subjective ground," and that one's *Gesinnung*, a subject's ethical disposition, is the result of a free choice. The subject's free acts are motivated by the law that the subject has freely chosen as the supreme ground of its acts. What one chooses, in effect, is to be the addressee of the law one already is. Since, as I said above, the one the law interpellates is not exactly the subject but rather what in the subject exceeds the subject (freedom), what one chooses is to harbor the other in the subject, freedom, to which the law addresses itself.

UNCONDITIONALITY AND ADDRESS

The law interpellates a freedom, a subject that must freely choose to be constituted by freedom, to be the one—the freedom—the law can address. The law as address (imperative) and the law as free origin (freedom) come together in the idea that one has freely chosen one's disposition. Structurally, a subject's free act of choosing its own disposition (*Gesinnung*) functions as the unconditioned beginning of the causality of freedom in oneself. This free act of choice introduces the boundary the imagination needs for the causality of freedom in the subject to cohere. Through its initial and free act, the subject becomes the author of its own disposition and thus responsible for it. The subject becomes the one that has chosen to harbor the causality of freedom acting in oneself and through oneself, a free causality the subject does not understand. By choosing a disposition that has the moral law as the supreme ground of motivation, the subject confers on the unconditioned law the power to be the cause and makes it the element that *initiates* the chain. Here, in the second *Critique*, the (practical) causality at stake is the causality of freedom that constitutes the subject. By analogy with the theoretical structure of the third antinomy, reason is able to envision the subject as beginning its own subjective itinerary, the itinerary of a subjectivity constituted and animated by the causality of freedom. Although the causality of freedom is unconditioned, the subject plays the role of the unconditioned by *beginning by itself,* by choosing to harbor the causality of freedom that is already in oneself.[109]

In offering an account of the constitution of the moral subject by the law, the second *Critique* is able to provide theoretical reason with the subjectivity it had to presuppose at the moment of introducing a causality through freedom in the third antinomy. With this the delineation of the causality of freedom in Kant's theoretical and practical philosophy may be said to run its full course. The effects of freedom could become manifest in the world, we recall, by the unwitting mediation of a subject constituted by freedom. In this theoretical sense, the causality of freedom acts through the subject, enabling reason to supplement natural causality with a causality through freedom.[110] As *bearer* of freedom or practical reason, the subject is the one that, by taking up the position of the unconditioned, could make freedom's effects reverberate in the causal chain. Structurally speaking, reason in the third antinomy envisions the subject as embodying a spontaneity able to start a series on its own. In playing the role of the unconditioned, the subject, I argued, enables a synthesis of causal linkage to form, however fleetingly and contingently. The subject thus establishes a relationship between the phenomenal series and what exceeds it, between what the understanding can cognize and the other of thought. In fact, subjectivity, I proposed, *is* that relationship. In the third antinomy, therefore, the position or relationship we call subject plays the role of a contingent and dynamic boundary that enables reason to conceive a cosmological synthesis of causal linkage. As the subject plays the function of unconditioned cause, reason may envision it retroactively as anchoring and reconfiguring the cosmological causal chain.[111]

In Kant's practical philosophy, in turn, the retroactive constitution of subjectivity is enabled by the subject's initial free choice of ethical disposition as the "ultimate subjective ground" for adopting maxims motivated by the law. More exactly, the free choice of *Gesinnung,* an unconditioned choice that is not intentional or conscious and does not appear as an event in the world, is what confers on the causality of freedom constituting the subject its power to begin. Or to formulate this in terms of Kant's qualification of the law as unconditioned, although the law is its own cause only the intervention of the subject can give it its power as cause by making of it the element that initiates and motivates its own subjective itinerary.[112] The circular character of this process, related to the circularity of respect (*Achtung*) I will examine in the next chapter, is only apparent. It reflects the retroactive functioning of causality at play in the third antinomy, a retroactivity that, we now see, also configures the practical causality through which subjectivity is produced.

What reason imagines retroactively (tracing back a subjective itinerary toward a first free motivation) as the subject's free choice of *Gesinnung*, a choice not recoverable through consciousness, marks the very emergence of autonomous subjectivity. Facticity would be the consciousness that the law is in us. What in cosmological causality was an unknown possibility, the existence of the unconditioned, finds its practical equivalent in the facticity of the law. If the unconditioned initiated the cosmological causal chain, facticity establishes that the law is present in us and has the ability to motivate freedom's causality in the subject. In choosing one's *Gesinnung*, one would come to choose, in effect, something that was already in oneself. According to Kant's insight into this originary *act* of the power of choice, autonomy would consist in authoring what one has received (a law that gives itself, that addresses a freedom). Freely choosing one's good disposition would mean giving oneself what is already in oneself, choosing to be the addressee one already is of the law, choosing to be the one (the freedom) to which the law addresses itself. This law that gives itself to us, that "thrusts itself upon us on its own" as a fact of reason,[113] will be, through the enigma of autonomy, the law we believe we give ourselves. Only in this sense may we say that the subject becomes the unconditioned beginning or "author" of the causality of freedom that animates its subjectivity. By venturing the possibility of this originary choice to be free, to begin by oneself and stand for the origin of what has no origin, the essay "On the Inherence of Evil" intimates a deeply Kantian notion of autonomy that Kant did not elaborate systematically in a single place.

4

AFFECT OF THE LAW

How does the causality of freedom affect the subject? What is the subject's relationship to the law? Although freedom is incomprehensible, it manifests itself through the moral law, of whose existence, insists Kant, we know.[1] This would seem to imply that the law is something we can experience, yet Kant defines the law as excluding any matter (any desired object or goal) that could move the power of desire. Surprising as it may sound to us, sensible beings, the desire of an autonomous subjectivity can only be motivated by the law. That the law should become the sole incentive for action implies, however, that its form must also play the motivating function of matter.[2] But how can the form of the law play the function of matter and move the faculty of desire (*Willkür*) without the help of sensibility? In order to do so the law must have some kind of impact on the subjectivity it constitutes. Kant's attempt to describe this impact as an exceptional kind of affect poses one of the most difficult challenges of his critical project. How does the subject experience the inexperienceable, the law? What is the law's impact on the subjectivity it affects and moves?

At the very heart of autonomy there is something that appears other but does not have its grounds outside me—it has neither empirical nor transcendent grounds. In order to account for the singularity of this other and of its relationship to the subject Kant introduces the notion he calls "respect" of the law (*Achtung*). Dieter Henrich describes respect as belonging to "that class of accomplishments in which an identification with something of one's own takes place which is at the same time encountered as the other."[3] In respect "I recognize a command," a power not foreign to me which "nonetheless . . . *appears* and *demands* respect."[4] I acknowledge a power in me which is other than me, even though "I subordinate myself to this command without being moved to do so by grounds other than those contained in it."[5] Jean-Luc Nancy evokes respect, in turn, as "the very alteration of the position and the structure of the subject," that is, as the way in which the subject "responds (but without *responding*) to the alterity of the law."[6] Kant's notion of respect expresses the impact of the law's otherness on the subject, but can that affect be conveyed without inflicting a violence on logical discourse, without stretching its resources to the extreme? Respect is, Kant writes, a unique feeling "brought about by an intellectual basis," a feeling "that is not of empirical origin and is cognized a priori."[7] What kind of feeling, then, is respect? Can one even consider this affect not based on presentations of the agreeable or disagreeable to be a feeling? And how could the singular feeling of respect influence the power of desire and determine the will without the mediation of sensibility?[8] With the term "respect" Kant names the law's capacity to motivate the will by itself, but explaining how that happens would be tantamount, he admits, to finding "the philosopher's stone."[9]

Kant's investigation of the moral affect he calls "respect" in the third chapter of the Analytic in the second *Critique*, "On the Incentives of Pure Practical Reason," focuses on the effect of the law on the subject, and on the subject's relationship to the law. This chapter begins by establishing the law's ability to determine and motivate the will: "What is essential in all moral worth of actions," writes Kant, "is that *the moral law must determine the will [Wille] directly*."[10] Understanding how the law determines action objectively is already a challenging task.[11] Beyond this objective determination, it is perhaps even more difficult to understand how the law can motivate the will (*Wille*) also subjectively, that is, "directly," without the mediation of any feeling.[12] How "a law can by itself and directly be a determining basis of the will," acknowledges Kant, "is an insoluble problem for human reason, and is one and the same problem as the one concerning how a free will is possible."[13] Indeed, how can the law become the only ethical motivation, literally "*elater animi*," the driver of the soul?[14] How are we to interpret Kant's claim that the form of the law moves the power of desire (*Willkür*), given that, as he tirelessly insists, the faculty of desire is generally affected only by presentations and the feelings they produce? If the form of the law cannot be contained by any presentation, and thus cannot arouse any feeling, how can it animate the subject and move it to act? Ultimately, if the law is defined by its empty form (as Kant claims), and the law's form has no power on sensibility, how do we even know the law exists?

It would seem, then, that in order to become the sole motivation of morality the law must have some kind of impact on the subject. In order to understand how the law of freedom works by giving rise to its own causality through the mediation of the subject (by being the cause of objects and events, as we saw in the third antinomy), then, one needs to explain how the law becomes the subjective or affective cause of the subject's choices. At stake here is the possibility of autonomy, for only by having freedom as its sole subjective cause could the subject be autonomous. The question Kant must thus address is how the impact or affect produced on the subject by a law that "thrusts itself upon us" as "the sole fact of pure reason"[15] becomes the only causality that animates the subject. As he explains in "On the Inherence of Evil" (the first essay in the *Religion*), the law was freely chosen by each of us in an *act* of choice that did not happen in time and which is therefore irrecoverable through memory or consciousness.[16] In explaining the affect produced by this choice—an affect that in the dislocated causality of respect also furthers the power of freedom acting in us—it is nevertheless not a matter of seeking an incentive produced and fueled by the law in order to promote obedience. What we must ask is, rather, what effect the law itself as incentive has on the subject's "mind."[17] What one needs to figure out, in sum, is how the law itself is a cause that acts on, in, and through the subject in ways the latter does not necessarily understand. Kant explains that impact in the form of the only feeling that would be moral and not pathological, the sole affect not belonging to sensibility but ascertainable a priori. This is the singular feeling he calls respect (*Achtung*).

The task of exploring the law's effect in terms of affect, as Kant sets out to do here, poses one of the riskiest challenges to his critical project, a challenge which is at once philosophical and poetic. On the success of this explanation depends the *Critique*'s ability to complete the system of freedom. The quandary to reckon with would seem to be partly logical: as soon as one begins to read the chapter "On the Incentives," one can detect a certain circularity in the causal relationship between the moral law and the will. Respect is an affect produced by the moral law as it determines the will. Respect is, *at the same time*, the affect through which the moral law determines our will. Respect appears, therefore, both as the effect and the cause of the determination of the will.[18] As Nancy puts it, "the imperative does not take place without respect . . . . It is respect of the imperative, the respect for it and the respect that it commands *ipso facto*, that gives us the law, or that gives us the law *as law*."[19] Furthermore, the law "arouses *respect* for itself"[20] as its effect, and yet, on the other hand, "no feeling for this law occurs at all."[21] Although the motivational force the law instills in the subject is not a feeling (it has no connection with sensibility), the affect produced by the "positive furtherance" of the law's causality "can now also be called a feeling of respect for the moral law."[22] What kind of "feeling," then, is respect?

In respect Kant discerns the interaction of two *moments*, a negative and a positive one. These two moments acting together—*Achtung* as *attentio* and *Achtung* as *reverentia*[23]—correspond to the two senses, negative and affirmative, he attributes to the notion of freedom: freedom *from* and freedom *to*. In a first, negative sense, the moral law impairs all sensible inclinations, striking down self-conceit, and restricts "psychological" self-love to the rational self-love which is the condition of agreement with the law. This restrictive action, which brings about pain, humbles and humiliates us. "Thus to this extent the effect of the moral law as an incentive is only negative."[24] As an incentive the law has "a negative effect on feeling . . . which is itself a feeling."[25] Respect in the negative sense manifests itself to sensibility in the form of humiliation provoked by the law's restraining effect on sensible motives, incentives over which the law (itself a practical incentive and the only moral one) must prevail. This "negative effect on feeling (disagreeableness) is, like all influence on feeling and every feeling in general, *pathological*."[26] We could also formulate this by pointing out that the effect of the moral law is perceived in a pathological way from the restricted perspective of consciousness. It is noteworthy that every time Kant refers to this negative effect he is careful to clarify that he is speaking from the finite perspective of consciousness. Hence his insistence that the rational subject affected by inclinations feels humiliated "as the effect of the consciousness of the moral law."[27] As the subject becomes conscious of the moral law, the affected subject feels humiliated. Although the unique feeling called respect is not produced by any sensible incentive, although "there is in the subject no *antecedent* feeling that would be attuned to morality," what makes respect possible is precisely the subject's sensibility and finitude: respect "presupposes this sensibility and hence also the finitude of such beings [i.e., rational beings] on whom the moral law imposes respect."[28] The fact that, as Kant notes, "sensible feeling . . . is indeed a condition of that sensation we call respect" means that we "feel" respect because of our sensibility, but "this sensation . . . must be called *brought about practically*."[29]

Kant's chapter on respect does indeed differentiate between the law's negative effect, a psychological feeling, and the positive effect through which the law advances its causality (an effect that, as we already anticipated, functions also as cause). Kant is very careful to clarify that the negative effect of the law on feeling, the law's restraining action, is perceived as pathological from the limited perspective of consciousness. In fact, Kant emphatically differentiates his positive conception of respect as affect—an affect that *signals* the subject's relationship with the law—from the way in which the subject perceives and presents the law's effect. When in this chapter he speaks about the negative presentation of the law's effect, the law is not referred to directly, but rather as it is "regarded subjectively," as a presentation of "our self-consciousness": "the presentation of something as *determining basis of our will* humbles us in our self-consciousness when we compare it with the sensible propensity of our nature."[30] In fact, Kant is explicit about the difference between the pathological "effect of the consciousness of the moral law" and the "practical feeling" that furthers the law's causality:

> Although as the effect of the consciousness of the moral law and consequently in reference to an intelligible cause—viz., the subject, of pure reason as supreme legislator—this feeling of a rational subject affected by inclinations is called humiliation (intellectual contempt), yet in reference to the positive basis of this humiliation, the law, it is at the same time called respect for the law. No feeling for this law occurs at all.[31]

Kant insistently signals, in sum, that he is speaking of our necessarily limited presentation of the law. It is important to keep this in mind so as not to reduce the idea of freedom as efficient cause, an idea into which one cannot have any insight, to what he terms psychological or "comparative" freedom. Significantly, the section that immediately follows the one on respect, "Critical Examination of the Analytic of Pure Practical Reason,"[32] devotes several pages to the distinction between practical and psychological freedom. Psychological freedom is driven by matter or by presentations, that is, by determining bases that belong in natural necessity even when those grounds are presented as internal. Kant firmly criticizes the assumption that actions are free because they are rooted in internal presentations, and he gives as examples automata and spin-tops, which once they have been set in movement do not need any external input to continue moving.[33] Indeed, whether a will is free does not depend on whether the power of desire is moved solely by internal determining grounds. In fact, the notion of autonomy does not rest on the distinction between internal and external,[34] but rather on the distinction between natural causality and causality through freedom, that is, on whether motivation is caused by empirical conditions or uncaused (empirically unconditioned). In the case of a conception of morality that reduces obligation to a threatening command, one would act, for example, out of fear. If one were to understand practical freedom as a psychological property instead of as "a transcendental predicate of the causality of a being that belongs to the world of sense,"[35] one would end up annulling transcendental freedom, and with it the moral law.

Kant's description of the law's negative impact on feeling is so compelling that it has dwelled in many readers' imaginations as the predominant definition of respect. Explaining the positive aspect of respect constitutes a more difficult challenge. Beyond having the negative effect of checking sensible impulses, "this law is, after all, something in itself positive, viz., the form of an intellectual causality, i.e., of freedom."[36] As the form of a causality through freedom "the moral law is an object of the greatest *respect* and thus also the basis of a positive feeling that is not of empirical origin and is cognized a priori. Therefore respect for the moral law is a feeling that is brought about by an intellectual basis" and whose necessity we can recognize.[37] Unlike respect in the negative sense, which affects sensibility, respect in the positive sense takes place in practical reason or, as Kant also puts it, in the intelligible subject (that is, in the intelligible otherness in subjectivity to which the subject has no access). In its positive effect the law takes the form of an intellectual causality, a causality through freedom. The effect of the law can become a positive feeling with an intellectual basis. This positive affect is one of the ways in which the free causality that acts in the subject but that the subject does not understand *signifies* itself. Freedom leaves its mark in the subjectivity it constitutes by legislating, by giving the law. Since respect in the positive sense is not rooted in sensibility, Kant hesitates to consider it a "feeling" or at least restrains his acknowledgment that this affect must be a feeling: "No feeling for this law occurs at all."[38]

Respect as a practical affect is associated with its ability to further freedom's causality, but when one tries to think it, respect seems to disturb the causal order, as I noted above. In my discussion on the law's causality in

Chapter 3 I underscored Kant's explicit attempt to avert accusations of circularity regarding the causality of freedom and the moral law.[39] In the case of the section on respect, however, far from avoiding a certain dislocation of causality, Kant, in fact, promotes it. In the process of elucidating the *"moral feeling"* of respect, the causal linkage between it and the law becomes circular: respect for the moral law is said to be an effect produced by the law which *at the same time* furthers the law's motivational force,[40] that is, the law's ability to determine the subject's will without the mediation of sensibility: "inasmuch as the law moves the resistance out of the way, in the judgment of reason this removal of an obstacle is esteemed equal to a positive furtherance of its [this law's] causality."[41] Here respect is qualified as that which furthers the law's influence on the will: "Thus the moral law . . . has influence on the sensibility of the subject and brings about a feeling that furthers the law's influence on the will"[42]; elsewhere respect is a feeling produced by the law. But as Kant also affirms a few lines below, respect for the law is a subjective determining basis, that is, an incentive, only as "regarded subjectively": "respect for the law is not an incentive to morality; rather, it is morality itself regarded subjectively as an incentive."[43]

These words offer us insight into why the causality of law and respect appears circular to us. Respect is morality itself, not an incentive to morality, but from a subjective viewpoint it is regarded as incentive. From that restricted subjective perspective, this causality would thus be perceived as follows: because one feels respect for the law, one's faculty of desire comes to desire the law. However, the law in the subject and the affect the law produces in the subject, respect, are one and the same. One could conclude, therefore, that the law does not exist out there, as something outside the subject and independent from it that would then be adopted by the subject. Rather, the law only exists in the subject and through the intervention of the subject. This circularity imprinted on respect corresponds to the retroactive functioning of causality at play in it, a retroactivity that, as we know, characterizes causal linkage as conceived in the third antinomy.[44] It is not the case, either, that there is in the subject a preexisting feeling that would predispose it toward the law ("there is in the subject no antecedent feeling that would be attuned to morality").[45] In fact, the subject emerges in relationship to the law, it is constituted by the affect of the law. Moreover, not only does the law leave a trace in the subject: the subject is itself that trace, as I argue in Chapter 5. This is what one can take Kant to mean when he says that respect is morality itself, that respect and the law (or respect for the law and morality) are the same, however much from the subject's restricted viewpoint respect may be perceived as an incentive. Though respect would seem to be an affect produced in the subject by the law, an affect that would then function as an incentive to morality, in effect the law itself does not exist outside the impact it produces in the subject, the affect called respect. This would explain why the causality of respect appears dislocated. The law in the subject and the effect the law produces in the subject are one and the same: a *being affected* unconditionally or, in Levinas's words, an "anarchic being affected" (*affection anarchique*)[46]—the subject itself.

BETWEEN

As an effect produced by the law respect is a sensible feeling. As that which furthers the law's causality, in turn, respect does not have its origin in sensibility, but rather in practical reason. What happens, then, *between* the law's restrictive effect and its becoming a positive "feeling"? Given that the negative effect of the law operates in sensibility (the law disarms sensible incentives of their motivational force) whereas its positive effect occurs in practical reason (the law becomes the only motivation), what is the connection between these two areas of influence, phenomenal and intelligible, Kant attributes to the law? Or to echo the terminology he introduces in the solution of the third antinomy, is there any difference between the law's effect on the subject's sensibility and the law's intelligible impact? "Here then," writes Kant in the *Grounding for the Metaphysics of Morals*, "is the extreme limit of all moral inquiry."

> To determine this limit is of great importance for the following considerations. On the one hand, reason should not, to the detriment of morals, search around in the world of sense for the supreme motive and for some interest that is conceivable but is nonetheless empirical. On the other hand, reason should not flap its wings impotently, without leaving the spot, in a space that for it is empty, namely, the space of transcendent concepts that is called the intelligible world, and thereby lose itself among mere phantoms of the brain. Furthermore, the idea of a pure intelligible world regarded as a whole of all intelligences to which we ourselves belong as rational beings (even though we are from another standpoint also

members of the world of sense) remains always a useful and permissible idea for the purpose of a rational belief, although all knowledge ends at its boundary.[47]

As we know, demarcating the intelligible by placing it off-limits secures the smooth functioning of theoretical reasoning, since that demarcation bounds the realm of objectivity (what the understanding can cognize) by introducing an empty space beyond in which reason can locate transcendental freedom.[48] But can one affirm, as the *Grounding for the Metaphysics of Morals*, the second *Critique*, and "On the Inherence of Evil" do, that the intelligible manifests itself in the world? And in affirming the existence of the intelligible, can one really prevent it from being reduced to the transcendent? The third antinomy locates the coexistence between nature and freedom in the subject, which in playing the role of the unconditioned would anchor the dynamic series of causal linkage. The second *Critique* situates unconditionality at the center of ethics, specifically in the notion that the only possible ethical motivation comes directly from the law. In so doing, both the third antinomy and the Analytic of Practical Reason elaborate freedom's causality in the subject (and through it in the world) as immanent. Respect attests to this subjectivity affected not only by what is given through the senses but also by unconditioned freedom and the law. A lot is therefore at stake in this last section of the Analytic, the section on respect.

Can there really be a connection between these two heterogeneous *spaces*, the sensible and the intelligible, when only one of them is defined by presentations and can be represented? Henrich equates the difficulty in understanding the relationship between these two moments of respect with the enigma of the facticity of the law, which he envisions chronologically or causally as necessarily preceding respect. He attributes the intricacy of this connection to the fact that Kant has to assign each of the moments he distinguishes in respect to a different faculty of the mind: again, the negative effect (respect as limitation and therefore as humiliation) takes place in "sensibility," whereas the positive one (respect as elevation) emerges from "the 'intellectual side' of moral life." Henrich contends, however, that the negative and positive manifestations of respect are not interdependent: "As a rational being I know how to esteem a power which I experience as a sensible being insofar as this power exercises force on me in an inexplicable fashion and hinders the unfolding of my inclinations. My reason experiences an expansion, my sensibility a limitation."[49] He concludes that in Kant's account the positive aspect of respect is merely the effect of evaluating rationally the worth or liberation of having an obstacle removed.[50] All Kant's theory would ultimately achieve, according to this view, is an evaluation of limited sensibility. But this expansion or elevation, I would respond, constitutes a psychological reward, and hence a sensible compensation. The fact is that the affect Kant calls respect in the positive sense is not exactly something one may perceive. One cannot adopt the distance necessary to perceive—let alone represent—anything, because (as I have argued so far) the effect or affect of the law is a *being affected*, that is, the subject itself.

It may well be the case, then, that an evaluation of the limits of experience is all Kant could possibly accomplish if he were to remain faithful to the limits of theoretical reason he had so painstakingly established in the first *Critique*. Kant's doctrine of respect indeed aspires to account for "the power and the demand of the law which encounters me,"[51] but beyond naming that power, beyond naming its impact on the subject, can one ever succeed in accounting for it? For Henrich that account would have to be that of "a positive relation of consciousness to the law" which "would be an act of identification and thus distance and unity at once."[52] Although this is an accurate description of the notion of consciousness as Fichte would soon formulate it, a notion which, as Henrich himself points out, is not yet present in Kant, what one could object to Henrich's critique is that the intelligible dimension of practical reason is not available to consciousness. The act of identification (of "distance and unity at once") Henrich rightly attributes to consciousness would do justice, according to him, to respect as a structure "in which an identification with something of one's own takes place which is at the same time encountered as the other."[53] But must not any account of the structure of respect that describes it in terms of identification be dialectic and remain enrooted in the restrictive perspective of consciousness?

The challenge confronting Kant's reasoning—as well as Henrich's interpretation—is that any positive or substantial account one may give of the causality through freedom or of the origin of the moral law must necessarily miss its object, since this causality presupposes an unconditioned element to which reason must restrict its access. That unconditioned element is, moreover, embodied by the subject. It inhabits the subject, so to speak, and in this sense it cannot be considered to exist outside. "Solely the concept of freedom permits us to find the unconditioned and intelligible for the conditioned and sensible without needing to go outside ourselves."[54] We could argue, therefore, that the only way in which Kant's account would do justice to the immanence of freedom or the unconditionality of the law is by failing to account for it. This would testify to the rigor of Kant's thinking, especially since he was explicitly aware that his critics and supporters alike could deem it inconsistent or interpret it as lack of philosophical restraint. Given that Kant's account of respect would prove one of the most controversial chapters in the second *Critique*, could he have had it in mind when in the ensuing "Critical Examination of the Analytic of Pure Practical Reason" that completes this chapter he observes that "what halfway through it seemed to me at times very precarious in view of extraneous other doctrines was, in the end, in an unexpected way perfectly harmonious with what . . . had turned up on its own—provided only that I left this precariousness out of sight and attended merely to my business until it was completed"?[55] In recommending that "in every scientific investigation one should with all possible exactness and frankness pursue one's course undisturbed, without being concerned about what the investigation might perhaps offend against outside its realm,"[56] could Kant be anticipating the criticism his loyalty to his own insight could potentially provoke?

But this is not only a question of loyalty to one's insights. Crucially at stake here is the need to keep noumenon negative, so that its unconditionality can function as a boundary. In the third antinomy that boundary (unconditioned freedom), embodied by the subject, allowed reason to form a synthesis of causal linkage that coheres as a contingent system in progress.[57] In the second *Critique* that boundary, the unconditionality of the law, makes the constitution of subjectivity conceivable, if not conceptualizable. Acknowledging limits, indeed the very problem that fuels the entire critical project, entails refraining from trespassing the bounds of what theoretical reason can know. We may thus reformulate our initial question on respect in the following terms: How does the ethical motivation furthered by the law manifest itself to the finite perspective of consciousness?

THE LAW'S THREATENING VOICE

Here is the argument I would like to rehearse. The otherness at the heart of autonomy is neither another form of heteronomy brought about by natural determinism, nor the voice of conscience (even though Kant refers to the notion of conscience in contexts I will study below). The power that is not mine I find in respect refers to the intelligible or what we have called the other of thought: to something I embody, something that acts in me. This relationship with an element of excess that inhabits me, a relationship that we here name subjectivity, is, I argue, what Kant conceives as respect. But again, can practical philosophy account for this otherness *within* the self from the limited perspective of consciousness without reducing it to a form of heteronomy (a source of pathological motivation) such as a coercive injunction or a fear-instilling voice of conscience?

Let us retake Henrich's contention that all Kant's theory of respect accomplishes is an account of limited sensibility. According to him, Kant's theory dissolves the structure of respect (in which "something of one's own takes place which is at the same time encountered as the other") "into the interplay of two acts which could equally well be experienced independent of each other."[58] "Therewith," he argues, "the intention of the moral consciousness is perverted into its opposite, and indeed in opposition to the intention which was contained in Kant's theory. There is no possibility for this theory to account for a positive relation of consciousness to the law . . . ."[59] But why would "the intention of the moral consciousness" be "perverted into its opposite," and what is the result of that perversion? According to Henrich, that perversion takes place as a consequence of the inability to explain rationally the unity of the two moments of respect. What I propose to do here is trace the origin of that perversion precisely back to the attempt at reducing the positive moment of respect—associated with a practical reason that must act—to a rational logic of coherence. One of the problems is that *reverentia* does not follow from *attentio*. *Attentio* and *reverentia* cannot be in a causal relation (unless one is thinking in terms of psychological causality), especially if *attentio* is understood only as a negative limitation, even if at certain points of his reasoning Kant seems to deduce the latter from the former. It may well be the case that what leads to a perversion of the moral consciousness is precisely the urge to establish a logical continuity between the two acts involved in respect. So long as the positive aspect of respect (what Henrich denominates elevation or *reverentia*) is considered a conscious act, so long as it is taken to be the object of rational explanation, it would seem one must run into a deformation of the law.

In fact, in the process of unraveling the effect of the law, the chapter on *Achtung* introduces another form of alterity that appears as a demotion of the unconditioned and formal law: the law is described as having a terrible gaze and voice.

> There is something so special in the boundless esteem for the pure moral law stripped of all advantage—as this law is presented to us, for compliance, by practical reason, whose voice makes even the boldest offender tremble and compels him to hide from his [own] sight—that one need not be surprised to find this influence of a merely intellectual idea on feeling unfathomable for speculative reason, and to have to settle for being capable nonetheless of this much insight a priori: that such a feeling is inseparably linked with the presentation of the moral law in every finite rational being.[60]

The law seems to have acquired a fearful voice that makes "even the boldest offender tremble and compels him to hide from his [own] sight." Werner Pluhar's choice to translate *"vor seinem Anblicke"* as "from his [own] sight" (instead of from the law's sight, as it is frequently translated) is particularly suggestive because it emphasizes the internal character of the law. What one would be compelled to hide from is not any externalized version of the law's gaze, but rather the very sight of oneself, of, as Kant will put it later, the shameful and dreary "inner spectacle of self-examination."[61] This translation underscores the law's manifestation in the form of a voice. In line with the dreaded confrontation with one's conscience in self-examination, this depiction of the law as voice is in consonance with Kant's eventual identification of the law with conscience, as well as with the usual representation of conscience as a voice.[62] Later in the chapter Kant will again refer to "respect for the law, which is linked with fear or at least worry about transgressing it."[63]

Does this mean that Kant betrays his initial conception of the law? This depiction of a threatening law would seem to contradict the law's spirit, its ability to determine and motivate the will directly. Following the law according to the spirit means furthering the law's ability to act as unconditioned, that is, to be its own condition, the sole motive for an action. In any instance of "fear or at least worry about transgressing" the law there would seem to be a shift from motivation to the idea that there is a missing substantial content or prescription one needs to obey. As I pointed out in Chapter 3, envisioning the law as missing content implies yielding to the desire for a substantial content—for a pre-existing idea of the good—that would provide the horizon that legitimizes one's choices. But if one aspired to find support for one's actions anywhere other than in the law, even if that elsewhere were the idea of the good, one would be motivated by pathological incentives. This is, in fact, what following a coercive or seductive law would imply, which is why Nancy insists that the law carries neither threat nor promise.[64] In seeking to allay the fear of being punished, one is in effect motivated by a desired object or goal, thus prioritizing heteronomy over autonomy. Acting according to the law and only because of the law means, in turn, taking the law as *causa sui* (as unconditioned), as an action's sole incentive. "*Autonomy* of the will is the sole principle of all moral laws and of the duties conforming to them; any *heteronomy* of the power of choice, on the other hand, not only is no basis for any obligation at all, but is, rather, opposed to the principle of obligation and to the morality of the will."[65] Thus, wouldn't the consciousness of the law, where the law is likely to be perceived as an alienating command, replace ethical obligation with something that in effect belies it, "something opposed to the principle of obligation and to the morality of the will"?

Should we, again, entertain the idea that in this chapter Kant belies his conception of a formal law by demoting it to a law of what Freud would call the superego? Some Kantian scholars have, in fact, sought to demonstrate that there is a productive proximity between Kant's moral law and Freud's superego.[66] Others have, in turn, detected a shift in Kant's understanding of the law in the paragraphs on respect I quoted above, which may be interpreted as a demotion of the unconditioned law to a law of the superego (*avant la lettre*) or conscience.[67] Even if one were to envision the superego as a productive thing,[68] ethical obligation is not reducible to it. Envisioning the ethical as a constraint on action only accounts for a *this side* of obligation, as I have argued elsewhere.[69] Kant's law is not associated with the internalization of external authority; if it were, it could be used to justify any unjustifiable act.[70] Any demotion of the law to a punishing agency would seem to indicate a desire to revive an absolute other that can function as the legitimizing horizon of one's acts.

UNCONDITIONED TOTALITY

In theoretical terms, if we were to reduce the law to the way one would imagine it to be from the limited scope of consciousness—as a kind of externally imposed and coercive obligation—we would make ethics depend on a transcendent object that would belie its immanence. In so doing, we would trespass the limits of theoretical reason and make it fall in contradiction with itself, as Kant explains in the Antinomy chapter of the first *Critique*. In fact, the Dialectic of the second *Critique* explores situations in which reason trespasses its limits by, for example, aspiring to reach an unconditioned totality. When it aspires to conceive of an absolute totality, "reason in its practical use fares not a whit better" than reason in its theoretical use.

> As pure practical reason it seeks for the practically conditioned (which rests on inclinations and natural need) likewise the unconditioned; moreover, it does not seek this unconditioned as the determining basis of the will, but, even when this determining basis has been given (in the moral law), it seeks the unconditioned totality of the *object* of pure practical reason, under the name of the *highest good*.[71]

The illusion the Dialectic seeks to reveal consists in replacing a conception of causality in which an unconditioned element contingently anchors a series (as happens in the third antinomy) with the attempt to form an unconditioned totality. In this different conception, the unconditioned would be the series as a totality, rather than an exceptional member of the series.[72] Here, in the illusion the Dialectic explores it is no longer a matter of seeking the unconditioned in the moral law and conferring on it the ability to be the will's only determination and motivation. Accordingly, the Dialectic of Practical Reason marks an explicit departure from the conception of freedom and the law expounded in the Analytic, as Alenka Zupančič points out.[73] This also implies a departure from the conception enabled in the third antinomy of a causality anchored contingently by an unconditioned role played by the subject.[74] For here, in the Dialectic of Practical Reason, "even when this determining basis is given (in the moral law)," pure practical reason "seeks the unconditioned totality" of its own object, "of the *object* of pure practical reason." Kant is right to emphasize the word "*object*," echoing his insistence in the Analytic that practical reason does not have an object. Yet in affirming that the concept of the good could only be derived from the law and not the other way around, the Analytic also exposes reason to the illegitimate temptation to step over its boundaries and attempt to derive that object. Hence the preliminary reminder Kant offers at the beginning of the Dialectic: "It will have been seen from the Analytic that if we [were to] assume, prior to the moral law, any object—under the name of a good—as determining basis of the will and then [to] derive the supreme practical principle from it, this would always bring about heteronomy and displace the moral principle."[75] There emerges, however, a practical antinomy that justifies reason's impulse to seek a concept of the good: the highest good is indeed to be derived from the law, but if one were to prove that the highest good is impossible, it would follow that the moral law is "fantastic and aimed at empty imaginary purposes, and hence itself false."[76]

If achieving the highest good were proved to be impossible, then the law would be false. Yet a human life is too short to attain the holiness necessary to fulfill the highest good. Attempting to solve this practical antinomy, the Dialectic sets out to imagine the conditions required for the highest good to be attained. Hence reason introduces the postulates of the immortality of the soul and of the existence of God. Regarding the former, only an immortal soul could be imagined to progress infinitely toward the highest good. Regarding the latter, imagining the outside viewpoint of God would provide the external position from which the soul's infinite progression toward goodness could be conceived as a whole, as a totality. Reason's aspiration to create an unconditioned whole as explored in the Dialectic leads it, in short, to posit an unlimited series (in the case of the infinite progress toward goodness of an immortal soul) and then conceive it as an unconditioned totality (by postulating the external viewpoint of God) in order to be able to imagine what would be required for the fulfillment of the highest good.

This "unavoidable illusion" of reason that arises from applying its idea of the totality of conditions, as well as "the principle of presupposing the unconditioned for every conditioned" to appearances, is the same illusion Kant denounces by revealing the antinomies reason falls into in the first *Critique*. Significantly, the attempt on the part of reason to create an unconditioned whole (as manifested in its attempt to conceive of the conditions in which the highest good would be fulfilled) is in consonance with the structure of the second dynamic conflict. In the fourth antinomy the aspiration to link the contingent with the necessary gives way to a thesis that affirms a necessary being completely outside the world of sense, a necessary being as a cause of the world that the antithesis then excludes.[77] This necessary being, adds Kant in his explanation, would be external to the series, it "would have to be thought as entirely outside the series of the world of sense (as *ens extramundanum*) and merely intelligible."[78] Fully independent from the series, completely outside, here the intelligible remains "a mere thought entity."[79] The necessary being introduced in the fourth antinomy could never become an unconditioned member of the series because of its independence from nature and causality. This antinomy's conception of the intelligible as being completely outside and thus as unrelated to the world—"merely a thought entity," a speculation—could never link the diachronic series with its outside, as does the third antinomy. The cosmological idea that prompted the fourth antinomy, writes Kant as he explains this antinomy's solution, urges us "to look for an intelligible object with which this contingency will cease."[80] But is the ceasing of contingency a requirement to form a whole, a condition for a dynamic synthesis to work? In fact, the third antinomy proves that a certain sense of completion can only be reached in a contingent way. The fourth antinomy's aspiration to link the contingent with the necessary can only be met by positing an intelligible being that lies completely outside the series.

The idea of an immortal soul that progresses infinitely toward holiness is structured like the antithesis of the fourth antinomy,[81] whereas the existence of God conceived as a fully external cause, position, and viewpoint follows the pattern of the thesis. The transcendental ideas of the soul and God were proved to be illusory in the chapters "On the Paralogisms of Pure Reason" and "The Ideal of Pure Reason," which, together with "The Antinomy of Pure Reason," form the Dialectic of the first *Critique*.[82] The highest good toward which morality tends, on the other hand, would seem to contradict Kant's conception in the Analytic of Practical Reason, where he affirms that that there is no preexisting good, that the good is derived from the law. According to this view, the otherness to which the subject is related would be either a punishing law or a necessary being like the one introduced and then denied in the fourth antinomy. As Kant remarks, concerning the fourth antinomy, "as soon as we posit the unconditioned . . . outside all possible experience, the ideas become *transcendent*."[83] The problem with this conception, then, is that it pushes aside the possibility of immanent ethical constitution. In the case of that necessary being, "we were unable, without the mediation of the first dynamical idea [the idea of freedom], to ascend to it from the world of sense. For had we wanted to attempt this, we would have had to venture a leap: we would have had to leave all that is given to us and soar to that of which again nothing is given to us whereby we could mediate the connection of such an intelligible being with the world of sense (because the necessary being was to be cognized as given *outside us*)."[84] The immanent view of the emergence of subjectivity is lost, in sum, when the other to which the subject is related, the other that constitutes the subject, is no longer an element of excess that has an impact on the subject, but rather a transcendent other that lies completely outside, unrelated to the same, or an other that is in dialectic relation to the same.[85]

But this is a problem the third antinomy had already solved. What makes the third antinomy unique, we recall, is that in it the unconditioned lies both outside and inside the series as an exceptional member. This unconditioned cause is the very role that subjectivity, itself animated by the causality of freedom, plays. As the locus of something that exceeds it, of something irreducible to it, the subject, a member of the series, takes the position of the uncaused or unconditioned cause, as I argued in Chapter 2. In the third antinomy it was therefore not a matter of achieving an unconditioned totality, but rather a contingent anchoring of the series by the unconditioned, an exceptional member that plays the role of boundary and relationship between the series and its outside. This is what the third antinomy does, and only in this third conflict does the mediation between the sensible and the intelligible become possible, as Kant reminds his reader a few pages after the section on respect.

> By contrast [with the necessary being of the second dynamical idea], this [sort of mediation] is entirely possible, as is now obvious, with regard to *our own* subject insofar as *on the one hand* this subject through the moral law (by virtue of freedom) determines [and thus cognizes] himself as an intelligible being and *on the other hand* he cognizes himself as active in accordance with this determination in the world of sense. Solely the concept of freedom permits us to find the unconditioned and intelligible for the conditioned and sensible without needing to go outside ourselves.[86]

The thesis of the fourth antinomy also advances the possibility of the intelligible, but locates that necessary being fully outside the series. Yet, as we learned in our exploration of the third antinomy, if a synthesis of causal linkage can be formed at all, it is only insofar as it is formed contingently: it is only by allowing for a certain contingency that a synthesis of events derived from their causes may be conceived.[87] The series cannot aspire to completion simply through the agency of an intelligible object or being lying completely outside the series, unrelated to it, as the thesis of the fourth antinomy stipulates. The transcendental idea of a necessary being the fourth antinomy explores is therefore transcendent.

ALTERATION IS NOT ALIENATION

But the risk of moving from an immanent vision of ethics to a transcendent one (as the fourth antinomy and the Dialectic of Practical Reason do) is also practical. How are we then to understand these two versions of ethics, the one expounded in the Analytic in which the law redoubles as form and motivation, and the transcendent version advanced by the Dialectic, where the possibility of the law of freedom hinges on the postulates of the immortality of the soul and the viewpoint of God? We may start by exploring the similar tension between an immanent and a transcendent vision of the law that some scholars detect in Kant's notion of respect, a tension arising between the two different senses Kant attributes to *Achtung*. As the affect that furthers the law's motivating power, the notion of respect provides practical insight into the impact of freedom's causality on the subjectivity it constitutes. As the fear of a threatening and fear-instilling law, a coercive agency that berates the self akin to the voice of conscience or to a superegoic illusion, respect functions as a heteronomous otherness, a framework that justifies one's pathological choices and belies autonomy. What I have proposed in this chapter is that these two different approaches to ethics do not necessarily signify a shift in Kant's conception, but should be interpreted, rather, in light of Kant's faithfulness to the limited perspective of consciousness and of theoretical reason. We should keep in mind, in short, that respect in the negative sense refers to the impact the law has on (phenomenal) consciousness. The terrible voice of the law is the way "this law is presented to us, for compliance"; "such a feeling is inseparably linked with the presentation of the moral law in every finite rational being," that is, from the presentation of the law produced from the limited perspective of consciousness. For duty, Kant clarifies, "demands submission, yet also does not seek to move the will by threatening anything that would arouse natural aversion in the mind and terrify."[88] The reference to the law's gaze and voice must be assigned to the restricted perspective of consciousness, that is, to the fact that all one can have of the law, when thinking about it, is presentations. Therefore, the apparent oscillation Kant's readers detect in this chapter between an empty law and a threatening law may indicate less a change in his conception of the law than his inclusion of a perspective of consciousness that bears witness to the faithfulness of the critical project to the finitude of the phenomenal world. The fourth antinomy and the postulates of practical reason would alert us to the risk a finite self runs of understanding itself as depending on totalities (of "dissolving," as Levinas puts it, in an all-encompassing horizon) rather than as always already affected by what makes others other.

Read in this way, what Kant's section on respect suggests is that the ethical notion of autonomous obligation that constitutes subjectivity must coexist with the finite consciousness and sensibility of the subject it produces, a consciousness from which one's ethical constitution is perceived, paradoxically, as heteronomy. Kant's ethics of freedom is not incompatible with affect—in fact, it is only conceivable in terms of affect. But it was necessary, at least conceptually, to differentiate the affect of freedom as motive from the sensible, heteronomous, and thus restricted perception of a threatening law. It was necessary, in sum, to differentiate between the relationship with an other (a constitutive excess) the subject incarnates and the dialectic of self-consciousness where ethical obligation may be recast as guilt. Autonomy, I argue in the next chapter, emerges at the meeting of the two.

5

AUTONOMY, OR BEING INSPIRED

Une respiration profonde jusqu'au souffle coupé par le vent de l'alterité.
—EMMANUEL LEVINAS, *AUTREMENT QU'ÊTRE OU AU-DELÀ DE L'ESSENCE*

How can transcendence withdraw from *esse* while being signaled in it?
—EMMANUEL LEVINAS, *OTHERWISE THAN BEING, OR BEYOND ESSENCE*

In *Otherwise than Being, or Beyond Essence* (1974) Emmanuel Levinas describes subjectivity as a *being disturbed* by a call that comes from elsewhere, by "a command exerted by the other . . . upon me."[1] That a command comes from the other or from elsewhere should surprise no one. What makes this event of the other extraordinary is that it is within the self: It is "a command exerted by the other in me upon me [*exercé par autrui en moi sur moi*]."[2] Though the demand does not originate in me, I, its addressee, become its locus of enunciation: the other "orders me by my own voice . . . by the mouth of him it commands [*m'ordonne par ma voix même . . . par la bouche de celui qu'il commande*]."[3] But since I find it in myself, I believe I am its origin. This is how I become autonomous. Autonomy consists in believing oneself the author of an order one has received.[4] But what is this order like? This "assignation to respond" is like "a trauma . . . that prevents its own representation, a deafening trauma, cutting the thread of consciousness that should have welcomed it in its present."[5] It is outside representation and causality. Thus, I only encounter this order in "the obedience itself,"[6] when I find myself responding without knowing to what. A response without condition, without discernible cause, "obedience precedes any hearing of the command,"[7] just "like an echo of a sound that would precede the resonance of that sound."[8]

This constitutive excess *in* the subject which is not reducible to the subject is what we may call unsatisfactorily "event of the other," or "event-other," tropes that name something for which we lack concepts and words.[9] How does this irreducible excess *arouse* subjectivity, and how does our ethical constitution appear to the necessarily limited perspective of self-consciousness we as subjects occupy? We only intuit this event when we find ourselves responding to something we cannot master: the event of the other disturbs the order of being and discourse. If the demand exists outside representation, if we only become aware it has been placed because of the disturbance it creates—our uncaused response—how can we speak about it, how can a disturbed discourse state it is disturbed? Acknowledging the limit imposed on his philosophical language by a constitutive excess, the challenge Levinas must meet, just like Kant in his chapter on respect,[10] is that of signifying ethical disturbance in the subject and the world without reducing it to a representation. But how? Again, can discourse express its own disturbance?

Subjectivity, according to Levinas, is a relationship with "illeity," an irreducible other that signifies outside all modalities and alternatives of being, and that, itself anarchy, refracts any notion of origin. As he argues in "Humanism and An-archy" (1968), there is a "pre-originary" or "beyond the ultimate" that would never become originary or ultimate. "*Inwardness*," he writes, "*is the fact that in being the beginning is preceded.*"[11] Subjectivity is an "anarchic being affected" (*affection anarchique*), a being affected without *arché* that, as such, embodies the trace of a disturbance that can never become origin. The event of the other thus signals itself as "a diachrony refractory to all synchronization."[12] Kant also conceives the subject of practical reason as constituted by the impact of an excess, an excess in the subject but irreducible to the subject that manifests itself in the form of a command that addresses the self. The alterity of the law, writes Nancy, is not the alterity of "any assignable other, whether a great Other or a little other, even though it determines the being-other of any other."[13] This alterity also determines the subject's relationship to the being-other of any other. If, according to Levinas, subjectivity is an-archic, can we reconcile Levinas's claim that any origin is preceded with Kant's conception of the unconditioned law as free beginning?

Let us embark on our study of subjectivity in *Otherwise than Being* by raising some of the questions we put forth to Kant in the previous chapters. How does an ethical excess arouse subjectivity? Who does the ethical demand address and how does it incite a response? Levinas is best known for his early attempts to address these questions, especially in the extended "defense of subjectivity" he undertakes in *Totality and Infinity: an Essay on Exteriority* (1961).[14] According to this earlier book, the ethical call that constitutes subjectivity as a different kind of freedom comes from an absolutely exterior other that exceeds the self's ability to conceptualize. Levinas names this other "face" (*le visage*), thus giving existence in discourse to what absolves itself from thought, what escapes the logic of coherence and the grasp of reason.[15] "The face is present in its refusal to be contained. In this sense it cannot be comprehended, that is, encompassed. It is neither seen nor touched—for in visual or tactile sensation the identity of the I envelops the alterity of the object, which becomes precisely a content."[16] Here "face" is already a figure, a trope naming something that cannot be conceptualized, namely, ethical orientation as it is motivated by the event of the other.[17] The face and its demand lack a place in differential logic, and thus are not inflected by the categories of thought. "Face" aspires to name what escapes visibility, what knowledge perceives as a void.

But in evoking an other which lies completely outside, isn't Levinas already positing that other? Does the "face" in *Totality and Infinity* name a true absence, or is it just one more speculative thought, a presupposed other? This is the question Jacques Derrida and Maurice Blanchot raised in the mid-1960s. In his 1964 response to Levinas, "Violence and Metaphysics," Derrida writes: "According to Levinas, there would be no interior difference, no fundamental and autochthonous alterity within the ego."[18] In other words, if the other is absolutely exterior, if it is separated from the self by an untraversable distance, how does one even know the other exists? Moreover, as Jean-François Lyotard points out, any affirmation of the other's absolute exteriority presupposes the closure of the subject.[19] In positing an exteriority that would interrupt ontological being, Levinas is still thinking within the horizon of being: he has not yet found the "new modality of speaking"[20] and the "exact trope"[21] that would allow him to point to what exceeds ontology. Though according to him the other that disrupts the self cannot be thought, positing something unrepresentable in terms of absolute exteriority to the self would still be a way of presupposing it.

Levinas was confronted with a difficult challenge, the challenge of evoking the outside of representation in representative language. But if the expression coming from the face interrupts the order of being, should not the possibility of philosophical language be interrupted too? How can rational discourse, which follows the logic of causality, evoke an event that "precedes" and "exceeds" consciousness? And if that interruption does not take place in chronological time but rather has *always already happened* in an immemorial past, how can it *happen* to an already constituted subject?[22] *Totality and Infinity* attempts to evoke the disturbance of being by means of a discourse—philosophical discourse—able to realize its own closure. Although this book aspires to signify an unrepresentable event that disrupts discourse, it does so by means of a discourse that is itself unaffected by the disturbance it announces. In spite of distinguishing the "Saying" from the thematization effected by the "Said," Levinas has not yet found the mode of speaking that would allow his own discourse to express the disturbance of ethics performatively by exposing itself as disturbed. Yet again, can discourse express ethical disturbance, even if it were to do so by displaying its own disturbance? Or, to quote Levinas, "how can transcendence withdraw from *esse* while being signaled in it? [*Comment la transcendance peut-elle se soustraire à l'esse tout en s'y signalant?*]"[23]

This is the question Levinas takes up in *Otherwise than Being* (1974).[24] If *Totality and Infinity* focused on the interruption of the self by a call, in *Otherwise than Being* ethical disturbance spreads to the whole order of discourse. This latter work strives to signify its own lack of closure as philosophical discourse, but this derangement (*dérangement*) cannot be simply stated. Only a discourse that has already achieved its own closure can affirm something. If what is affirmed is the impossibility of a closure that statement must be false.[25] As Levinas himself acknowledges, "to conceive the *otherwise than being* requires, perhaps, as much audacity as skepticism shows, when it does not hesitate to affirm the impossibility of statement while venturing to *realize* this impossibility by the very statement of this impossibility."[26] Yet perhaps one could signify the disruption of discourse through rhetorical operations that perform closure as an absence, as a constitutive impossibility. This is what *Otherwise than Being* proposes to do: no less than signifying what cannot be represented as a present absence. As Levinas puts it, "we must stay with the extreme situation of a diachronic thought."[27]

Something similar happens with the discursive construction we call "sub-ject." In *Otherwise than Being* ethical excess does not affect an already con-stituted subject, because there is no pre-existing subject to be affected.[28] If the event-other may be said to disrupt anything, one is affirming so in on-tic time, from the perspective of consciousness in which the "subject" con-stitutes itself anticipatorily and retroactively. The expression "constituting oneself" does not imply any initiative, and the temporality indicated by the term "retroactive" is not chronological, though it may appear so from the ontic perspective of autonomy. "A linear regressive movement," remarks Levinas, "a retrospective back along the temporal series toward a very re-mote past, would never be able to reach the absolutely diachronous pre-original which cannot be recuperated by memory and history."[29] The "alteration without alienation or election"[30] of the same—the impact of the event-other—belongs in a "past that was never present" or in a past "not be-longing to the order of presence."[31] This dislocated temporality (if we may refer to it in these terms) "cannot be recuperated by reminiscence not be-cause of its remoteness, but because of its incommensurability with the pres-ent."[32] In this pre-originary "past" the same has always already been "affected" without choice; the hope for subjective closure or unicity is an ontic illu-sion. This "diachronous" temporality is irrecoverable from the "stance" of autonomy because the correlative emergence of consciousness, autonomy, and ontic time is premised on a reduction that has already missed the oth-erness of the event, the alteration of the same that precedes and exceeds self-consciousness and constitutes subjectivity as heteronomy.[33]

Levinas will indeed address the reversion of heteronomy into autonomy, but that account does not take place until chapter five of *Otherwise than Be-ing*. Though the book gestures to it from the beginning,[34] chapters one to four are devoted to the heteronomous constitution of the subject, a consti-tution that "happens" (or has always already happened) beyond the limits of theoretical reason, outside of knowledge. Indeed, as Levinas remarks, the event of the other appears to consciousness as a paradox "in that I am obliged without this obligation having begun in me," something which "is impos-sible in a consciousness" and which consciousness translates as "an anach-ronic upheaval [*un bouleversement anachronique*]."[35] It is "as though" one's response could not start by welcoming the order ("awaiting" or "welcom-ing" would presuppose a subject's initiative), but rather consisted in "obey-ing this order before it is formulated." Or, he adds, "as though it were formulated before every possible present, in a past that shows itself in the present of obedience without being recalled, without coming from memory, being formulated by him who obeys in his very obedience."[36] The challenge *Otherwise than Being* takes up, once again, is that of expressing in language the reverberation of a constitutive event exceeding representation without reducing it as would a discourse that closes upon itself. "It is necessary [*il faut*] that within the temporalization that is recoverable, . . . a lapse of time without return, a diachrony refractory to all synchronization, a transcending diachrony, signals itself."[37]

SUBSTITUTION AND SKIN

In the mid-1960s Levinas evokes the event of the other as the impact it has in the world, and in the world of the self. With his introduction of the "trace" Levinas finds the "new modality" of saying that allows him to name the derangement the ethical inserts in the world.[38] The *trace* (of the other-event) is a disturbance in the order of discourse. In disturbing discourse, the trace disrupts the ontological order of the self. In fact, with the trace Levinas will be able to show how the autonomous order of the self can only be achieved as a retroactive effect (I will return to this). As he evokes it, "the trace . . . is not the residue" of something that was present and can be "tracked down."[39] Rather, the "trace is the presence of that which properly speaking has never been there, of what has always already passed by. . . . Someone has already passed. His trace does not *signify* his past, as it does not *signify* his labor or his enjoyment in the world; it is the very disturbance imprinting itself (we would be tempted to say *engraving* itself [*se gravant*]) with an irrecusable gravity."[40] And then, in *Otherwise than Being*, he writes: "There is the trace of a withdrawal which no actuality has preceded, and which becomes present only in my own voice . . . ."[41] As we will see, the command presents itself in the "saying" of the one it commands, in the voice of its addressee.

The trace disturbs the order of being and discourse. Yet, as I pointed out above, discourse cannot affirm its own disturbance, because a disturbed discourse should have lost its ability to affirm anything. If discourse could convincingly say "I am disturbed" then it would not be disturbed (it would already have achieved the very closure it pretends to lack). Is there, again, any way of signifying the ethical without reducing it to representation? If we identify discourse with differential representation, a discourse that can account for the disturbance of discourse is an impossibility. Yet not all language is enacted by consciousness[42] (and it is against the reduction by consciousness of all experience to differential representation that Levinas levels his critique of representation).[43] Conceptual representation does not embrace all that can be signified. Discourse can only express its own disturbance by inflicting a violence on its own language so as to signify something that exceeds its ability to represent. The derangement of discourse can only be expressed—and this is very important—through an element irreducible to conceptualization. As we will see, the trace of the other is not found in what language says, but rather in the ways language acts, in a discourse that performs its own being disturbed.

As we continue exploring how that event-other withdraws from the representations in which it signals itself, let us consider the figure of the trace from the viewpoint of rhetoric. A rhetorical reading privileges the performative dimension of language—its "saying"—over its constative statements—the "said" (I will soon turn to what Levinas means by the terms "saying" and "said"). This rhetorical perspective will also help us discern which tropological and logical operation could account for what Levinas calls "substitution."[44] What kind of trope is the "trace"? The "trace" is a catachresis, a trope that belongs in the family of metaphor. Both metaphor and catachresis are operations of substitution, and the boundaries between them are not always clear. As Patricia Parker observes in her now classic essay "Metaphor and Catachresis," the distinction between the transfer of terms in metaphor and catachresis depends on whether or not a prior term exists: in metaphor the proper term is displaced by the figural one, whereas in catachresis the figural term becomes the proper term.[45] In a metaphor, a figure replaces an already existing term (a Grecian urn, for example) in order to express it otherwise ("still unravish'd bride of quietness," to quote Keats). Catachresis, in turn, substitutes itself for a non-existing term (the "face" of a clock, the "mouth" of a cave, the "eye" of a storm).[46] Catachresis is a trope that allows differential language to evoke or name something that belongs in a different representative space. (One could argue this happens also in metaphorical substitution, where the existing or real term could already be a figure, and the transfer is likely to add an element of excess).[47] Significantly, eighteenth-century French rhetoric also denominates the literal exception to language catachresis signals ("an ex-ception to essence")[48] simply with the term "substitution" (*suppléance*).[49] In taking the place of an absent term, the figural term becomes the primary meaning.[50] Catachresis is, in other words, the very operation of substitution for what is absent.[51] In substituting itself for a non-existing term, catachresis names and signals an absence.

The trace names the event of the other catachrestically: "trace" is a signifier that does not fill the void it names (we will have to remain alert, however, to the risk of fixing the absence or void).[52] Furthermore, in signaling something that eludes representation, catachresis signifies representation's limits. As a substitution in which the figural term points to the absence of a real term, we may consider catachresis to express the index of rhetoricity, signification as such.[53] How does *Otherwise than Being* make this happen? The "face" that in *Totality and Infinity* stood for an outside other becomes in *Otherwise than Being* "a failing of all presence,"[54] a "space signifying emptiness,"[55] a lapse, "a trace of itself."[56] Now the face "shines" in the trace.[57] This shift of emphasis from "face" to "trace" allows Levinas to evoke an other still irreducible but no longer outside.[58] Departing from the emphasis on the other's absolute exteriority as it was figured in the face-to-face relation, *Otherwise than Being* refers to the alterity-relation as a disruption within oneself, as the "Other-within-the-Same" (*l'Autre-dans-le-Même*).[59] The exteriority of the other as implied in *Totality and Infinity* has become irrecoverable:[60] "The order that orders me does not leave me any possibility of resetting things the right way around with impunity, of going back up to the exteriority of the Infinite . . . ."[61] Unable to take a distance from the other, for the other is in the same, the subject is described as "obsessed" with "proximity." Levinas's term "obsession" expresses the way in which subjectivity, a "relationship irreducible to consciousness," nevertheless signals itself in consciousness as an affection whose source does not become a representable theme.[62] Traversing consciousness "against the current [*à countrecourant*]," inscribing itself in consciousness as "*foreign*, to signify a heteronomy," "a delirium overtaking the origin, rising earlier than the origin, prior to *arché*, to the beginning,"[63] obsession is "a relationship with exteriority 'prior' to the act that would open up that outside, a relationship which, precisely, is not act."[64] This act opening up an outside would be equivalent, in terms of Kant's first *Critique*, to the opening by theoretical reason of a negative noumenal space beyond experience in which to locate transcendental ideas. The diachronic retroaction Levinas calls "obsession" overtakes the origin because, according to him, every origin is preceded.[65] In going beyond the origin, obsession would be pre-originary. Levinas's sensibly affected subject, an "anarchic being affected," is a diachrony overtaking any origin, without stopping at any synchronic cause. Obsession, "a relationship with the outside, prior to the act that would open up that outside,"[66] refracts any synchronicity[67] a beginning or originary cause could provide. (Recall that in Kant's essay "On the Inherence of Evil" the subject's adoption of its originary disposition [*Gesinnung*] was figured as a subjective act of free choice that did not happen over time. Levinas's conception of a subjectivity affected by the anarchic trace of the other will soon inspire us to consider in a different light the originary—and thus synchronic—free act of choice by virtue of which Kant's subject of practical reason may be considered to be autonomous.)

The trace does not stand for the event of the other. Instead, the trace points to the impact the other has on the subject. The event of the other manifests itself only as alteration or disturbance of the same. In saying that the event of the other manifests itself only as a disturbance of the same, we are characterizing the subject in terms of a metonymic relation: the signifiers "event of the other," its impact or "trace" in the world, and the "subject" that bears that trace displace signification through a relation of contiguity. This displacement of signifiers is supported by the trope "trace." Furthermore, the disturbance of the event-other is engraved in a subject like a trauma to which one responds unwittingly, without having decided to respond.[68] And in fact, in replacing one signifier with another (from face to trace to skin to other-within-the-same), Levinas's text enacts rhetorically the displacement that the event of the other-within—"the provocation that has never presented itself, but has struck traumatically [*frappé de traumatisme*]"[69]—unleashes in consciousness. Replicating the structure of a trauma also allows Levinas's text to account for the impact of the ethical event retroactively, from the temporality of consciousness, though the event itself remains inaccessible. Levinas's allusions to trauma in this signification process are eloquent, because the signifying and affective dimensions are inextricably linked: paradigmatic substitutions depend on affect because they are (at least partly) ruled by the unconscious.[70] It might well be the case, then, that the subject's "obsession" and "traumatism," as well as its being held "hostage" in its own skin, constitute the affective expression of the subject's relationship to the other. Levinas also refers to this "being affected" through expressions of bodily sensibility—"cellular irritability," suffocating in one's skin—affects that cannot be experienced through the senses, yet powerfully evoke sensible bodily disturbance.

Levinas thus refers to the relationship with the other as a disruption within oneself, as the Other-within-the-Same (*l'Autre-dans-le-Même*), where the other is now, in another Levinasian trope, under one's skin, as if inhabiting the self. The more constrained by a skin inhabited by the other, the more deeply the self must breathe, taking the other in (*inspiring* the other) as its skin becomes tighter. Being "in one's skin" no longer refers to a subject safely contained within a form that allows it to coincide with itself.[71]

> In its own skin. Not at rest under a form, but tight in its skin [*mal dans sa peau*], encumbered and as it were stuffed by itself [*encombré et comme bouché par soi*], suffocating under itself, insufficiently open, forced to detach itself from itself [*astreint à se dé-prendre de soi*], to breathe more deeply, all the way [*jusqu'au bout*], to dispossess itself to the point of losing itself.[72]

"The expression 'in one's skin,'" then, is "not a metaphor for the in-itself."[73] "In one's skin" comes to refer to an interval, "to a recurrence in the dead time or the *meanwhile* [*l'entre-temps*] which separates inspiration from expiration, the diastole from the systole of the heart beating dully against the walls of one's skin. . . . This recurrence is 'incarnation.'"[74] We may ask, what is it that recurs "in the interval," that replaces all metaphors standing "for the in-itself"? What "recurs" in the interval is no other than the subject. In "the unconditionality of the accusative,"[75] "expelled from being, . . . without out a foundation, reduced to itself, and thus without condition,"[76] the subject is no longer an "in itself." "In its own skin," the subject is not "at rest under a form, but tight in its skin [*mal dans sa peau*]."[77] A "recurrence which is not self-consciousness, . . . not self-coinciding," the subject "in the interval, one without attributes,"[78] "in its bearing as same" is "more and more extended to the other."[79]

The trope "skin" is so stretched that it is on the verge of being turned inside out, just as happens with the form "subject."[80] "Encumbered and as it were stuffed with itself [*encombré et comme bouché par soi*], suffocating under itself, insufficiently open, forced to detach itself from itself, to breathe more deeply, all the way, forced to dispossess itself to the point of losing itself,"[81] the form subject is invested with a *surplus* of signification or an excess of presence (in terms of rhetoric, it is overdetermined). Here we should pay attention to what is happening in language, to a rhetoric operation *Otherwise than Being* performs time and again (the diachronic series of signifiers is about to be anchored by an operation of substitution and thus signification is *about to* cohere). The metonymic displacement from other, to trace, to other-within-the-same, to the subject's tight skin is beginning to shade into a relation of substitution in the form of catachresis. By what Levinas calls an "inversion of being," the subject "in the interval,"[82] "emptying itself of itself,"[83] *substitutes itself* for the other by "the extraordinary and diachronic reversal [or reverting: *renversement*] of the same into the other."[84] Subjectivity is *substitution*.[85]

From the viewpoint of rhetoric, the subject emerges as a catachresis. In substituting itself for the other (for an absence), the figural term "subject" becomes the primary meaning—it is impossible to go back up to the exteriority of the other.[86] Levinas even wonders:

> Do the being encumbered with oneself and the suffering of constriction in one's skin [*constriction dans sa peau*], better than metaphors, follow the exact trope of an alteration of *essence*, which reverses or inverts itself [*qui s'inverse—ou s'invertit—*] into a recurrence where the expulsion of self outside of itself [*de soi hors soi*] is its substitution for the other—which would mean, properly speaking, the Self emptying itself of itself [*se vidant de lui-même*]?[87]

The subject as "exact trope"? What would be the exact trope the subject becomes by "emptying itself from itself" in "its substitution for the other"? A trope beyond any particular trope ("better than metaphors"), the subject's "alteration of essence" in substitution—in the "reversal of the same into the other"—is "signification itself."[88] I already pointed out that catachresis—a trope that substitutes itself for an absence it names—indicates the limits of representation. What makes catachresis an index of rhetoricity—an "exact trope"[89]—is its emptiness, an emptiness that signals something that eludes representation and thus has the potential to introduce a boundary.[90] Catachresis is, moreover, the area in which the diachronic axis of metonymy (of the signifier's displacement or indefinite regression) interacts with the synchronic axis of metaphor (or unconditioned position), as we have just seen.[91]

It is important to understand that the meeting of the diachronic and the synchronic does not take place as a punctual crossing, but rather as an extended area of interaction where diachrony is contingently and repeatedly anchored, which "inverts itself into a recurrence." Think, for example, of the coming together of the two operations in the counterintuitive expression "diachronic reversal of the same into the other,"[92] where "reversal," which at first view seemed to indicate a synchronic operation akin to substitution, is qualified as "diachronic." Notice how in the lines quoted above this dynamic interaction between predominantly diachronic sequences ("encumbered with oneself," "suffering of constriction in one's skin," which express the *overdetermination* of the form "subject") and predominantly synchronic substitutions ("expulsion of self outside itself," "its substitution for the other," "the Self emptying itself of itself") hinges on the "trope of an alteration of essence" inverting itself "into a recurrence." Let us quote again:

> Or do the being encumbered with oneself and the suffering of constriction in one's skin, better than metaphors, follow the exact trope of an alteration of *essence*, which reverses or inverts itself into a recurrence in which the expulsion of self outside of itself is its substitution for the other— which would mean, properly speaking, the Self emptying itself of itself?[93]

Observe, finally, how this operation of "inverting into a recurrence," which hinges between diachronic and synchronic movements, performs ("incarnates") the meeting of the diachronic and the synchronic I just described as catachresis. "This recurrence is 'incarnation.'"[94] The term "recurrence," which Levinas uses to qualify subjectivity, also indicates an important tropological function, since it points to the unceasing substitution of the subject, indicating that the operation of substitution is not only or not entirely synchronic. What are the implications of this interplay between the diachronic and the synchronic? When that interaction happens, when a metonymic series of figures shades into a metaphoric substitution, what occurs is an anchoring effect—a fleeting and contingent bounding of signifiers— that allows signification to cohere.

BECOMING A SIGN

This anchoring of diachrony is constitutive: it produces signification. And the signification that emerges here, in substitution, is subjectivity. Emptied out of itself and filled with the other, the subject makes signs of its "anarchic being affected [*affection anarchique*]."[95] The subject makes "signs of signification itself [*faire signe de signification même*]" "to the point of becoming a sign [*faire signe en se faisant signe; faire ainsi signe au point de se faire signe*],"[96] a sign that signifies signification as such. Levinas expresses this "inversion of Being into a sign"[97] also as a "saying that says the saying itself [*Dire disant le dire même*]."[98] This "saying as such" or "saying itself" is not a "saying" without a "said"[99]—saying and said are inseparable in Levinas.[100] The subject as sign that "says the saying as such" does not express any preceding conceptual unity, but rather gives a signification to what cannot be represented. In this way, what does not have a location within differential representation and remains heterogeneous to it (and for our purposes, heterogeneous to ontic time) is signified as an absence. Hence Levinas's insistence on the need for a "diachrony without synthesis"[101] and on the trope of the trace as "irreversible lapse."[102]

Yet that the subject "says the saying itself [*dire . . . le dire même*],"[103] that the subject "makes signs by becoming itself a sign,"[104] does not mean it finds repose or an identity in its very position or "figure as sign [*Dire ainsi, c'est faire signe de cette signifiance même . . . en se faisant signe sans se reposer dans sa figure même de signe*]."[105] Contrary to the effect of identification that occurs as self-consciousness (as one *regains* self-consciousness), I become a sign "without having anything to identify myself with, but the sound of my voice or the figure of my gesture—the saying itself [*sans avoir rien à quoi m'identifier, sinon au son de ma voix ou à la figure de mon geste—au dire même*]."[106] As a sign of its embodying a relationship with the other, subjectivity does not express any preceding conceptual unity, but rather names the "null place [*non-lieu*]"[107] of what cannot be represented. In becoming a sign of signification as such the subject functions as the "intermediary [*truchement*]," mediation, or relationship between what can be represented and what remains incommensurable to the present, heterogeneous to representation:

The inscription of the order in the for-the-other of obedience is an anarchic being affected [*affection anarchique*], which slips into me [*se glissa en moi*] "like a thief" through the outstretched nets of consciousness [*à travers des filets tendus de la conscience*]. This trauma has surprised me completely; the order *has never been represented*, for it has never presented itself, not even in the past coming in memory, to the point that it is I who says only, and after the event [*après coup*], this unheard-of [*innouïe*] obligation. This ambivalence is the exception and subjectivity of the subject, its very psyche, a possibility of inspiration. It is the possibility of being the author of what had been breathed in me *unbeknownst to me* [*ce qui m'avait été à mon insu insuflé*], of having received, one knows not from where, that of which I am author. . . . The unheard-of saying [*le dire inouï*] is enigmatically in the anarchic response, in my responsibility for the other. The trace of infinity is this ambiguity in the subject, in turns beginning and intermediary, a diachronic ambivalence which ethics makes possible.[108]

Notice that here the subject is not exactly a self-same in relationship with the other, but rather the *meeting* of self and other, a relationship between same and other, an "Other-within-the-same." In embodying the relationship to the other, the "anarchic affection" and "anarchic being affected" (*affection anarchique*)[109] we call "subject" emerges as a "sign" of the other that inhabits and animates it, as sign of its own substitution and unconditionality.[110] That the subject becomes a sign of its being affected means the subject is singular. Its being singular, according to Levinas, would precede the distinction between universal and particular.[111]

Becoming a sign of signification, a "saying that says the saying itself," or responding "me voici" ("here I am" in the accusative) before an order has been placed (for "obedience precedes any hearing of the command"),[112] this is how the subject bears witness to (*témoigne*) the event of the other-within. In becoming a sign, subjectivity bears witness to that of which no knowledge is possible, "of which no theme, no present, has a capacity".[113] "'Here I am' [*me voici*] as a witness of the Infinite, but a witness that does not thematize what it bears witness of, and whose truth is not the truth of representation, is not evidence."[114] The witness "by its own voice"[115] testifies to the impact of the other—indeed, to its own subjectivity as alterity-relation—and it does so as if responding to a trauma. Believing it acts in its own name, the subject acts in the name of the other, in the name of a disruption one cannot reduce to identity or agency. In bearing witness to its own substitution, the subject expresses (its being a relationship with) the other—it speaks in the name of the other in the most literal sense.[116] We can now hear the full resonance of the words with which we began: the command of the other speaks "by the mouth of the one it commands," "by my own voice."[117]

BELIEVING ONESELF THE AUTHOR

The subject *substitutes itself* for the other: the subject takes the position of the unconditioned (Kant) or emerges in substitution (Levinas). In both cases, subjectivity contingently embodies the relationship between two incommensurate realms. And in enunciating "by its own voice" a command it finds in itself the subject becomes autonomous, representable, a member of the social and political community. We are at last ready to consider the enigma of Kant's moral law of freedom from a fresh perspective. Doing full justice to Kant's unconditioned and incomprehensible law, Levinas speaks of a command which is unprecedented, unheard of, and unheard (*inouï*). Since this order has been "breathed in unbeknownst to me," without my being aware that it has been placed in me, since it has "slipped in me 'like a thief,'" sneaking "through the outstretched nets" of my consciousness and my conscience (*conscience* in French has both meanings), I find this order in myself. But I do not discover the order through knowledge. If I intuit a demand has been placed, it is only insofar as I find myself already responding and wonder what it is I am responding to. "Obedience precedes [*précédant*] any hearing of the command."[118] Anarchic and unconditioned, this order without precedent is inseparable from the "inspired" being ("the for-the-other of obedience") in which it inscribes itself, and from the response it provokes. The subject does not exactly receive a demand that exists out there or that may appear as an inaccessible command. The demand has never presented itself, for it is unable to become phenomenon "without entering into conjunction with the very subject" it affects and constitutes, "without closing itself up in finitude and immanence."[119] Thus, finding itself unwittingly responding, the subject has always already been constituted by a demand that only appears retroactively in the subject's response. The order is "*affection anarchique*," an anarchic *affect* and a *being affected* without origin, for which no previous signifier can account. The expression "*affection anarchique*" refers to an unconditioned affect, an assignation to responsibility that, as trace, comes to coincide with the "being affected" or subjectivity it motivates and moves. By inscribing itself in me (in a way that evokes the Kantian self-donation of the law), the order singles me out. This obligation I have not chosen "calls for a unique response not inscribed in universal thought, the unforeseeable response of the chosen one."[120]

What makes subjectivity singular, unique, is its having been chosen: "election by subjection."[121] Can we consider Kant's practical subject of the law to be singular in this sense, too? Is the subject of practical reason the one who chooses or is it, rather, the chosen one? In his essay "On the Inherence of Evil," Kant acknowledges that the law has been freely chosen in an act of choice to which one has no conscious access.[122] Because the choice was not an act in time, one can be aware neither of what was chosen nor of having chosen it. That the law was chosen freely could perhaps be conjectured from its reverberation in one's acts. More exactly, the effect of the law would be the affect produced by the law in the subject Kant calls respect (*Achtung*), an affect moving the power of desire that constitutes the law's motivational force, its ability to further itself. Although Kant's autonomous subject must have chosen the law as its ultimate source of motivation, although that free choice is inscrutable to the very subject who made it, does not the fact that one chooses the law imply that one must have been addressed and chosen by the law in the first place? "Election by subjection." Chosen, singular, without condition, the subject—the subjected one—is "sub-jectum,"[123] the one that supports and serves as ground, the one that, in substituting itself for the other—a substitution that is not an act—may be taken as unconditioned cause but not as stable ground. Its unconditionality would be an "unconditionality of the accusative,"[124] for is this not the sense of being enjoined? This subject "without a foundation, reduced to itself, and thus without condition,"[125] may be envisaged as unconditioned cause, as what anchors signification, in the contingent sense I attributed to the immanent system in progress the third antinomy achieves.[126] If we consider Kant's moral law in the double sense of free beginning and address,[127] the subject of practical reason, the one that has adopted its own ethical disposition (*Gesinnung*) in a free act of the power of choice, would be, in effect, the one that has been chosen.

As I wrote above, following Nancy, reason's being practical is not something reason itself would reveal but rather something that befalls reason as a fact, as the fact of reason (*factum rationis*), of which neither reason nor the subject is the origin.[128] The law is what in the subject exceeds and addresses the subject. This subjectivity being exceeded, addressed, motivated, and enjoined by the law chimes with Levinas's evocation of subjectivity as "alteration without alienation or election."[129] The obligation I have not chosen "calls for a unique response not inscribed in universal thought, the unforeseeable response of the chosen one [*l'élu*]."[130] One does not elect because one has been elected. Autonomy entails the responsibility of casting one's singularity, the fact that one has been chosen, as one's free act. Only in this sense may we say that Kant's practical subject becomes the unconditioned beginning or "author" of the causality of freedom that animates its subjectivity.[131] Significantly, the idea of becoming autonomous by virtue of authoring something without origin—something that cannot be authored, unconditioned—plays an important role in the task of universalization, both in Kant and in Levinas. The task of universalization calls for the intervention of the one—the subject—that the imperative, from its alterity, addresses and enjoins: "Act . . . ."[132] At stake here is not a self-positing or self-legislating subject but rather a "subject posited as deposed," in Levinas's words. "The subject posited as deposed—me—I universalize myself."[133]

The very "possibility of finding, anachronously, the order in the obedience itself, and of receiving the order out of oneself" is, writes Levinas, a "reverting of heteronomy into autonomy."[134] What does this "reconciliation" of autonomy and heteronomy mean and how does it happen? The demand does not originate in me (heteronomy) but I receive it out of myself (autonomy).[135] And, in fact, Levinas, who describes "this reverting of heteronomy into autonomy" also as the impact of the infinite on the finite—as "the very way in which the infinite passes itself"—finds this *passing of the infinite* remarkably expressed in "the metaphor of the inscription of the law in consciousness."[136] This metaphor, he suggests, reconciles autonomy and heteronomy.[137] Levinas's text bears the traces of this reverting of heteronomy into autonomy. At this point, it begins to introduce a distance, the distance that emerges retroactively with self-consciousness and autonomy. What was an "inscription of the order in the for-the-other of obedience" is expressed, let us quote these words again, by the "metaphor of the inscription of the law in consciousness." As we will see shortly, the "reverting of heteronomy into autonomy" is also a reverting of proximity and obsession into the distancing from oneself that enables consciousness and representation. In fact, if we read Levinas's text closely, it seems as if this passage from a "reverting [*retournement*]" to a "reconciliation" were effected by the "metaphor of the inscription of the law in consciousness" itself. What one may perceive as a "reversion" in which autonomy prevails is in fact a "reconciliation" between the two (Levinas's choice of the term "conciliant," however striking at first, is exact): autonomy is inseparable from heteronomy, the two interact and hence exist in generative tension, even if the perspective of consciousness loses sight of the latter, even if the "reconciling" of the two "in the present is ambiguity."[138]

The subject bears witness to this ambiguity "in the present." To witness, writes Levinas, is to be inspired in the common sense of the word. Being inspired means, as we know, finding in myself something that was not in me before. Since I find it in myself, I believe I am its origin. What I find in myself comes from elsewhere, it does not originate in me (or in what I identify myself with as "me"), yet I can consider myself its author. Inspiration is "the possibility of being the author of what had been breathed in me *unbeknownst to me* [*ce qui m'avait été* à mon insu *insufflé*], having received, one knows not from where, that of which I am author."[139] As the subject becomes the author of a demand coming from elsewhere, "autonomy and heteronomy are reconciled."[140] Autonomy is the possibility "of receiving the order out of oneself,"[141] believing I am its origin, and saying it "by my own voice."[142]

When Levinas alludes to inspiration and the reconciliation of heteronomy and autonomy, he introduces in his account the birth of consciousness, which had been absent up to this point. Autonomy would constitute a perception, from the limited perspective of a self-conscious rational subject, of the derangement provoked by the event of the other outside temporality and representation. Autonomy acquires the status of founding principle, we may say, by occluding ethical heteronomy from the very self-consciousness it inaugurates. Far from betraying the primacy of ethics as first philosophy, then, Levinas throws unprecedented light on Kant's idea of autonomy. When he refers to the "reverting of heteronomy into autonomy" Levinas points to the distancing of the subject from itself. This distancing, which in Levinas's account becomes possible by believing oneself the author of an order one has received,[143] allows for self-consciousness.

Autonomy manifests itself to reason, not to ethical experience. Its manifestation is contemporaneous with the distancing from oneself that enables consciousness and self-consciousness. In distancing oneself, in redoubling oneself as subject and object of thought, one in fact plays out the illusion of "producing" oneself as a complete and bounded whole.[144] Autonomy is therefore an illusion, the reduction or narrowing of scope that characterizes one's perception of oneself as self-conscious being. Although the self is indeed constituted by another, obligated in an anarchic way, autonomy emerges as the effect of looking at oneself from the distance of reason and representation, which is the only position we can occupy as self-conscious subjects. Or to put this more exactly: it is in calling oneself "autonomous" that one retroactively (and thus also anticipatorily) constitutes oneself as subject. But again, the expressions "calling oneself" or "constituting oneself" do not imply any initiative, and the term "retroactive" is not chronological. These are just ways of telling ourselves something that has *always already happened* outside causality and temporality, "diachronically." However strange this retroaction may appear to logic, the conscious subject is a retroactive construction.

Levinas conceives the subject as a retroactive construction, and in so doing he throws light on Kant's idea of autonomy.[145] Yet, if we represent ourselves as autonomous, as self-legislating, how are we then to explain our feeling obligated, or our motivation to act ethically?[146] Since we do not choose to respond to the ethical event because our response is independent from any intentional or rational decision, we may tend to misinterpret ethical obligation as a constraint on action.[147] And since ethical excess is not translatable to consciousness, it is only too easy to distort ethical obligation by recasting its alterity as an authoritarian threatening agency that judges and condemns and inflicts guilt. Guilt fills the lapse left by the absence from representation of the ethical demand, and gives obligation a "content." In Chapter 4, speaking about Kant's moral law, I argued that the reduction of the law to a threatening source of coercion is the result of a necessary perspective, that of consciousness, which inevitably must reduce. Autonomy would be inconceivable (and perhaps intolerable?) without that reduction, without first authoring what comes from elsewhere or has no origin, and then reverting into an experience of heteronomy which is understood negatively as something being imposed from the outside which internalizes itself (fate, conscience, a coercive command). The reduced perspective of consciousness conceives of the illusion that the subject *becomes* its own cause, the origin of the law, by externalizing that cause (that is, by attributing it to a coercive outside element such as, say, fate) in a way that makes it at once external and internalized. What reason can only grasp, in other words, is the "recurrence" in which the subject may be envisioned retroactively as playing the role of the unconditioned (and thus as contingently enabling the closing or completion of the series) by virtue of the fact that the other inhabits it. As I proposed in the foregoing chapters on Kant, the subject embodies precisely a relationship between two heterogeneous spaces, the intelligible and the phenomenal. All reason can perceive of that relationship is the impact the intelligible has on the phenomenal, whether it be the impact of the other on the subject, where the subject as relationship is precisely that impact and trace (motivation as "cause" of the subject's itinerary in Kant's practical philosophy), or the ability to supplement natural causality as the thesis of the antinomy formulates it (synthesis of causal linkage).

Certain passages of Kant's writing on ethics—such as those in the second *Critique* which verse on respect as a negative effect—have been read as reducing the law to a threatening, guilt-instilling command.[148] It may well be the case, in fact, that the principle of autonomy that founds the acting subject of modern liberal politics is paradoxically fueled by self-beratement and guilt, as I have argued elsewhere.[149] Moreover, the ability to conceive of a subject that is autonomous by virtue of its self-legislating reason (itself an inaccurate or at least incomplete interpretation of Kant's notion of autonomy)[150] depends on establishing a clear distinction between "self" and "other," what is "interior" and what is "outside," a distinction which is suspended in the Levinasian "other-within-the-same," and which Kant considered irrelevant when used to ascertain whether autonomy is at play.[151] Perhaps counterintuitively, this prevailing notion of autonomy is inseparable from the logic of identity and difference. Yet, as I have suggested, subjectivity in Levinas does not depend on difference, it does not occur within the logic of identity, a logic that would encompass any temporary interruption. "The one-self [*soi-même*]," he clarifies, "does not rest in peace under its identity, and yet its restlessness is not a dialectical scission, nor a process of equalizing difference."[152] Subjective constitution is therefore not linked to the problem of alterity, if we understand "alterity" dialectically in terms of altruism or "concern" for the other. Rather, subjectivity is related to the enigma of sameness, which Levinas describes as a "claim laid on the same by the other in the core of the same . . . , beyond the logic of same and other, of their insurmountable adversity."[153] One could, in fact, say that the "problem" of the other still belongs in the "logic of same and other, of their insurmountable adversity." Within this antagonism, the other's resistance—an ontic event—would oppose the self's powers by force, whereas ethical resistance suspends the freedom of a self who "can no longer have power." Levinas indeed underscores the suffering inflicted on others by the self by virtue of the "violence of the encounter with the non-I,"[154] by virtue of the confrontation and struggle that define identity. Identity presupposes difference between other and self—hence "identity politics" requires an "ethics of difference," hence too altruistic concern for the other verges on its negation, on the assimilation of the non-I by the I. When Levinas speaks of subjectivity as "substitution offered in the place of another," he immediately clarifies: "Not a victim offering itself in his place, which would suppose there is a reserved region of subjective will behind the subjectivity of substitution."[155] So long as one takes into account only the modern liberal logic of the prevailing "autonomous" subject, the logic of the antagonism between self and other of which altruism is only another expression, one must miss the question of subjective constitution. Levinas is not concerned with the difference between self and other, but rather with the lapse opened within a self affected by the event of the other, an event that reverberates in the subjects that are its trace.[156]

THE THIRD WAS ALREADY THERE

In inspiration, in the conciliation of heteronomy and autonomy—in what we may call auto-heteronomy—the third comes into view in *Otherwise than Being*.[157] The third was already there. It was in Levinas's writings at least since the 1954 essay "Ego and Totality," it is briefly mentioned in "Substitution," the core chapter of *Otherwise than Being*, and the moment of its most extended appearance in this book—*Otherwise than Being*, chapter five, 156ff.— is repeatedly cross-referenced from the beginning. The third was already there, in the alterity-relation, because it inheres in the other: "The third party looks at me in the eyes of the Other."[158] The entry of the third in Levinas's text marks the passage *in thought* from the constitutive excess I have been calling event-other to a human other. What the third makes *appear* is an other who is another subject related to others: "Justice requires the contemporaneousness of representation. It is thus that the neighbor becomes visible, and, looked at, presents himself, and there is also justice for me."[159] The entry of the third is also the moment in which the subject can become an other: "But justice can be established only if I, always evaded from the concept of the ego, always desituated and divested of being, always in non-reciprocatable relationship with the other, always for the other, can become an other like the others."[160] Though *Otherwise than Being* evokes at length the self's substitution for the other—for this is the sense of subjectivity as the "other-within-the-same"—its account of subjectivity is not complete until the other appears in the otherness of another person. The third was already in the other, the other was already plural, and so was the same as the one-for-the-other, but the third takes center stage in Levinas's argument only at this moment. Also at this moment the reader realizes that the subject's response to the other that "orders me by my own voice" has (had already) become an action in the world: the subject speaks for the other and no longer for itself, or rather, the subject speaks for the other in speaking for itself. This same with an other within is therefore not "one" because the "other" within is not "one" either. "If proximity ordered to me only the other alone, there would have not been any problem. . . . A question would not have been born, nor consciousness, nor self-consciousness."[161] If the other were one, the problem of life in community, of social and political life, would not have emerged, but neither would have self-consciousness or autonomy: there would have been no subject.

Let us take a closer look at Levinas's words: "If proximity ordered to me only the other alone, there would not have been any problem . . . ."[162] What, then, is the "problem" born with the third? Proximity "is troubled and becomes a problem from the entry of the third."[163] But the third has always been there (it can only be evoked retroactively).[164] And the problem that emerges—that is constructed retroactively—with the third and self-consciousness is no other than the subject. And with the subject come to light philosophy, knowledge, science, reciprocity, rationality, representation, and political agency. "We have to follow down the latent birth of knowing [and of essence, and of the said, and of a question] in proximity."[165] The conciliation of heteronomy and autonomy is possible because rationality and cognition were "in proximity"—in ethical substitution—from the start, demanded by the event of the other.[166]

Self-consciousness is rooted in differential representation: it occurs within the highly productive logic of identity and difference, an antagonistic logic able to institute conflict and ultimately encompass it as a temporary interruption. Self-consciousness misses the excess that founds it, its own subjectivity.[167] Since autonomy necessitates self-consciousness, the emergence of autonomy—and with it of the power to decide and act—is premised on losing sight of the excess that constitutes it, of the *causality* (to express it in Kantian terms) acting in it. Only as the autonomous subject misrecognizes the origin of the law, only as caught in the play of reciprocity it misses the other and thus itself, does its social articulation come into view. What I have here called (ethical) subjectivity is, in turn, a form of signification related to the enigma of sameness.[168] A lapse in representation, a trace of the other that exceeds it, the subject substitutes itself—"not an act"[169]—for the other while believing itself—and acting as—the autonomous cause of that excess.

From the theoretical perspective enabled by autonomy and the third, the ethical subject that emerges by substituting itself for the excess-other that constitutes it can be envisaged as anchoring signification. Whether conceived as unconditioned (Kant) or as substitution (Levinas), subjectivity emerges as the anchoring of the diachronic that allows causality and signification to cohere contingently. When read side by side with subjectivity as substitution, the link between Kant's theoretical and practical approaches to freedom gains momentum: the ethical subject that emerges by substituting itself for the excess-other that constitutes it (as *Otherwise than Being* evokes and performs it) embodies the relationship between two incommensurate spaces, the relationship Kant calls unconditioned cause. In the midst of the "diachrony without synthesis" or anarchic relationship we call subjectivity, the subject's substitution brings on contingent moments of synchrony. With substitution, then, fleeting effects of *"essence"* can arise. If the bounding effected by the unconditioned in Kant allows objectivity to emerge, the objectivity arising from substitution, and coming to view with the third, is the articulation of social justice and of political community.[170] *"Essence* as synchrony: *togetherness-in-a-place."*[171]

"The third party . . . is of itself the limit of responsibility."[172] As "the limit of responsibility" comes into play, the constitution of society becomes visible. This limitation of responsibility allows for synchronization and thus for "the intelligibility of a system."[173] With the third there is synchrony, and a synthesis can take place, but a synthesis that should be understood (as we did with the third antinomy) as the contingent and fleeting formation of a system in progress. The essence that emerges here—the being that becomes an object for thought—is precarious and does not function as a principle. "Here, one tries to express the unconditionality [*l'incondition*] of the subject, which does not have the status of a principle. It is a condition that confers sense on being itself, and welcomes its gravity. It is as resting on a self, *supporting* the whole of being [*tout être*], that being gathers itself [*se rassemble*] into a unity of the universe and *essence* is assembled into an event."[174] Sense, or signification emerges in the subject's unconditionality, that is, in its recurrent substitution for the other. It is sense that determines essence and not the other way around: "a sense [*le sens*] that is not measured by being or not being, with being determining itself, on the contrary, on the basis of sense."[175] This conception of a sense whose incondition determines being marks a momentous change in thinking Levinas attributes to Kant.[176]

"Subject" names the relationship with an incommensurable otherness whose exteriority is irretrievable:[177] thus does autonomy emerge.[178] Subjectivity thus embodies the interaction between two positions. On the one hand, as "a relationship with the outside prior to the act that would open up that outside,"[179] the subject, other-within-the-same, is heterogeneous and singular.[180] The subject takes the place of the unconditioned or substitutes itself for the other.[181] In substituting itself for the other that inhabits it, the unconditioned subject contingently and recurrently anchors the diachronic series. By virtue of the relationship it embodies with an outside (by virtue, that is, of its heterogeneity to representation), this subject signifies the void that bounds representation. A lapse Levinas expresses as the "meanwhile" between inspiration and expiration, between two heart beats, the subject— "sub-jectum"—supports the symbolic field. This bounding process reconfigures what it articulates time and again. The contingent system cohering here, "togetherness-in-a-place," manifests itself as "dwelling of the others,"[182] the space "inhabited by the others that look at me,"[183] "what is incumbent on me from all sides."[184] At the same time, as autonomous, the subject is a member of society, "an other like the others" whose position is representable. Its representability must nonetheless be qualified. Subjectivity, "comparable and incomparable,"[185] can no longer be reduced to differential logic because its autonomy is auto-heteronomy. The singular site of a relationship on which autonomy rests, each irreplaceable subject must act.

NOTES

INTRODUCTION: THE SUBJECT OF FREEDOM

1. Immanuel Kant, *Critique of Practical Reason*, trans. Werner S. Pluhar (Indianapolis, IN: Hackett, 2002), 46, Ak. 5: 31.

2. Emmanuel Levinas, *Totalité et infini: essai sur l'exteriorité* (Paris: Livre de Poche, 1990), 219, translated by Alphonso Lingis as *Totality and Infinity: An Essay on Exteriority* (Pittsburgh, PA: Duquesne University Press, 1969), 200. Emmanuel Levinas, *Autrement qu'être ou au-delà de l'essence* (Paris: Livre de Poche, 2004), 232, translated by Alphonso Lingis as *Otherwise than Being, or Beyond Essence* (Pittsburgh, PA: Duquesne University Press, 1998), 148.

3. This obligation is aroused neither by coercive commands nor by a heightening of conscience. See, for example, Kant, *Critique of Practical Reason*, 111, Ak. 5: 86, and Levinas, *Autrement qu'être*, 159 / *Otherwise than Being*, 101.

4. The following studies on the presence of Kant's theoretical and practical philosophy in Levinas's thinking fruitfully approach them side by side: Jean-François Lyotard, "Levinas's Logic," in *Face to Face with Levinas*, trans. Ian McLeod, ed. Richard A. Cohen, 117–58 (Albany: SUNY Press, 1986); Etienne Feron, "Intérêt et désintéressement de la raison: Levinas et Kant," in *Levinas en contrastes*, ed. Michel Dupuis, 83–105 (Brussels, Belgium: De Boeck-Wesmael, 1994); Jere Paul Surber, "Kant, Levinas, and the Thought of the 'Other,'" *Philosophy Today* 38, no. 3 (1994): 294–316; Catherine Chalier, *What Ought I to Do? Morality in Kant and Levinas*, trans. Jane Marie Todd (Ithaca, NY: Cornell University Press, 2002); Peter Atterton, "From Transcendental Freedom to the Other: Levinas and Kant," in *In Proximity: Kant and the Eighteenth Century*, ed. Melvyn New, Richard Bernasconi, and Richard A. Cohen, 327–53 (Lubbock: Texas Tech University Press, 2001); Paul Davies, "Sincerity and the End of Theodicy: Three Remarks on Levinas and Kant," in *The Cambridge Companion to Emmanuel Levinas*, ed. Simon Critchley and Robert Bernasconi,

161–87 (Cambridge: Cambridge University Press, 2002). Peter Atterton's illuminating essay, "From Transcendental Freedom to the Other," studies the relationship between Kant's transcendental idea of freedom and Levinas's other in a way that is particularly relevant to my own approach. Catherine Chalier's *What Ought I to Do?* is the first extended analysis of the proximity and difference between Kant and Levinas. The areas of closeness and distance between the two thinkers in her account reflect Levinas's own assertions about his different notions (good and evil, autonomy and heteronomy, the face, sensibility, reason, causality, anarchy, happiness, religion, etc.). Chalier's original title in French, *Pour une morale au-delà du savoir*, offers a more accurate idea of the direction of her study. My own study underscores, in turn, the structural proximity between Kant and Levinas in what concerns the constitution of subjectivity, its function, and the emergence of autonomy. The most important areas of convergence, those in which I propose Levinas casts light on Kant's theory, come to view when *Otherwise than Being* is read as a work whose language rhetorically expresses the ethical disturbance of which Levinas speaks (see the rhetorical reading I propose of *Otherwise than Being* in Chapter 5).

5. For a compelling account of Levinas's criticism of Kant, see Chalier, *What Ought I to Do?*, especially the chapter "Intelligible Character and Anarchy" (110–31). See also Gabriela Basterra, "Tragic Autonomy Meets Ethical Heteronomy," in *Seductions of Fate: Tragic Subjectivity, Ethics, Politics* (New York: Palgrave Macmillan, 2004), 131–68.

6. For a thorough account of the evolution of Kant's notion of autonomy, see Susan Meld Shell, *Kant and the Limits of Autonomy* (Cambridge, MA: Harvard University Press, 2009). This prevailing notion of a free subject is well described by Robert B. Pippin in his "Introduction: 'Bourgeois Philosophy' and the Problem of the Subject," in *The Persistence of Subjectivity: On the Kantian Aftermath* (Cambridge: Cambridge University Press, 2005), 1–23.

7. I want to express my deepest gratitude to Helen Tartar, the first editor of this book, for making it happen with her unique vision. In memoriam.

8. Immanuel Kant, *Critique of Pure Reason*, trans. Werner S. Pluhar (Indianapolis, IN: Hackett, 1996), 442–559, A 406–567/B 433–595.

9. Kant, *Critique of Pure Reason*, 342, A 288–89/B 344–45.

10. Kant, *Critique of Practical Reason*, 65, Ak. 5: 46.

11. Jean-Luc Nancy, "Le Katègorein de l'excès," in *L'impératif catégorique* (Paris: Flammarion, 1983), 18–19, translated by James Gilbert-Walsh and Simon Sparks as "The *Kategorein* of Excess," in *A Finite Thinking*, ed. Simon Sparks, 133–51 (Stanford, CA: Stanford University Press: 2003), 142.

12. Kant, *Critique of Practical Reason*, 5, Ak. 5: 3–4. The entire line reads: "Now the concept of freedom, insofar as its reality is proved by an apodeictic law of practical reason, forms the *keystone* of the whole edifice of a system of pure reason, even that of speculative reason."

13. The subjectivity constituted by freedom I study here is not reducible to self-consciousness or identity. Identity emerges in the realm of differential representation and is thus based on the dialectic of subject and object, of the "I" and the "non-I." Even though this logic of identity and difference brings forth self-consciousness, agency, reciprocity, universality, and autonomy, it paradoxically depends on the self-division that results from internalizing essentialized figures of otherness (see Basterra, *Seductions of Fate*, especially "Tragic Modern Subjectivity"). In turn, the Kantian and Levinasian subjectivity I study here exceeds the field of differential representation that would produce it as identity, and is therefore larger than the self-conscious identity it includes and exceeds. Unlike self-conscious identity, which depends on a dialectic relation to the other, the subjectivity at stake in Kant's and Levinas's ethical accounts concerns the same (the subject) constituted by an excess of which subjectivity is itself the trace.

14. Jean-Luc Nancy, "Le Katègorein de l'excès," 19 / "The *Kategorein* of Excess," 142 (translation modified). Nancy's entire paragraph reads: "No doubt *pure reason* is not only an expression that is foreign to our sensibility but one whose concepts need to be submitted—perhaps more than any other concepts—to critique or to the deconstruction of metaphysics. Yet it could well be that a new task announces itself thus: the task of thinking 'pure reason' *in terms of* [*à partir de*] its being-practical, and of the duty that constitutes it [*qui le constitue*, that is, that constitutes its being practical: *son être-pratique*] or enjoins it."

15. Emmanuel Levinas, "Transcendence and Evil" (1978), in *Of God Who Comes to Mind*, trans. Bettina Bergo, 122–34 (Stanford, CA: Stanford University Press, 1998), 123. See Atterton, "From Transcendental Freedom to the Other," 327–33.

16. See, for example, Levinas's turn to Kant's thinking in the concluding paragraph of "Substitution," the core chapter of *Otherwise than Being*: "If one had the right to retain one trait from a philosophical system and neglect all the details of its architecture . . . , we would think here of Kantism, which finds a sense [*un sens*] to the human without measuring it by ontology . . . , outside the immortality and death ontologies stumble upon. The fact that immortality and theology would be unable to determine the categorical imperative signifies the novelty of the Copernican revolution: sense that is not measured in terms of being or not-being, with being determining itself, on the contrary, on the basis of sense." Levinas, *Autrement qu'être*, 205 / *Otherwise than Being*, 129 (translation modified).

17. Emmanuel Levinas, "Is Ontology Fundamental?" (1951), trans. Alphonso Lingis, in *Basic Philosophical Writings*, ed. Robert Bernasconi, Simon Critchley, and Adriaan Peperzak, 1–10 (Bloomington: Indiana University Press, 1996), 10. See also Emmanuel Levinas, "The Primacy of Pure Practical Reason" (1971), trans. Blake Billings, in *Man and World* 27 (1994): 445–53.

18. Monique David-Ménard, *La folie dans la raison pure: Kant lecteur de Swedenborg* (Paris: Vrin, 1990). All translations from this book are mine.

19. Joan Copjec, "Sex and the Euthanasia of Reason," in *Supposing the Subject*, ed. Joan Copjec, 16–44 (London: Verso, 1994), 19–20.

20. Kant, *Critique of Pure Reason*, 519, A 509/B 537.

21. Kant, *Critique of Pure Reason*, 554, A 561/B 589n.

22. Kant, *Critique of Pure Reason*, 319, A 255/B 310–11.

23. Kant, *Critique of Pure Reason*, 473, A 444–45/B 472–73.

24. Kant, *Critique of Pure Reason*, 473, A 445/B 473.

25. Kant, *Critique of Pure Reason*, 537–38, A 536/B 564, and 544, A 547/B 557.

26. Nancy, "Le Katègorein," 19 / "The *Kategorein*," 142.

27. Gilles Deleuze, *Kant's Critical Philosophy: The Doctrine of the Faculties*, trans. Hugh Tomlinson and Barbara Habberjam (London: Athlone, 1984), 28.

28. As Richard Velkley explains (speaking of Dieter Henrich's approach to Kant's practical reason as an account of motivation rather than as a theory of agency), "Rousseau's great contribution, according to Kant, was to show not how human reason as free accounts for our actions in the world, but how it can be *self*-determining and thus give itself, and even *be* itself, an end, without dependence on a natural order or a higher being. Hence Kant's turn to freedom is inseparable from the project of justifying *reason as such*, in the light of the collapse of all traditional metaphysics of nature and being (of which collapse Kant was convinced well before 1781)." Richard L. Velkley, "Introduction: Unity of Reason as Aporetic Ideal," in Dieter Henrich, *The Unity of Reason: Essays on Kant's Philosophy*, ed. Richard L. Velkley (Cambridge, MA: Harvard University Press, 1994), 216–17n38.

29. Kant, *Critique of Practical Reason*, 68, Ak. 5: 49.

30. Kant, *Critique of Practical Reason*, 66, Ak. 5: 46.

31. Alenka Zupančič, *L'éthique du réel: Kant avec Lacan* (Caen, France: Nous, 2009), 62–72. This book is not a translation of Zupančič's earlier *Ethics of the Real: Kant, Lacan* (New York: Verso, 2000). Rather, as the author indicates, it is written directly in French, and constitutes a largely reworked version of the book in English. Most of my references here are to *L'éthique du réel* (my translation), unless otherwise noted.

32. Nancy, "Le Katègorein," 26 / "The *Kategorein*," 147.

33. See Zupančič, *L'éthique du réel*, 68.

34. Immanuel Kant, "On the Inherence of the Evil alongside the Good Principle, or, On the Radical Evil in Human Nature," in *Religion within the Bounds of Bare Reason*, trans. Werner S. Pluhar (Indianapolis: Hackett, 2009), 21, Ak. 6: 21. Henceforth I abbreviate the title of this essay as "On the Inherence of Evil."

35. Kant, *Religion within the Bounds of Bare Reason*, 26, Ak. 6: 25.

36. Kant, *Critique of Practical Reason*, 46, Ak. 5: 31.

37. Levinas, *Autrement qu'être*, 232 / *Otherwise than Being*, 148.

38. Zupančič, *L'éthique du réel*, 74–75.

39. Kant, *Critique of Practical Reason*, 98, Ak. 5: 75 (translation modified).

40. See Zupančič, *L'éthique du réel*, 80.

41. Kant, *Critique of Practical Reason*, 138, Ak. 5: 108. For Kant's explanation of the two ways in which we may think of the unconditioned, see *Critique of Pure Reason*, 451, A 417–18/B 445–46.

42. Kant, *Critique of Practical Reason*, 138, Ak. 5: 108.

43. See Zupančič, *L'éthique du réel*, 77–84.

44. Kant, *Critique of Pure Reason*, 451, A 417–18/B 445–46.

45. For an illuminating account of the relationships and differences between affect, emotion, drive, and trauma, see Charles Shepherdson, *Lacan and the Limits of Language* (New York: Fordham University Press, 2008), 81–100. Chalier has, in turn, dealt with the relationship between sensibility and reason in Kant and Levinas in *What Ought I to Do?*, 85–109. On the presence of affect in reason, see Michel Henry, *The Essence of Manifestation*, trans. Girard Etzkorn (The Hague: Martinus Nijhoff, 1973).

46. Levinas initiated his philosophical writing within the phenomenological tradition, and his first three books—*The Theory of Intuition in Husserl's Phenomenology* (1930), *Existence and Existents* (*De l'existence à l'existant*, 1947), and *En découvrant l'existence avec Husserl and Heidegger* (1949)—analyze the philosophies of Husserl and Heidegger both as source of inspiration and as object of criticism. Levinas's own singular relationship with phenomenology, which plays an active role in his philosophy of subjectivity, exceeds the limits of this book. It is important to note, however, that at the end of *Otherwise than Being* Levinas points to the need to "venture . . . beyond phenomenology" (Levinas, *Autrement qu'être*, 281/ *Otherwise than Being*, 183). *Otherwise than Being* ventures "beyond phenomenology" by means of "the strange discourse conducted here about the signification in the-one-for-the-other." In this discourse of the subjective, "in the hyperbole, the superlative, the excellence of signification from which they derive," notions "lose the consistency that the theme in which they manifest themselves offers them" (*Autrement qu'être*, 281/ *Otherwise than Being*, 183 [translation modified]). Levinas's adjective "strange" (*l'étrange discours*) and the nouns "hyperbole," "superlative," and "signification" convey the sense of exceeding or surpassing notions and themes. How this exceeding may be enacted in language, and this surpassing signified, is the question that underlies the tropological approach to *Otherwise than Being* I am proposing here, which focuses on the ways in which Levinas's language acts. For a clarifying analysis of the evolution of Levinas's phenomenology, see Bettina Bergo, "What Is Levinas Doing? Phenomenology and the Rhetoric of an Ethical Un-conscious," *Philosophy and Rhetoric* 38, no. 2 (2005): 122–44.

47. Levinas, *Autrement qu'être*, 232/ *Otherwise than Being*, 148.

48. Emmanuel Levinas, "Humanism and An-archy" (1968), in *Collected Philosophical Papers*, trans. Alphonso Lingis, 127–39 (Pittsburgh, PA: Duquesne University Press, 1998), 133.

49. Levinas, "Humanism and An-archy," 132. "The thesis and antithesis of the third Kantian antinomy," he continues, "imply the priority of the thesis, since the situation is not limited to themes: the thesis and antithesis present themselves to the consciousness that thematizes them to itself in the identity of the *said*, the logos; they both present themselves to a freedom for adoption or refusal. Absolute non-freedom could not show itself in any way." Levinas, "Humanism and An-archy," 132.

50. I refer the reader to four insightful studies on post-Kantian thought and freedom after Kant: Dieter Henrich, *Between Kant and Hegel: Lectures on German Idealism*, ed. David S. Pacini (Cambridge, MA: Harvard University Press, 2003); Pippin, *The Persistence of Subjectivity*; John Llewelyn, *The HypoCritical Imagination: Between Kant and Levinas* (New York: Routledge, 2000); and Andrew Cutrofello, *Continental Philosophy: A Contemporary Introduction* (London: Routledge, 2005).

51. Kant addresses the paradox of transcendental apperception and inner sense at the end of the 1787 edition of the "Deduction of the Pure Concepts of Understanding," *Critique of Pure Reason*, 192–96, B 153–59. See my summary of it in the opening section of Chapter 1.

52. Levinas, *Autrement qu'être*, 281 / *Otherwise than Being*, 183.

53. Levinas, *Autrement qu'être*, 185 / *Otherwise than Being*, 117.

54. Levinas, *Autrement qu'être*, 245 / *Otherwise than Being*, 157 (translation modified).

55. Levinas, *Autrement qu'être*, 245 / *Otherwise than Being*, 157 (translation modified).

56. Levinas, *Autrement qu'être*, 188n / *Otherwise than Being*, 119n22.

57. Levinas, *Autrement qu'être*, 183 / *Otherwise than Being*, 116.

1. NEGATION AND OBJECTIVITY: METHODOLOGICAL PRELUDE

1. David-Ménard, *La folie dans la raison pure*. All translations from this book are mine.

2. Kant, *Critique of Pure Reason*, 71–72, A 19/B 33 (beginning of "Transcendental Aesthetic") and 105–6, A 50/B 74 (beginning of "Transcendental Logic"). In Kant's critical project there are actually four faculties at play, one passive and three active: sensibility, the imagination, the understanding, and reason. Each of these faculties produces different types of presentation. As they function in the *Critique of Pure Reason*, sensibility produces intuitions, the imagination mediates between sensibility and the understanding and produces figurative synthesis, the understanding produces concepts, and reason produces ideas. See Gilles Deleuze, *Kant's Critical Philosophy*, 9.

3. Kant, *Critique of Pure Reason*, 105–6, A 50/B 74.

4. As Gilles Deleuze convincingly argues, the pair that informs Kant's analyses in first *Critique* is not the disjunction between appearances and essence or appearances and things-in-themselves, but rather the conjunction of apparitions and conditions of apparition or sense of the apparition ("Synthesis and Time" [Vincennes seminar on Kant, March 14, 1978]). Kant's *Critique* focuses on the conditions of our relationship with what affects us and appears to our senses (empirical things and events), the conditions through which we can know and make sense of what appears, and the limits at which knowledge ends.

5. Kant, *Critique of Pure Reason*, 71–72, A 19/B 33.

6. "For only by means of such pure forms of sensibility can an object appear to us, i.e., can it be an object of empirical intuition. Hence space and time are pure intuitions containing a priori the condition for the possibility of objects as appearances, and the synthesis in space and time has objective reality." Kant, *Critique of Pure Reason*, 145, A 89/B 121–22.

7. Kant groups the categories according to the four logical functions involved in all possible judgments: quantity, quality, relation, and modality (see table of functions of judgments in *Critique of Pure Reason*, 124, A 70/B 95). Categories or pure concepts of understanding derive their validity from their reference to space and time. The categories of quantity are *unity*, *plurality*, and *allness* or *totality*; the categories of quality are *reality*, *negation*, and *limitation*; the categories of relation are those of *inherence* and subsistence (*substantia et accidens*), of *causality* and dependence (cause and effect), and of *community* (interaction between agent and patient); finally, the categories of modality are *possibility*-impossibility, *existence*-nonexistence, and *necessity*-contingency (see table of categories in *Critique of Pure Reason*, 132, A 80/B 106).

8. Kant, *Critique of Pure Reason*, B 151–54. This mediating activity of the imagination is what Kant calls schematism, and through it the imagination relates categories to determinations in time (*Critique of Pure Reason*, 216–17, A 144–45/B 183–85).

9. Kant, *Critique of Pure Reason*, 152, A 97.

10. See Deleuze, *Kant's Critical Philosophy*, 8, 14. As Deleuze points out, the notion of representation is ambiguous. One must distinguish between the representation and what presents itself to us, that is, what appears in intuition: a phenomenon as a manifold of sensations in space and time. "What presents itself is thus not only empirical phenomenal diversity in space and time but the pure a priori diversity of space and time themselves. Space and time are pure intuition, the only thing sensibility presents a priori. So intuitions would be presentations and it will be the process of synthesis that produces representation. Within the framework of the first *Critique* representation is defined as knowledge, as the synthesis of that which is presented" (8).

11. Categories are "conditions under which alone their manifold [of sensible intuitions] can come together in one consciousness." Kant, *Critique of Pure Reason*, 185, B 143.

12. Kant, *Critique of Pure Reason*, 158, A 107.

13. Kant, *Critique of Pure Reason*, 177, B 132.

14. Kant, *Critique of Pure Reason*, 178, B 133.

15. "Hence the original and necessary consciousness of one's own identity is at the same time a consciousness of an equally necessary unity of the synthesis of all appearances according to concepts." Kant, *Critique of Pure Reason*, 159, A 108. Or, as Kant clarifies in the second edition, "only because I can combine a manifold of given presentations *in one consciousness*, is it possible for me to present the *identity itself of the consciousness of these presentations*," of the consciousness across these presentations. Kant, *Critique of Pure Reason*, 178, B 133.

16. Kant, *Critique of Pure Reason*, 196, B 159. Kant raises this question and offers an explanation to it at the end of the 1787 edition of the "Deduction of the Pure Concepts of Understanding," *Critique of Pure Reason*, 192–96, B 153–59.

17. Kant, *Critique of Pure Reason*, 194, B 155.

18. When we think of ourselves, writes Kant, "we intuit ourselves only as we are inwardly *affected*; and this seems contradictory, because we [despite being active] would then have to relate to ourselves as passive." Kant, *Critique of Pure Reason*, 192, B 152–53.

19. These forms are irreducible to each other because Kant conceives of them as heterogeneously determined: inner intuition emerges in spatio-temporal determination and has the sequential form of figurative synthesis, whereas the unity of transcendental apperception is a condition for conceptual determination done by the understanding.

20. Kant, *Critique of Pure Reason*, 194–95, B 156. "We must concede," continues Kant, "that, as far as inner intuition is concerned, our own [self as] subject is cognized by us only as appearance, but not in terms of what it is in itself." Kant, *Critique of Pure Reason*, 194–95, B 156.

21. Kant, *Critique of Pure Reason*, 196, B 159.

22. See Deleuze's development of this idea in Gilles Deleuze, *Difference and Repetition*, trans. Paul Patton (New York: Columbia University Press, 1994), 85–87.

23. In his lecture "The Question of Subjectivity" (January 9, 1976), Levinas praises Kant's transcendental ideas because they go beyond knowledge toward something they cannot reach: "Thus the Kantian ideas are forms of thinking that overflow knowledge and point toward a subjectivity awakened by what it could not contain." Emmanuel Levinas, *God, Death, and Time*, trans. Bettina Bergo, 149–52 (Stanford, CA: Stanford University Press, 2000), 149. In another lecture, "Kant and the Transcendental Ideal" (January 16, 1979), Levinas emphasizes the importance of Kant's rational ideas, because in them "he admits the existence of thoughts that speak of being and that are obligatory for reason, *but that do not rejoin being*. . . . What Kant therefore discovers in the *Critique of Pure Reason*, and particularly in the Transcen-

dental Dialectic, is the fact that *thinking*, without falling into arbitrariness, and indeed in order to satisfy the needs of reason, *can fail to reach being*." Levinas, *God, Death, and Time*, 153–54. However, in his 1978 essay "Transcendence and Evil," Levinas criticizes Kant for adding to the transcendental ideal of freedom the postulates of God and the immortality of the soul, a move that, for Levinas, constitutes a return to ontology. See Levinas, "Transcendence and Evil," 123.

24. Kant, *Critique of Pure Reason*, 371, A 326–27/B 383. Leaving to the understanding the task to determine empirical objects by referring phenomena to the synthetic unit of the category, "pure reason reserves for itself solely the absolute totality in the use of the concepts of understanding, and seeks to take the synthetic unity thought in the category up to the absolutely unconditioned." Kant, *Critique of Pure Reason*, 371, A 326/B 383. "Accordingly, reason refers only to the use of understanding. Reason refers to that use [expressly] . . . in order to prescribe to understanding the direction leading to a certain unity—a unity of which the understanding has no concept and which aims at collating [arranging and holding together] all acts of understanding, in regard to every object, in an *absolute whole*." Kant, *Critique of Pure Reason*, 371, A 326/B 383.

25. An idea is thus "a necessary concept of reason for which no congruent object can be given in the senses." Kant, *Critique of Pure Reason*, 371, A 327/B 372.

26. Kant, *Critique of Pure Reason*, 370, A 326/B 382.

27. Kant, *Critique of Pure Reason*, 445, A 409/B 436. The words "condition" and "conditioned" refer here to the sequence or successive series through which the imagination and the understanding represent the manifold of intuition.

28. In empirical cognition that closure is given by the object-concept to which the understanding refers the manifold.

29. In his lecture "The Radical Question: Kant Against Heidegger" (February 6, 1976), Levinas underscores the lack of reference to being in Kant's transcendental ideas as an important contribution: "That meaning might signify without reference to being, without recourse to being, without a comprehension of being given is . . . the great contribution of the Transcendental Dialectic in the *Critique of Pure Reason*." Levinas, *God, Death, and Time*, 60.

30. These three categories correspond to the three syllogisms of relation (categorical, hypothetical, and disjunctive). "And hence we shall have to search for an *unconditioned*, first, of the *categorical* synthesis in a subject; second, of the *hypothetical* synthesis of the members of a series; third, of the *disjunctive* synthesis of the parts in a system." Kant, *Critique of Pure Reason*, 368, A 323/B 379.

31. Kant, *Critique of Pure Reason*, 376, A 334/B 391. The psychological idea of the soul, the cosmological idea of the world as a totality, and the theological idea of God are the ideas of traditional metaphysics. These ideas give rise to the three metaphysical disciplines whose integrity Kant contests: rational psychology, rational cosmology, and transcendental theology.

32. In the Dialectic Kant shows that the three branches of special metaphysics—psychology, cosmology, and theology—are therefore respectively ridden with paralogism (by affirming the being of the soul), antinomy (by assuming the existence of the world), and transcendent ideas (by presupposing the being of God).

33. This is how Kant describes the four cosmological ideas and their antinomies: "Absolute completeness of the composition of the given whole of all appearances" (first idea), "Absolute completeness of the division of a given whole in [the realm of] appearance" (second idea), "Absolute completeness of the arising of an appearance as such" (third idea), "Absolute completeness of the dependence of the existence of the changeable in [the realm of] appearance" (fourth idea). Kant, *Critique of Pure Reason*, 450, A 415/B 443.

34. Kant, *Critique of Pure Reason*, 443, A 407/B 434.

35. Kant, *Critique of Pure Reason*, 458, A 426/B 454, A 427/B 455.

36. Kant, *Critique of Pure Reason*, 514–15, A 503–4/B 531–32.

37. See David-Ménard, *La folie dans la raison pure*, 29–30.

38. Kant, *Critique of Pure Reason*, 513, A 501–2/B 529–30.

39. Kant, *Critique of Pure Reason*, 515, A 504/B 532.

40. Kant, *Critique of Pure Reason*, 514, A 503/B 531.

41. Kant, *Critique of Pure Reason*, 515, A 505/B 533.

42. David-Ménard, *La folie dans la raison pure*, 30–31.

43. "Thus of two dialectically opposed judgments both can be false, because one judgment not merely contradicts the other but says something more than is required for contradiction." Kant, *Critique of Pure Reason*, 515, A 504/B 532.

44. Kant, *Critique of Pure Reason*, 514, A 503/B 531.

45. Kant, *Critique of Pure Reason*, 514–15, A 503–4/B 531–32.

46. Kant, *Critique of Pure Reason*, 514–15, A 503–4/B 531–32.

47. Kant, *Critique of Pure Reason*, 514–15, A 503–4/B 531–32.

48. It prevents the conflict from being locked into a binary structure ("either infinite or finite") and allows for a third alternative: rather than being either infinite nor finite, the world may be simply non-infinite. In fact, for all we know, the world may even *not be* at all—there is a possibility that the world does not have a separate existence in itself.

49. Kant, *Critique of Pure Reason*, 515, A 504/B 532.

50. David-Ménard, *La folie dans la raison pure*, 29–30, 35, and Copjec, "Sex and the Euthanasia of Reason," 29–30.

51. Kant, *Critique of Pure Reason*, 515, A 504/B 532, and 515, A 504/B 532.

52. Beyond denying the world is infinite, the second judgment adds something more than is needed for the contradiction, the finitude of the world, thus leaving out the possibility of a simply non-infinite world, a world not characterized empirically by means of magnitude.

53. Kant, *Critique of Pure Reason*, 515, A 504/B 532.

54. David-Ménard, *La folie dans la raison pure*, 30, 35, and Copjec, "Sex and the Euthanasia of Reason," 29–30.

55. Kant, *Critique of Pure Reason*, 514–15, A 503–4/B 531–32, emphasis added.

56. Kant, *Critique of Pure Reason*, 515, A 504–5/B 532–33.

57. Kant, *Critique of Pure Reason*, 515, A 504–5/B 532–33. As Kant remarks when criticizing Zeno's detractors, trying to deny two propositions contradicting each other is absurd.

58. Kant, *Critique of Pure Reason*, 515, A 504–5/B 532–33.

59. Kant, *Critique of Pure Reason*, 515, A 504–5/B 532–33.

60. Again, the problem was not whether the world was infinite or finite as the dialectic or contrary conflict presented it, because in fact the world is not.

61. Kant, *Critique of Pure Reason*, 515, A 505/B 533.

62. Kant, *Critique of Pure Reason*, 515, A 505/B 533.

63. Kant, *Critique of Pure Reason*, 517, A 508/B 536.

64. As Joan Copjec points out, "Kant avoids the skeptical impasse by refusing the answer to the question 'Is the world finite or infinite?' and by negating instead the assumption implicit in the question: the world *is*." Copjec, "Sex and the Euthanasia of Reason," 30.

65. Kant, *Critique of Pure Reason*, 370, A 326/B 382.

66. Kant, *Critique of Pure Reason*, 510–11, A 497–98/B 525–26.

67. Kant, *Critique of Pure Reason*, 515, A 504–5/B 532–33.

68. See Copjec, "Sex and the Euthanasia of Reason," 30–31.

69. Copjec, "Sex and the Euthanasia of Reason," 30–31.

70. Kant, *Critique of Pure Reason*, 517, A 508/B 536.

71. Kant, *Critique of Pure Reason*, 445, A 409/B 436.

72. Kant, *Critique of Pure Reason*, 445, A 409/B 436.

73. Kant, *Critique of Pure Reason*, 451, A 416/B 444. When trying to form an "all," reason's work of synthesis is bound to fail, because it enters into contradiction with the seemingly endless empirical regression. Indeed, we do not even know if completing the series would be possible in sensibility (in our sensible intuition of phenomena)—"whether this completeness [demanded by the synthesis] is possible in sensibility is still a problem." Kant, *Critique of Pure Reason*, 451, A 417/B 444.

74. Kant, *Critique of Pure Reason*, 518–19, A 509–10/B 537–38. A constitutive principle, in turn, is "the principle of the absolute totality of the series of conditions considered as given in objects" (A 509–10/B 537–38), an absolute totality that could only be grasped in simultaneity and not in succession.

75. Kant, *Critique of Pure Reason*, 519, A 509/B 537.

76. Kant, *Critique of Pure Reason*, 515, A 504–5/B 532–33. As Kant had initially clarified, in order to achieve this completeness, reason "demand[s], for a given conditioned, absolute totality on the side of the conditions," "according to the principle that *if the conditioned is given, then the entire sum of conditions and hence the*

absolutely unconditioned (through which alone the conditioned was possible) *is also given*." Kant, *Critique of Pure Reason*, 445, A 409/B 436.

77. Kant, *Critique of Pure Reason*, 518, A 509/B 537.

78. Kant, *Critique of Pure Reason*, 519, A 509/B 537.

79. Once Kant has proved that the world is an impossible concept, a concept that defeats itself, he devotes the rest of section 8 to explaining the distinction between progression and regression, and between infinite regression and indeterminate regression—"regression extending indeterminably far (*in indefinitum*)." Kant, *Critique of Pure Reason*, 521, A 512/B 540. Kant's introduction of indeterminate regression here prepares the basis for the second, affirmative solution to the antinomy I paraphrase below.

80. Kant, *Critique of Pure Reason*, 519, A 509/B 537.

81. Kant, *Critique of Pure Reason*, 527, A 520/B 548.

82. Kant, *Critique of Pure Reason*, 527, A 521/B 549.

83. From this follows that we can only define empirical synthesis as incomplete (Kant, *Critique of Pure Reason*, 519, A 510/B 530), but since synthesis requires completeness defining it as incomplete is a contradiction in terms.

84. Kant, *Critique of Pure Reason*, 527, A 521/B 549.

85. It is in order to guard against this possible misunderstanding that Kant has to state his solution twice, according to Copjec ("Sex and the Euthanasia of Reason," 31).

86. Kant, *Critique of Pure Reason*, 528, A 521/B 549.

87. Copjec, "Sex and the Euthanasia of Reason," 31.

88. Kant, *Critique of Pure Reason*, 528, A 522/B 550.

89. Immanuel Kant, *Logic*, trans. John Richardson (London: Printed in Stationers' Court for W. Simpkin and R. Marchall, 1819), 145, § 22.

90. See David-Ménard, *La folie dans la raison pure*, 29.

91. For the distinction between dialectic conflict and analytic opposition, see also John Llewelyn's "Antinomy as Dialectic Imagination in Hegel's Critique of Kant" (*The HypoCritical Imagination*, 69–87), Llewelyn's own reading of Hegel's critique of Kant's mathematical antinomies in the *Science of Logic*, especially the section titled "Analytical and Dialectic Opposites" (81–85).

92. David-Ménard, *La folie dans la raison pure*, 32. This paragraph and the next few paragraphs gloss David-Ménard's explanations.

93. "Even when this concept of contradiction is only provisional, since it doesn't distinguish the logical viewpoint from the transcendental viewpoint, it is enough to make of the antinomy, by contrast, the symptom of a problem: the face to face of reason with itself, this strange discord, does not establish the truth of any of the two propositions." David-Ménard, *La folie dans la raison pure*, 31.

94. David-Ménard, *La folie dans la raison pure*, 37.

95. In this paragraph I have glossed David-Ménard's explanation in *La folie dans la raison pure*, 38.

96. Kant, *Critique of Pure Reason*, 514–15, A 503–4/B 531–32.

97. Kant, *Critique of Pure Reason*, 515, A 504/B 532.

98. Exclusion was thus already present in the antinomy, albeit as a failed operation, because the assumed subject that was excluded had been illegitimately introduced.

99. David-Ménard, *La folie dans la raison pure*, 33.

100. David-Ménard, *La folie dans la raison pure*, 33n, 34.

101. Kant, *Critique of Pure Reason*, 514–15, A 503–4/B 531–32.

102. David-Ménard, *La folie dans la raison pure*, 37.

103. David-Ménard, *La folie dans la raison pure*, 39–40. I gloss David-Ménard's argument in the rest of this section.

104. Kant, *Critique of Pure Reason*, 510, A 497/B 525.

105. David-Ménard, *La folie dans la raison pure*, 39–40.

106. At the very moment in which Kant reveals the falsity of thesis and antithesis in the mathematical antinomy, he renames antinomic conflict and contradiction respectively as dialectic and analytical opposition: "Permit me to call this sort of opposition *dialectical* but that of contradiction *analytical opposition.* Thus of two dialectically opposed judgments both can be false, because one judgment not merely contradicts the other but says something more than is required for contradiction." Kant, *Critique of Pure Reason*, 514–15, A 503–4/B 531–32.

107. Kant, *Critique of Pure Reason*, 515, A 504–5/B 532–33, see quotation below.

108. David-Ménard, *La folie dans la raison pure*, 41.

109. Kant, *Critique of Pure Reason*, 515, A 504–5/B 532–33.

110. David-Ménard, *La folie dans la raison pure*, 40.

111. Kant, *Critique of Pure Reason*, 513, A 501/B 529.

112. David-Ménard, *La folie dans la raison pure*, 29–30.

113. David-Ménard, *La folie dans la raison pure*, 8.

114. David-Ménard, *La folie dans la raison pure*, 58.

115. Since limits are set up through negation, it may come as a surprise to realize that the first *Critique* speaks about negation and nothingness only in passing (David-Ménard, *La folie dans la raison pure*, 58). But in effect, David-Ménard proposes, the first *Critique* articulates "through a redefined negation a theory of rational illusions in relation to a theory of the constitution of the object." The core of the first *Critique* nevertheless unravels the relationship between negation and existence at length, as David-Ménard points out. The transitional chapters between the Analytic and the Dialectic of Pure Reason constitute, according to her, a study of the power of negation. First, the extended critique of Leibniz in the Amphiboly offers a detailed analysis of real conflict. Then the last pages of the Analytic deal with the table of categories of nothing, by opposition to which "something" may be defined (28). Allowing something to form in the place of nothing, suggests David-Ménard, means allowing something to take shape in the place of the idea of the world, and this is

what the Dialectic accomplishes negatively in its second chapter, "The Antinomy of Pure Reason," by exploring several forms of negation: conflict and contradiction, dialectic and analytic opposition, and—indirectly—indefinite judgment.

116. Kant, *Critique of Pure Reason*, 343–45, A 290–92/B 346–49.

117. David-Ménard, *La folie dans la raison pure*, 28, 42.

118. David-Ménard, *La folie dans la raison pure*, 45.

119. David-Ménard, *La folie dans la raison pure*, 44–46.

120. The term transcendental here does not refer to the Kantian sense of transcendental ideality, where things-in-themselves would be the support (the real) of appearances. The only truly constitutive transcendental object from the perspective of my study, freedom, functions in the other transcendental sense David-Ménard means here, which Judith Butler sums up as "one in which the condition is not external to the object it occasions." Distinguishing between the two senses of the transcendental is crucial. As Butler writes, "In the Kantian vein, 'transcendental' can mean: the condition without which nothing can appear. But it can also mean: the regulatory and constitutive conditions of appearance of any given object. The latter sense is the one in which the condition is not external to the object it occasions, but is its constitutive condition and the principle of its development and appearance. The transcendental thus offers the criterial conditions that constrain the emergence of the thematizable." Judith Butler, "Competing Universalities," in Judith Butler, Ernesto Laclau, and Slavoj Žižek, *Contingency, Hegemony, Universality: Contemporary Dialogues on the Left* (London: Verso, 2000), 147. Freedom is imagined by reason as being both outside and inside the object it constitutes. In fact, freedom does not exist except in the object it constitutes. Freedom in the subject is, however, an irreducible other, an element of excess.

121. Kant, *Logic*, 145, § 22, quoted in David-Ménard, *La folie dans la raison pure*, 33.

122. Kant, *Logic*, 145, § 22.

123. David-Ménard, *La folie dans la raison pure*, 34.

124. Kant, *Logic*, 145, § 22.

125. Kant, *Logic*, 145, § 22.

126. Kant, *Logic*, 145, § 22.

127. David-Ménard, *La folie dans la raison pure*, 34. She also writes: "The logical rigor of indefinite judgment is the very work of the transcendental" (34).

128. Kant, *Critique of Pure Reason*, 317, B 307.

129. On the difference between negative judgment and indefinite judgment, and between the positive and negative uses of noumenon, see David-Ménard, *La folie dans la raison pure*, 69–70, and also Slavoj Žižek, *Tarrying with the Negative: Kant, Hegel, and the Critique of Ideology* (Durham, NC: Duke University Press, 1993), 111–12.

130. See Kant, *Critique of Pure Reason*, 317, B 307: "If by noumenon we mean an object of nonsensible intuition and hence assume a special kind of intuition, viz.,

an intellectual one—which, however, is not ours and into the possibility of which we also have no insight—then that would be the noumenon in the *positive* meaning of the term."

131. Kant, *Critique of Pure Reason*, 317, B 307.

132. "And although . . . there may indeed be beings of the understanding to which our sensible power of intuition has no reference whatever, yet our concepts of understanding, as mere forms of thought for our sensible intuition, do not in the least extend to them. Hence what is called noumenon by us must be meant as such only in the *negative* signification." Kant, *Critique of Pure Reason*, 318, B 309.

133. Kant, *Critique of Pure Reason*, 342–43, A 288/B 344, quoted in David-Ménard, *La folie dans la raison pure*, 70.

134. Kant, *Critique of Pure Reason*, 342–43, A 288/B 344.

135. Kant, *Critique of Pure Reason*, 343, A 288–89/B 345.

136. Kant, *Critique of Pure Reason*, 342, A 288/B 344.

137. Kant, *Critique of Pure Reason*, 318–19, A 254–55/B 310–11.

138. Kant, *Critique of Pure Reason*, 342, A 288/B 344, quoted by David-Ménard, *La folie dans la raison pure*, 69.

139. Kant, *Critique of Pure Reason*, 341, A 286/B 342–43.

140. Kant, *Critique of Pure Reason*, 319, A 255/B 310.

141. Kant, *Critique of Pure Reason*, 319, A 255/B 310.

142. Kant, *Critique of Pure Reason*, 317, B 308.

143. Kant, *Critique of Pure Reason*, 319, A 255/B 310–11.

144. David-Ménard, *La folie dans la raison pure*, 69.

145. Kant, *Critique of Pure Reason*, 322, A 259–60/B 315.

146. David-Ménard writes: "The noumenon is not an absolute nothingness (*néant*)" (*La folie dans la raison pure*, 69).

147. David-Ménard, *La folie dans la raison pure*, 69.

148. Kant, *Logic*, 145, § 22.

149. Kant, *Logic*, 146, § 22.

150. Kant, *Critique of Pure Reason*, 319, A 255/B 311.

2. UNCONDITIONED SUBJECTIVITY

1. An abbreviated version of the argument in this chapter and in Chapter 5 appeared in Gabriela Basterra, "Subjectivity at the Limit: Kant, Velázquez, Levinas," *Diacritics* 40, no. 4 (2012): 46–70. I want to express my gratitude to Andrew Cutrofello, Clive Dilnot, Andrew Parker, and Eyal Peretz for their generous readings and invaluable comments.

2. The subjectivity at stake here is not associated with the transcendental idea of the soul critiqued in "On the Paralogisms of Pure Reason," the first chapter of the

Transcendental Dialectic. As we shall see, the mode of understanding the role of the subject in the third antinomy that I advance in this chapter both does justice to and expands the double-reference theory Kant offers as a solution to the dynamic antinomy.

3. Kant, *Critique of Pure Reason*, 554, A 561/B 580.

4. Kant, *Critique of Pure Reason*, 558, A 566/B 594n.

5. Kant, *Critique of Pure Reason*, 533, A 530/B 558.

6. Kant, *Critique of Pure Reason*, 473, A 444/B 472.

7. Kant, *Critique of Pure Reason*, 473, A 445/B 473.

8. Kant, *Critique of Pure Reason*, 551–52, A 557/B 586.

9. Kant, *Critique of Pure Reason*, 533, A 530/B 558.

10. In the thesis of the third antinomy the unconditioned functions in the second of the two senses Kant attributes to the term. In his introduction to the "System of Cosmological Ideas" at the beginning of the Antinomy chapter in the *Critique of Pure Reason*, Kant distinguishes between two ways of thinking of the unconditioned. "Either one thinks of it as consisting merely in the whole series, in which therefore all members would without exception be conditioned and only their whole would be absolutely unconditioned; and then the regression is called infinite. Or the absolutely unconditioned is only a part of the series, a part to which the remaining members of the series are subordinated but which itself is not subject to any other condition" (Kant, *Critique of Pure Reason*, 451, A 417–18/B 445). In the second case, the one at stake in my analysis here, "there is a first member of the series, which is called . . . with regard to causes, absolute self-activity (freedom)" (Kant, *Critique of Pure Reason*, 452, A 418/B 446). At the end of this chapter I analyze how this second conception of the unconditioned (which is the one at play in the theses of the antinomic ideas) interacts, in the third antinomy, with the first way of understanding the unconditioned mentioned by Kant.

11. Kant, *Critique of Pure Reason*, 319, A 255/B 310.

12. Kant, *Critique of Pure Reason*, 319, A 255/B 310–11.

13. Kant, *Critique of Pure Reason*, 534, A 531/B 559.

14. Kant, *Critique of Pure Reason*, 515, A 505/B 533.

15. "The regression in the series of the world's appearances, as a determination of the world's magnitude, proceeds *in indefinitum*." Kant, *Critique of Pure Reason*, 528, A 521/B 549. See my analysis of Kant's solution to the first antinomy in Chapter 1.

16. Kant, *Critique of Pure Reason*, 533, A 530/B 558.

17. Kant, *Critique of Pure Reason*, 473, A 445/B 473.

18. As Kant puts it, "In the dynamical regression . . . we are not concerned with the possibility of an unconditioned whole composed from given parts, or the possibility of an unconditioned part for a given whole; here we are concerned, rather, with the derivation of a state from its cause, or the derivation of the contingent ex-

istence of substance itself from necessary existence." Kant, *Critique of Pure Reason*, 554, A 561/B 589.

19. Kant, *Critique of Pure Reason*, 553, A 559/B 587.

20. Kant, *Critique of Pure Reason*, 559, A 566/B 594.

21. Kant, *Critique of Pure Reason*, 534, A 531/B 559. This paragraph continues: "Thus reason is satisfied; for the unconditioned is put prior to appearances, and yet the series of appearances, as always conditioned, is not thereby confused and—contrary to the principles of understanding—cut off."

22. Kant, *Critique of Pure Reason*, 534, A 531/B 559.

23. "In the preceding subsection we considered the changes of the world of sense in their dynamical series, where each change is subject to another as its cause. Now, however, we employ this series of states only as a guidance in order to arrive at an existence that can be the highest condition of all that is changeable, viz., the *necessary being*. Our concern here is not unconditioned causality, but the unconditioned existence of substance itself. Hence the series that we have before us is in fact only the series of concepts, and not that of intuitions insofar as one intuition is the condition of the other." Kant, *Critique of Pure Reason*, 553, A 559/B 587.

24. Kant, *Critique of Pure Reason*, 554–55, A 561/B 589.

25. That the unconditioned introduced by the thesis of the fourth antinomy is outside the series is not evident from the formulation of the thesis, which reads: "There belongs to the world something that, either as its part or as its cause, is an absolutely necessary being" (Kant, *Critique of Pure Reason*, 479, A 452/B 480). The Comment on the Thesis, however, anticipates that "the pure cosmological proof can establish the existence of a necessary being only if it simultaneously leaves undecided whether this being is the world itself or a thing distinct from it" (Kant, *Critique of Pure Reason*, 482, A 456/B 484). Kant's solution (section 4: "Solution of the Cosmological Idea of Totality in the Dependence of Appearances as Regards Their Existence as Such"), of which the passage just quoted is part, concludes, in effect, that "the necessary being would have to be thought as entirely outside the series of the world of sense" (Kant, *Critique of Pure Reason*, 555, A 561/B 589).

26. Kant, *Critique of Pure Reason*, 557–58, A 565/B 593.

27. Kant, *Critique of Pure Reason*, 558, A 566/B 594.

28. Kant, *Critique of Pure Reason*, 558, A 566/B 594.

29. Kant, *Critique of Pure Reason*, 535–36, A 533/B 561.

30. One can perceive, in fact, a certain oscillation in Kant's text as to whether the unconditioned member of the series is freedom or an effect of freedom. Although the third antinomy introduces the transcendental idea of freedom, freedom is a causal term, even if an exceptional one: an uncaused cause that is thus a beginning by itself. The thesis refers to it as a "causality through freedom" (that is, initiated by freedom) in this sense, whereas the explanation and the solution also refer to freedom's own intelligible causality, imagining, by analogy, that freedom could have

an intelligible cause. In any case, whether the unconditioned is considered to be freedom, an act of freedom, or an effect of freedom, what matters is that it introduces a causality through freedom in the natural causal series. Occasionally in Kant's explanation, especially when he is referring to the entire dynamic antinomy, one can also detect a certain oscillation as to whether or not the unconditioned is a member of the sensible series, despite his explicit affirmations that it is.

31. Kant, *Critique of Pure Reason*, 538, A 537/B 565. In his following statement Kant anticipates part of his explicit solution to the third antinomy: "Hence the effect can be considered as free with regard to its intelligible cause, and yet with regard to appearances be considered simultaneously as resulting from these according to the necessity of nature."

32. Kant, *Critique of Pure Reason*, 551–52, A 557/B 586.

33. Although the unconditioned is itself a member of the causal chain, its condition or cause lies outside the chain—or so we reason from our necessarily limited empirical perspective, thus attributing the unconditioned an absent cause. It is therefore not the case that the intelligible lies out there as an absolutely exterior other unrelated to phenomena, as happens in the fourth antinomy. Rather, it is present in the empirical world through its effects.

34. Kant, *Critique of Pure Reason*, 516, A 506/B 534.

35. See, for example, Kant, *Critique of Pure Reason*, 534–35, A 531–32/B 559–60.

36. What we need to ask, in other words, is how reason here is exceptionally permitted to imagine the unconditioned, how that uncaused member potentially allows the series of presentations to attain some completion, and what kind of completion that might be.

37. Kant, *Critique of Pure Reason*, 514, A 502/B 530.

38. Kant, *Critique of Pure Reason*, 535, A 533/B 561.

39. Kant, *Critique of Pure Reason*, 536, A 533/B 561.

40. Kant, *Critique of Pure Reason*, 534, A 531/B 559.

41. See section titled "Boundary Concepts" in Chapter 1.

42. Kant, *Critique of Pure Reason*, 537–38, A 536/B 564.

43. Kant, *Critique of Pure Reason*, 538, A 537/B 565.

44. Kant, *Critique of Pure Reason*, 552–53, A 558/B 586: "Now, to show that this antinomy rests on a mere illusion and that nature at least does *not conflict* with the causality from freedom—this was the only goal that we were able to accomplish, and it was, moreover, our one and only concern."

45. In just a few pages Kant qualifies this coexistence of nature's and freedom's causalities in the subject from three slightly different perspectives: as "a two-fold side" (intelligible and sensible) from which the subject's causality may be considered (*Critique of Pure Reason*, 539, A 538/B 566), as the two characters of any efficient cause (539–40, A 539/B 567), and as two viewpoints from which "the human being" cognizes itself (544, A 547/B 557). While in the first two cases the subject con-

stitutes the object or theme of speculative reason and of Kant's explanation, in the third it becomes both the subject and the object of knowledge, a thinking subject reflecting upon itself.

46. Kant, *Critique of Pure Reason*, 541, A 541/B 569.

47. Kant, *Critique of Pure Reason*, 537, A 534/B 562.

48. Kant, *Critique of Pure Reason*, 535, A 533/B 561.

49. Kant, *Critique of Pure Reason*, 548, A 552/B 580.

50. See Chapter 3.

51. "Hence reason is the permanent condition of all the voluntary actions under which the human being appears. Each of these actions, even before it occurs, is predetermined in the human being's empirical character. But in regard to the intelligible character, of which the empirical character is only the sensible schema, no *before* or *after* holds, and every action—regardless of its time relation to other appearances—is the direct effect of the intelligible character of pure reason." Kant, *Critique of Pure Reason*, 549, A 553/B 581.

52. Kant, *Critique of Pure Reason*, 549, A 554/B 582.

53. Kant, *Critique of Pure Reason*, 551, A 556/B 584.

54. Kant, *Critique of Pure Reason*, 551, A 556/B 584.

55. Kant, *Critique of Pure Reason*, 548, A 552/B 580.

56. Kant, *Critique of Pure Reason*, 548, A 552/B 580.

57. Kant, *Critique of Pure Reason*, 541, A 541/B 569.

58. Kant, *Critique of Pure Reason*, 541, A 541/B 569.

59. "For in that world they are always predetermined—although only by means of the empirical character (which is merely the appearance of the intelligible character)—by empirical conditions in the previous time, and are possible only as a continuation of the series of natural causes." Kant, *Critique of Pure Reason*, 541, A 541/B 569.

60. "Reason begins the series in such a way that nothing begins in reason itself, but that reason, as unconditioned condition of any voluntary action, permits no conditions above itself that precede the action as regards time—although reason's effect does begin in the series of appearances, but in the series can never amount to an absolutely first beginning." Kant, *Critique of Pure Reason*, 549, A 553–54/B 581–82.

61. How the subject is constituted by freedom and the relationship of the subject to freedom are further explored in the second *Critique* and especially in the *Religion*, in both cases largely in theoretical terms of causality.

62. Kant, *Critique of Pure Reason*, 535, A 533/B 561.

63. Kant, *Critique of Pure Reason*, 540, A 539/B 568.

64. See Kant, "The Antinomy of Pure Reason," section 1, "System of Cosmological Ideas," *Critique of Pure Reason*, 445–53, A 409–20/B 436–48.

65. Regarding the ending of the series, "we do not have to worry whether or not the series ceases" (Kant, *Critique of Pure Reason*, 446, A 410/B 436), because then it becomes an empirical series determined by the understanding.

66. See table of functions of judgments in Kant, *Critique of Pure Reason*, 124, A 70/B 95.

Quantity of Judgments: Universal, Particular, Singular
Quality: Affirmative, Negative, Infinite
Relation: Categorical, Hypothetical, Disjunctive
Modality: Problematic, Assertoric, Apodeictic

Categories or pure concepts of understanding derive their validity from their reference to space and time. The categories of quantity are unity, plurality, and all-ness or totality; the categories of quality are reality, negation, and limitation; the categories of relation are those of inherence and subsistence (*substantia et accidens*), of causality and dependence (cause and effect), and of community (interaction between agent and patient); finally, the categories of modality are possibility-impossibility, existence-nonexistence, and necessity-contingency. (See table of categories in Kant, *Critique of Pure Reason*, 132, A 80/B 106.)

67. Kant, *Critique of Pure Reason*, 446, A 409–10/B 436.

68. Kant, *Critique of Pure Reason*, 447, A 412/B 439. Since "future time, on the other hand, is not a condition for arriving at the present," reason is not concerned with it, or with whether or not the series of consequences (which would be empirical, and thus cognizable by the understanding) has an end. Kant, *Critique of Pure Reason*, 446, A 410/B 437.

69. Kant, *Critique of Pure Reason*, 448, A 412/B 439.

70. Kant, *Critique of Pure Reason*, 448, A 412/B 439. In the case of space, Kant clarifies that "here the side of the conditions is not in itself distinct from the side on which the conditioned lies, and hence in space regression and progression seem to be the same. Yet, because one part of space is not given by another part but is only bounded by it, we must regard each bounded space as being also conditioned insofar as it presupposes another space as the condition of its boundary, and so on for the other spaces. As regards bounding, therefore, the progression in space is also a regression, and the transcendental idea of the absolute totality of the synthesis in the series of conditions concerns also space" (Kant, *Critique of Pure Reason*, 448, A 412–13/B 439–40). In other words, each spatial region lying on either side of a boundary could be envisioned as conditioning the region on the other side.

71. For an excellent analysis of Kant's understanding of causality in the second analogy of experience, see Béatrice Longuenesse, "Kant on Causality: What Was He Trying to Prove?," in *Kant on the Human Standpoint* (Cambridge: Cambridge University Press, 2005), 143–83.

72. In an early essay, "Is There a Cause of the Subject?," Slavoj Žižek observes that a "cause is real" in the sense that it resists symbolization, and yet "cause is simultaneously the retroactive product of its own effects." Slavoj Žižek, "Is There a Cause of the Subject?," in *Supposing the Subject*, ed. Joan Copjec, 84–105 (London:

Verso, 1994), 102. As Žižek explains, an event does not become a *real cause* immediately (if we think of it in terms of chronological time). Rather, one must wait for effects to appear for them to be then attributed to a cause. Only thus does the cause become real, trauma, cause.

73. When the Comment on the thesis of the third antinomy introduces the possibility of different beginnings in the midst of the natural sequence, this seems to be suggesting as much. See Kant, *Critique of Pure Reason*, 477, A 450/B 478.

74. Hence the following Comment on the thesis: "Now, to be sure, we have in fact established this necessity of a first beginning, issuing from freedom, only insofar as this is required for making comprehensible an origin of the world, whereas all subsequent states can be taken to be a succession according to mere natural laws. Yet, having once proved thereby (although not gained insight into) the power of beginning entirely spontaneously a series in time, *we are now also permitted to let different series begin spontaneously, even in the midst of the course of the world*, as regards [not time but] causality." Kant, *Critique of Pure Reason*, 477, A 450/B 478. Emphasis added.

75. Kant, *Critique of Pure Reason*, 549, A 553–54/B 581–82. In the *Critique of Practical Reason* one can also find what at first view appears to be a circular relation between freedom, the moral law, and autonomy, as well as in the notion of "respect" (*Achtung*) as the effect produced by the law *and* the affect that produces the law. I deal with this in Chapter 4.

76. Kant, *Critique of Pure Reason*, 473, A 444–45/B 472–73.

77. Kant, *Critique of Pure Reason*, 473, A 445/B 473.

78. Kant, *Critique of Pure Reason*, 451, A 417/B 445. Accordingly, "there is a first member of the series, which is called . . . with regard to causes, absolute *self-activity* (freedom)." Kant, *Critique of Pure Reason*, 452, A 418/B 446.

79. Kant, *Critique of Pure Reason*, 451, A 417/B 445. Kant distinguishes between two ways of thinking of the unconditioned in his introduction to the "System of Cosmological Ideas" at the beginning of "The Antinomy of Pure Reason" chapter. See Kant, *Critique of Pure Reason*, 451–52, A 417–18/B 445–46.

80. Kant, *Critique of Pure Reason*, 452, A 418/B 445n. Of this type of unconditioned, the unconditioned totality of a series, Kant remarks: "The absolute whole of a series of conditions for a given conditioned is always unconditioned; for outside the series there are no further conditions in regard to which this whole could be continued. However, this absolute whole of such a series is only an idea—or, rather, a problematic concept whose possibility must be examined, viz., in reference to the way in which it may contain the unconditioned, which is the transcendental idea that is in fact at issue." Kant, *Critique of Pure Reason*, 451–52, A 418/B 445n.

81. Kant, *Critique of Pure Reason*, 475, A 447/B 475.

82. Kant, *Critique of Pure Reason*, 319, A 255/B 310.

83. See the last section of Chapter 1.

84. Kant, *Critique of Pure Reason*, 319, A 255/B 311.

85. The Comment on the Antithesis ventures a remote possibility of conceiving of a "transcendental power of freedom," but such a power "would at any rate have to be solely outside the world (although to assume, outside of the sum of all possible intuitions, a further object that cannot be given in any possible perception always remains a bold presupposition)." Kant, *Critique of Pure Reason*, 478–79, A 451/B 479.

86. Couldn't we venture, indeed, that in the third antinomy two conceptions of unconditionality interact? Although Kant initially distinguishes these two ways of thinking of the unconditioned as a disjunction ("Either . . . Or . . ."), and thus seemingly as mutually exclusive (see Kant, *Critique of Pure Reason*, 451, A 417/B 445), here, in the third antinomy, they would seem to collaborate in a unique way. As we know, the mathematical antinomy drops and the thesis of the fourth antinomy, as it turns out in the solution, is only conceivable if the unconditioned is considered to be fully outside the world of sense. In introducing an unconditioned that is heterogeneous but related to the series, the thesis of the third antinomy uniquely invites us to conceive it as the site of the relationship between the series and something in excess of it, other than it. Perhaps this interplay of two different conceptions of the unconditioned accounts for the oscillation one can perceive in Kant's explanation as to whether or not the unconditioned is a member of the sensible series, despite the occasions in which he explicitly affirms it is.

87. As one moves from the *Critique of Pure Reason* to the *Critique of Practical Reason*, however, limits still apply. The methodology of Kant's main ethical works—*Grounding for the Metaphysics of Morals*, *Critique of Practical Reason*, *Religion within the Bounds of Bare Reason*, and *Metaphysics of Morals*—is still theoretical. What changes are the object of the critique and the direction of the inquiry. If the first *Critique* examined reason's relationship to empirical objects (and thus had to start from experience to reach concepts and then principles), the second *Critique* explores reason's relationship to desire and the will, and can thus move from the principle of unconditioned causality, to concepts that determine the will, to the sensible subject of that will. See Kant, *Critique of Practical Reason*, 24–25, Ak. 5: 16.

88. Deleuze, *Kant's Critical Philosophy*, 28.

3. CAUSALITY OF FREEDOM

1. Kant, *Critique of Pure Reason*, 541, A 541/B 569.

2. Kant, *Critique of Practical Reason*, 65, Ak. 5: 46.

3. According to Kant, the unknown cause of phenomena has effects in the world "insofar as this intelligible character is indicated by the empirical character as the intelligible character's sensible sign." Kant, *Critique of Pure Reason*, 544, A 546/B 574. Emmanuel Levinas reformulates this in the form of a question: "How can transcendence withdraw from *esse* while being signaled in it?" Levinas, *Autrement qu'être*, 23 / *Otherwise than Being*, 10.

4. "For in the present critique we shall, starting from principles, proceed to concepts and then, if possible, from these to the senses, whereas in the case of speculative reason we started from the senses and had to end with the principles. Now, the basis for this lies again in this: that we are now concerned with a will and have to examine reason not in relation to objects but in relation to this will and its causality; and thus the principles of the empirically unconditioned causality must come at the beginning, and only thereafter can the attempt be made to establish our concepts of the determining basis of such a will, of their application to objects and finally to the subject and his sensibility. The law of the causality from freedom, i.e., some pure practical principle, here unavoidably comes at the beginning and determines the objects to which alone it can be referred" (Kant, *Critique of Practical Reason*, 24–25, Ak. 5: 16).

In what concerns the activity of the different faculties, in the first *Critique* the understanding is the active faculty of knowledge, the one that legislates, and reason trespasses its own boundaries by introducing transcendental ideas. In introducing freedom in the third antinomy, however, reason bounds what can be cognized. In the second *Critique* the legislating faculty is reason, and here the critique must inquire how practical reason—a reason that does not reason—moves the power of desire. See Deleuze, *Kant's Critical Philosophy*.

5. Kant, *Critique of Practical Reason*, 5, Ak. 5: 4.

6. Kant, *Critique of Practical Reason*, 68, Ak. 5: 49.

7. Kant, *Critique of Practical Reason*, 66, Ak. 5: 46.

8. "And so, even though we do not indeed grasp the practical unconditioned necessity of the moral imperative, we do nevertheless grasp its *incomprehensibility* [*Unbegreiflichkeit*]. This is all that can be fairly asked of a philosophy which strives in its principles to reach the very limit of human reason." Kant, "Concluding Remark," in *Grounding for the Metaphysics of Morals with On a Supposed Right to Lie Because of Philanthropic Concerns*, 3rd ed., trans. James W. Ellington (Indianapolis: Hackett, 1993), 62, Ak. 4: 463 (translation modified). In *Critique of Practical Reason* (12, Ak. 5: 7), Kant refers also to freedom's "utter *incomprehensibility* [*Unbegreiflichkeit*]."

9. Immanuel Kant, *Opus Postumum*, trans. Eckart Förster, ed. Eckart Förster and Michael Rosen (Cambridge: Cambridge University Press, 1993), 214, Ak. 22: 55. The complete sentence reads:

> In man there dwells an active principle, arousable by no sensible representation, accompanying him not as soul (for this presupposes a body) but as spirit, which, like a particular substance, commands him irresistibly according to the law of moral-practical reason, [and which], by its own actions, pardons or condemns man's commissions and omissions. In virtue of this property of his, the moral man is a *person*; that is, a being capable of rights, who can encounter wrong or can consciously do it, and who stands under the categorical imperative; free indeed, but yet under laws to which he

submits himself (*dictamen rationis purae*) and who carries out divine commands according to transcendental idealism.

10. Nancy, "Le Katègorein," 18 / "The *Kategorein*," 142.

11. Nancy, "Le Katègorein," 19 / "The *Kategorein*," 142. The law, writes Nancy, "belongs in the condition of possibility of a reason that proves to be by itself practical" (translation modified).

12. Kant, *Grounding for the Metaphysics of Morals*, 55, Ak. 4: 455–56.

13. Kant, *Grounding for the Metaphysics of Morals*, 55, Ak. 4: 456.

14. Kant, *Critique of Practical Reason*, 37, Ak. 5: 25, and 167, Ak. 5: 132.

15. Speaking about the categorical imperative in the *Grounding for the Metaphysics of Morals*, Kant contemplates the possibility that duty may be an empty concept: "Now if all imperatives of duty can be derived from this one imperative as their principle, then there can at least be shown what is understood by the concept of duty and what it means, even though there is left undecided whether what is called duty may not be an empty concept." Kant, *Grounding for the Metaphysics of Morals*, 30, Ak. 4: 421.

16. Kant, *Critique of Practical Reason*, 131, Ak. 5: 103.

17. Kant, *Critique of Practical Reason*, 23, Ak. 5: 15.

18. Kant, *Critique of Practical Reason*, 23–24, Ak. 5: 15.

19. Kant, *Critique of Practical Reason*, 24, Ak. 5: 16.

20. See Zupančič, *L'éthique du réel*, 68.

21. Kant, *Critique of Practical Reason*, 5, Ak. 5: 4.

22. Kant, *Critique of Practical Reason*, 5, Ak. 5: 4n.

23. Kant, *Critique of Practical Reason*, 5, Ak. 5: 4n.

24. Kant, *Critique of Practical Reason*, 7, Ak. 5: 5.

25. Kant, *Opus Postumum*, 223, Ak. 21: 16.

26. Kant, *Opus Postumum*, 223, Ak. 21: 16.

27. Kant, *Opus Postumum*, 223, Ak. 21: 16.

28. Nancy, "Le Katègorein," 30 / "The *Kategorein*," 150.

29. Kant, *Critique of Practical Reason*, 5, Ak. 5: 4n.

30. Nancy, "Le Katègorein," 18–19 / "The *Kategorein*," 142.

31. As Kant clarifies, the moral law is not a precept but a rule ("a rule that determines the will a priori merely with regard to the form of its maxims" [*Critique of Practical Reason*, 45, Ak. 5: 31]), an affirmation which is in consonance with Kant's insistence that the concept of freedom is a "regulative principle of reason" (*Critique of Practical Reason*, 67, Ak. 5: 48).

32. Kant, *Critique of Practical Reason*, 49, Ak. 5: 34.

33. "Only a formal law, i.e., one that prescribes to reason nothing more than the form of its universal legislation as the supreme condition of maxims, can be a priori a determining basis of practical reason." Kant, *Critique of Practical Reason*, 86, Ak. 5: 65. Cf. Kant, *Grounding for the Metaphysics of Morals*, Ak. 4: 444–45.

34. Kant, *Critique of Practical Reason*, 40, Ak. 5: 27.

35. Kant, *Grounding for the Metaphysics of Morals*, 61, Ak. 4: 462.

36. Emphasis added. Notice how Kant's language in this paragraph underscores the theoretical perspective from which its statements are advanced: "pure reason which *thinks* this ideal," "nothing remains *for me*," and "*I think* of reason" (emphasis added).

37. Kant, *Critique of Pure Reason*, 318–19, A 254–55/B 310–11.

38. Kant, *Critique of Practical Reason*, 45, Ak. 5: 31.

39. See Kant, *Critique of Practical Reason*, 37–38, Ak. 5: 25, and 40, Ak. 5: 27.

40. See Zupančič, *L'éthique du réel*, 62–63, 80.

41. Kant, *Religion*, 33, Ak. 6: 30.

42. Zupančič, *L'éthique du réel*, 61.

43. Kant, *Critique of Practical Reason*, 14, Ak. 5: 8–9, and 78–94, Ak. 5: 57–71.

44. Perhaps this is what Levinas has in mind when he writes, in *Otherwise than Being*, that after the death of God (that is, after the end of the long and venerable philosophical tradition that had the idea of the good as its horizon), it is an impulse ("assignation," "a relation") that arouses a value, and not the other way around. "From the Good to me, there is assignation: a relation that 'survives' the 'death of God.' The death of God perhaps signifies only the possibility to reduce every value arousing an impulse to an impulse arousing a value." Levinas, *Autrement qu'être*, 196 / *Otherwise than Being*, 123.

45. See Olivia Custer, *L'exemple de Kant* (Leuven, Belgium: Peeters, 2012).

46. Kant, *Critique of Practical Reason*, 97, Ak. 5: 74.

47. Kant, *Grounding for the Metaphysics of Morals*, 19–48, Ak. 4: 406–45. In this work, Kant offers four formulations of the categorical imperative, usually referred to as the formula of universal law ("Act only according to that maxim whereby you can at the same time will that it should become a universal law" [30, Ak. 4: 421, see also 42, Ak. 4: 437, and 43, Ak. 4: 439]), the formula of the law of nature ("Act as if the maxim of your action were to become through your will a universal law of nature" [30, Ak. 4: 421, see also 42, Ak. 4: 437]), the formula of the end in itself ("Act in such a way that you treat humanity, whether in your own person or in the person of another, always at the same time as an end and never simply as a means" [36, Ak. 4: 429]), and the formula of the kingdom of ends ("Act in accordance with the maxims of a member legislating universal laws for a merely possible kingdom of ends" [43, Ak. 4: 439, see also 39–40, Ak. 4: 433–34]). The first and second formulations (Ak. 4: 421) are generally considered to be the same, following Kant's own enumeration of three aspects of the categorical imperative by analogy with the categories of the understanding, which he sums up as follows: "There is a progression here through the categories of the *unity* of the form of the will (its universality), the *plurality* of its matter (its objects, i.e., its ends), and the *totality* or completeness of its system of ends." Nevertheless, gesturing toward the only formulation that will prevail

in the second *Critique*, he clarifies: "But one does better if in moral judgment he follows the rigorous method and takes as his basis the universal formula of the categorical imperative: Act according to that maxim which can at the same time make itself a universal law." Kant, *Grounding for the Metaphysics of Morals*, 41–42, Ak. 4: 436–37. For Paul Guyer's interpretation of the categorical imperative in the *Grounding for the Metaphysics of Morals*, which argues for the importance of considering Kant's four formulations as distinct, see Paul Guyer, *Kant's System of Nature and Freedom: Selected Essays* (Oxford: Oxford University Press, 2005), 146–68.

48. Kant, *Grounding for the Metaphysics of Morals*, 30, Ak. 4: 421, see also 42, Ak. 4: 437, and 43, Ak. 4: 439.

49. See Jacob Rogozinski, *Le don de la Loi: Kant et l'énigme de l'éthique* (Paris: Presses Universitaires de France, 1999), and Custer, *L'exemple de Kant*, 268, among others.

50. See, for example, Kant, *Critique of Practical Reason*, 45–46, Ak. 5: 31.

51. Dieter Henrich's approach to practical philosophy, on the other hand, has at its center a study of motivation, rather than a theory of agency. See especially *The Unity of Reason*. See also Velkley's "Introduction," 12, and 216–17n38.

52. See, for example, Rogozinski, *Le don de la Loi*, 9.

53. Kant, *Critique of Practical Reason*, 45, Ak. 5: 30.

54. The imperative would be the condition of possibility of praxis, or, as Nancy puts it, "the transcendental of praxis," where "transcendental indicates non-transcendence." Nancy, "Le Katègorein," 19 / "The *Kategorein*," 142.

55. As Dieter Henrich explains in "Ethics of Autonomy," "The doctrine of the unknowability of freedom leads to the theory of the categorical imperative as a *fact* of reason. Whoever grasps its facticity while trying to hold on to the unconditionality and rationality of this fact of *reason* will arrive at this doctrine of respect for the law." This, continues Henrich, is the logical order of Kant's moral theory. Chronologically, Kant first develops his theory of respect in 1781, and then the theory of the fact of reason after 1785. Dieter Henrich, "Ethics of Autonomy," trans. Louis Hunt, in *The Unity of Reason*, 89–121, 108, and 231n24.

56. Nancy, "Le Katègorein," 19 / "The *Kategorein*," 142.

57. Nancy, "Le Katègorein," 19 / "The *Kategorein*," 142.

58. Nancy, "Le Katègorein," 19 / "The *Kategorein*," 142.

59. Nancy, "Le Katègorein," 19 / "The *Kategorein*," 142. The fact of reason, writes Nancy, "befalls reason as that which befalls a passive matter, from the outside of reason, from an outside that exceeds all passivity and yet should not be identified with activity (since activity is prescribed, it is the end). The imperative is inactive; it is imperative. It exceeds the distinction between active and passive, between spontaneous and receptive [*le couple de l'actif et du passif, du spontané et du réceptif*]." Nancy, "Le Katègorein," 21–22 / "The *Kategorein*," 144 (translation modified).

60. Kant, *Critique of Practical Reason*, 46, Ak. 5: 31. "The *factum rationis*," writes Nancy, "is not an empirical intuition: if it were, it would submit the imperative to a sensible condition. This does not constitute an argument grounded on a moralistic disdain for the sensible (nothing could be more foreign to Kant), but rather an argument grounded on the *condition* that would thus impose itself on an unconditioned injunction. The *factum* is that the imperative does not depend on any fact." Nancy, "Le Katègorein," 21 / "The *Kategorein*," 143.

61. Deleuze, *Kant's Critical Philosophy*, 28.

62. Nancy, "Le Katègorein," 18–19 / "The *Kategorein*," 142.

63. Nancy, "Le Katègorein," 25–26 / "The *Kategorein*," 147 (translation modified).

64. Nancy, "Le Katègorein," 26 / "The *Kategorein*," 147.

65. Kant, *Critique of Pure Reason*, 535, A 533/B 561.

66. Kant, *Critique of Pure Reason*, 541, A 541/B 569.

67. Kant, *Critique of Pure Reason*, 548, A 552/B 580.

68. Nancy, "Le Katègorein," 13–14 / "The *Kategorein*," 138. What the imperative prescribes, in short, is *"the act of legislation* (hence it prescribes 'universally')."

69. Nancy, "Le Katègorein," 19 / "The *Kategorein*," 142.

70. Nancy, "Le Katègorein," 20 / "The *Kategorein*," 143.

71. Nancy, "Le Katègorein," 20 / "The *Kategorein*," 143. "The imperative injunction absolutely links reason [*conjoint absolument la raison*] to that which exceeds it absolutely."

72. Kant, *Opus Postumum*, 212, Ak. 22: 53.

73. See the previous section, "The Law's Letter."

74. Nancy, "Le Katègorein," 30 / "The *Kategorein*," 150.

75. Nancy, "Le Katègorein," 30 / "The *Kategorein*," 150.

76. Kant, *Critique of Pure Reason*, 535, A 533/B 561.

77. Immanuel Kant, *The Metaphysics of Morals*, in *Ethical Philosophy*, trans. James W. Ellington (Indianapolis, IN: Hackett, 1983), 22, Ak. 6: 222.

78. Nancy, "Le Katègorein," 31 / "The *Kategorein*," 151 (translation modified).

79. See Chapter 5.

80. Consider, for example, this passage on the concept of freedom as a regulative principle of reason:

> Although through this [principle] I do not at all cognize the object to which such a causality is attributed, as to what this object is, I nonetheless remove the obstacle inasmuch as on the one hand, in the explanation of events in the world and hence also of the actions of rational beings, I do justice to the mechanism of natural necessity by going back from the conditioned to the condition *ad infinitum*, while on the other hand I keep open for speculative reason the place that is vacant for it, namely the intelligible, in order to transfer the unconditioned there. However, I was not able to *realize* this *thought*, i.e.,

to convert it into *cognition* of a being acting in this way, not even as regards merely its possibility. Pure practical reason now fills this vacant place with a determinate law of causality in an intelligible world (causality through freedom), viz., the moral law. Although speculative reason does not gain anything through this as regards its insight, it does gain something as regards *securing* its problematic concept of freedom, which is here provided with *objective reality* that, although only practical, is yet indubitable. (Kant, *Critique of Practical Reason*, 67–68, Ak. 5: 48–49. See also 4, Ak. 5: 3.)

81. Nancy, "Le Katègorein," 13 / "The *Kategorein*," 137.

82. On Kant's conception of radical evil, see Richard J. Bernstein's clarifying chapter "Radical Evil: Kant at War with Himself," in *Radical Evil: A Philosophical Interrogation* (Cambridge, UK: Polity Press, 2002), 11–45.

83. The itinerary reason has to follow as it traces back the origin of the subject's ethical disposition takes the form of a regression over an unconditioned causal chain in which the most immediate ground for a particular action would be conditioned by a preceding ground, similarly to what happens in the third antinomy. That the first subjective basis for the adoption of maxims is "inscrutable [*unerforschlich*] to us" (Kant, *Religion*, 21, Ak. 6: 21) means that reason's presentations in search of it would regress indefinitely without ever reaching the unconditioned initiating cause, which would be an act of freedom.

84. Kant, *Religion*, 24–25, Ak. 6: 23–24.

85. Kant, *Religion*, 25, Ak. 6: 24.

86. Kant, *Religion*, 25, Ak. 6: 24.

87. Since all rational human beings are tempted by the incentives of self-love as corresponds to their sensible nature, Kant calls this subordination of the law to other motives "humanity."

88. Kant, *Religion*, 40, Ak. 6: 36.

89. Kant, *Religion*, 39, Ak. 6: 35.

90. Kant, *Religion*, 40, Ak. 6: 37.

91. See, for instance, Kant, *Religion*, 33, Ak. 6: 30:

The *wickedness (vitiositas, pravitas)*, or, if one prefers, the *corruption (corruptio)* of the human heart is the propensity of the power of choice to [pursue] maxims whereby one is to put the incentive from the moral law second to other (nonmoral) ones. It can also be named the *perversity (perversitas)* of the human heart, because it reverses the moral order in regard to the incentives of a *free* power of choice; and although legally good (lawful) actions can always still consist with this [wickedness], yet the way of thinking is thereby corrupted in its root (as far as the moral attitude is concerned), and the human being is therefore designated as evil.

92. Nancy, "Le Katègorein," 16 / "The *Kategorein*," 140.

93. Kant, *Critique of Practical Reason*, 23, Ak. 5: 15.

94. Kant, *Religion*, 41, Ak. 6: 37.

95. Kant, *Religion*, 26, Ak. 6: 25. Although both *Wille* and *Willkür* are often translated as "will," here I have referred to *Wille* as "will" and to *Willkür* as "power of choice," following Pluhar's translation of the *Critique of Practical Reason*. John Silber offers a clarifying explanation of the sense of each in Kant:

> Unlike *Willkür*, . . . *Wille* does not make decisions or adopt maxims; it does not act. Rather it is the source of a strong and ever present incentive in *Willkür*, and, if strong enough to be adopted by *Willkür* into the maxim of its choice, *Wille* "can determine the *Willkür*" and then "it is practical reason itself." *Wille* expresses the possibility of autonomy which is presupposed by transcendental freedom. The *Wille* represents the will's own demand for self-fulfillment by commanding *Willkür*, that aspect of the will which can either fulfill or abnegate its freedom, to actualize its free nature by willing in accordance with the law (and condition) of freedom. The most important difference between *Wille* and *Willkür* is apparent here. Whereas *Willkür* is free to actualize either the autonomous or heteronomous potentialities of transcendental freedom, *Wille* is not free at all. *Wille* is rather the law of freedom, the normative aspect of the will, which as a norm is neither free nor unfree. Having no freedom of action, *Wille* is under no constraint or pressure. It exerts, instead, the pressure of its own normative rational nature upon *Willkür*. (John R. Silber, "Ethical Significance in Kant's *Religion*," in Immanuel Kant, *Religion within the Limits of Reason Alone*, trans. T. M. Greene and H. H. Hudson, lxxix-cxlii [New York: Harper Torchbooks, 1960], civ.)

96. Kant, *Religion*, 26–27, Ak. 6: 25.

97. Kant, *Religion*, 21, Ak. 6: 21.

98. Kant, *Religion*, 31, Ak. 6: 29.

99. Kant, *Religion*, 26, Ak. 6: 25. What happens, though, when evil prevails over the law? In the General Comment Kant appends to this essay (because in it reason, he acknowledges, extends itself beyond its bounds), he asks: Can one reverse the corrupted subjective ground of one's actions, restore the original priority of the law in the foundation of one's maxims, and thus, by having the law as the only incentive, restitute the moral order of one's itinerary? Is it possible, in short, to rechoose one's *Gesinnung*? Here Kant introduces an extraordinary idea. One may reverse the supreme basis of one's maxims "through a single immutable decision" (Kant, *Religion*, 54, Ak. 6: 47). The originary free choice of *Gesinnung* that did not happen in time may be repeated (54, Ak. 6: 47). Restituting the moral law as the only source of motivation "must be brought about through a *revolution* in the attitude [*Gesinnung*] in the human being (a transition to the maxim of the attitude's holiness); and he can become a new human being only through a kind of rebirth, as if through a new

creation . . . and a change of heart" (54, Ak. 6: 47). Reading these lines, one may be tempted to assume that the subject's repetition of its initial choice of *Gesinnung* (a choice not made in time) would consist in a conscious decision in time. One would gain consciousness of one's sensible motivations, it would seem, and in so doing make sure that one's disposition is not corrupted again. Kant affirms, however, that the repetition of this choice is not conscious. Deliberately refraining from attributing to the subject any intentionality, Kant insists on the fact that, just as happens in regard to our initial free choice of disposition, we can gain no conscious access to the repetition of that choice. There is therefore no way to know with certainty whether the basis of a subject's adoption of maxims is changed, "neither through direct consciousness nor through the proof of the life he has led thus far; for the depth of the heart (the subjective first basis of his maxims) is inscrutable to himself" (58, Ak. 6: 51). On this Kantian rebirth in which one gives oneself one's disposition, which Kant also explores in the *Anthropology from a Pragmatic Point of View,* see Jean-Louis Chrétien, *The Unforgettable and the Unhoped For,* trans. Jeffrey Bloechl (New York: Fordham University Press, 2002), 114–15. See also Zupančič, *L'éthique du réel,* 34–40, for a highly suggestive reading of this passage.

100. Kant, *Religion,* 26, Ak. 6: 25.

101. Kant, *Religion,* 26–27, Ak. 6: 25.

102. Kant, *Religion,* 22, Ak. 6: 22.

103. Kant, *Religion,* 22, Ak. 6: 22.

104. The origin or initiating cause from which all effects would descend would thus be a *"rational origin,"* and not a *"temporal origin."* In the case of rational origin one considers only "the effect's *existence,"* whereas in the case of temporal origin one refers to an "event," that is, to "the effect's *occurrence,"* which has "its *cause in time."* "When the effect is referred to a cause that is still linked with it according to laws of freedom," the power of choice that has produced a certain effect is thus "linked with its determining basis not in time but merely in the presentation of reason." Kant, *Religion,* 44, Ak. 6: 40. Hence that determining basis is an uncaused cause, since "it cannot be derived from a *preceding* state." Kant, *Religion,* 44, Ak. 6: 40.

105. It is not exactly the case, therefore, that freedom's causality is structured by its own intelligible temporality. Rather, presentations of reason are independent from time, whereas actions that can be referred to their natural cause, that is, evil actions, constitute an "event in the world." As regards presentations of reason, "to search for the temporal origin of free actions as free actions (just as for natural effects) is therefore a contradiction." Kant, *Religion,* 44, Ak. 6: 41.

106. "Since this adoption is free, its basis (why, e.g., I have adopted an evil maxim rather than a good one) must be sought not in any incentive of nature, but always in turn in a maxim; and since this maxim must likewise have its basis, while yet apart from a maxim no *determining basis* of the free power of choice is to be or can

be adduced, one is referred back ever further *ad infinitum* in the series of subjective determining bases." Kant, *Religion*, 21, Ak. 6: 21n.

107. Kant, *Religion*, 26, Ak. 6: 25.

108. Kant, *Religion*, 26, Ak. 6: 25.

109. Kant, *Religion*, 26, Ak. 6: 25. By becoming the author or cause of its own itinerary, the subject gives motivational force and direction ("moral order") to what could otherwise be perceived as a deterministic causal series in which the moral order of grounds (the priority of the law over psychological incentives) has been reversed. In this way the subject emerges as autonomous, as having initiated its own itinerary through a free choice, and as striving to keep that itinerary from reversing the moral order, that is, from incorporating heteronomous incentives.

110. Kant, *Critique of Pure Reason*, 473, A 444/B 472.

111. See Chapter 2.

112. Zupančič, *L'éthique du réel*, 68.

113. Kant, *Critique of Practical Reason*, 46, Ak. 5: 31.

4. AFFECT OF THE LAW

1. Kant, *Critique of Practical Reason*, 5, Ak. 5: 4, and 68, Ak. 5: 49.

2. See Chapter 3.

3. Dieter Henrich, "Ethics of Autonomy," trans. Louis Hunt, in *The Unity of Reason*, 110.

4. Henrich, *The Unity of Reason*, 108.

5. Henrich, *The Unity of Reason*, 108.

6. Nancy, "Le Katègorein," 25–26 / "The *Kategorein*," 147 (translation modified).

7. Kant, *Critique of Practical Reason*, 97, Ak. 5: 73.

8. See John Llewelyn, "Respect as Effective Affectivity: Michel Henry on Kant," in *The HypoCritical Imagination*, 153–169. See also Michel Henry, *The Essence of Manifestation*, 644–46.

9. Kant, *Critique of Practical Reason*, 95, Ak. 5: 72.

10. Kant, *Critique of Practical Reason*, 94, Ak. 5: 72.

11. See Chapter 3.

12. Kant writes: "The objective determining basis must therefore always and quite alone be also the subjectively sufficient determining basis of an action if this action is not merely to fulfill the *letter* of the law without containing the law's *spirit*." Kant, *Critique of Practical Reason*, 95, Ak. 5: 72.

13. Kant, *Critique of Practical Reason*, 95, Ak. 5: 72. Cf. Kant, *Grounding for the Metaphysics of Morals*, Ak. 4: 456, 459, 461.

14. Kant, *Critique of Practical Reason*, 94–95, Ak. 5: 72.

15. Kant, *Critique of Practical Reason*, 46, Ak. 5: 31.

16. See Chapter 3.

17. Kant, *Critique of Practical Reason*, 95, Ak. 5: 72.

18. A compelling explanation of the apparent circularity of the causality of respect (that also examines Kant's approach to respect in the *Religion*) can be found in Silber, "Ethical Significance in Kant's *Religion*," civ, cvi-vii. See also Zupančič, *L'éthique du réel*, 68.

19. Nancy, "Le Katègorein," 23 (my translation; this particular line is missing from the English translation, where it should have appeared on 145).

20. Kant, *Critique of Practical Reason*, 98, Ak. 5: 74.

21. Kant, *Critique of Practical Reason*, 98, Ak. 5: 75.

22. Kant, *Critique of Practical Reason*, 98, Ak. 5: 75. This circularity is pointed out and criticized by Michel Henry in *The Essence of Manifestation*, as John Llewelyn explains (*The HypoCritical Imagination*, 155). On this dislocated causality, see also Zupančič, *L'éthique du réel*, 68.

23. See Henrich, *The Unity of Reason*, 109-11.

24. Kant, *Critique of Practical Reason*, 95, Ak. 5: 73.

25. Kant, *Critique of Practical Reason*, 95, Ak. 5: 73.

26. Kant, *Critique of Practical Reason*, 98, Ak. 5: 75.

27. Kant, *Critique of Practical Reason*, 98, Ak. 5: 75 (translation modified).

28. Kant, *Critique of Practical Reason*, 99, Ak. 5: 76.

29. Kant, *Critique of Practical Reason*, 99, Ak. 5: 76. Emphasis added.

30. Kant, *Critique of Practical Reason*, 98, Ak. 5: 74. Kant never put together a systematic theory of self-consciousness, though many of his reflections presuppose self-consciousness. As Dieter Henrich has demonstrated, the theory of self-consciousness that develops the concept of "self" as it has reached us in the writings of Kierkegaard, Heidegger, and Sartre originates in Fichte's *The Science of Knowledge* (1794–1795), twelve years before Hegel's *Phenomenology of Spirit*. For an initial insight into the complexity of self-consciousness as analyzed by Fichte and by Henrich himself, see Dieter Henrich, "The Paradoxical Character of the Self-Relatedness of Consciousness," in *Between Kant and Hegel*, 246-62.

31. Kant, *Critique of Practical Reason*, 98, Ak. 5: 75. The affect that accompanies the subject's relationship with the law of freedom is not even reducible to the sublime, at least not within the context of the second *Critique*. "Something that does approach this feeling is *admiration*, and this as an affect, amazement, can apply also to things, e.g., sky-high mountains, the magnitude, multitude, and distance of the celestial bodies, the strength and swiftness of many animals, etc. But none of this is respect" (Kant, *Critique of Practical Reason*, 100, Ak. 5: 76). If the affect of respect were identifiable with the sublime, it would still be produced by psychological (not rational) freedom. Amazement at "sky-high mountains" or at "the magnitude, multitude, and distance of the celestial bodies," reminiscent of the famous *"starry sky above me"* line in the conclusion to this second *Critique* and later qualified in the *Critique of Judgment* as the sublime (*Critique of Judgment*, trans. Werner S. Pluhar

[Cambridge: Cambridge University Press, 1987], Ak. 5: 269, 272, 365) defines in this passage what respect *is not*. Respect (in the positive sense) is indeed not the same as, and is not reducible to, the feeling produced by "*the starry sky above me*," in spite of the fact that this line equates the "admiration and reverence" produced by "*the starry sky above me and the moral law within me*" (Kant, *Critique of Practical Reason*, 203, Ak. 5: 162). Here we should be aware, once again, that what produces "admiration and reverence" is not the starry sky or the moral law themselves, but rather one's contemplation of each. "Two things fill the mind with ever new and increasing admiration and reverence, the more frequently and persistently one's meditation deals with them: *the starry sky above me and the moral law within me*." I can meditate no better about the moral law than I can about the starry sky. Kant does not miss this opportunity to insist on the limit-setting goal that fuels his critical project: theoretical reason can only produce knowledge of what is given to the senses. Those limits apply to the entire use of pure reason, and therefore also to its practical use.

32. Kant, *Critique of Practical Reason*, 114, Ak. 5: 89.

33. Kant, *Critique of Practical Reason*, 123, Ak. 5: 97.

34. As Kant writes, "in the question concerning that freedom on which we must base all moral laws and the imputation conforming to them, it does not matter at all whether the causality determined according to a natural law is necessary through determining bases lying within the subject or outside him, or, in the first case [i.e., determining bases lying inside the subject], through instinct or through determining bases thought by means of reason" (*Critique of Practical Reason*, 121, Ak. 5: 96).

35. Kant, *Critique of Practical Reason*, 120, Ak. 5: 94.

36. Kant, *Critique of Practical Reason*, 97, Ak. 5: 73.

37. Kant, *Critique of Practical Reason*, 97, Ak. 5: 73.

38. Kant, *Critique of Practical Reason*, 98, Ak. 5: 75.

39. See Kant's footnote on *Critique of Practical Reason*, 5, Ak. 5: 4, quoted in Chapter 3.

40. See Zupančič, *L'éthique du réel*, 68.

41. Kant, *Critique of Practical Reason*, 98, Ak. 5: 75.

42. Kant, *Critique of Practical Reason*, 99–100, Ak. 5: 76.

43. Kant, *Critique of Practical Reason*, 100, Ak. 5: 76.

44. See Chapter 2 and Gabriela Basterra, "Subjectivity at the Limit: Velázquez, Kant, Levinas," *Diacritics* 40, no. 4 (2012): 46–70.

45. Kant, *Critique of Practical Reason*, 99, Ak. 5: 76.

46. Levinas, *Autrement qu'être*, 232 / *Otherwise than Being*, 148.

47. Kant, *Grounding for the Metaphysics of Morals*, 61, Ak. 4: 462.

48. See Chapters 1 and 2.

49. Henrich, *The Unity of Reason*, 110.

50. "The positive factor in respect exists for feeling only mediately insofar as humiliated sensibility is the ground of a rational evaluation of worth." Henrich, *The Unity of Reason*, 110.

51. Henrich, *The Unity of Reason*, 111.

52. Henrich, *The Unity of Reason*, 111.

53. Henrich, *The Unity of Reason*, 110.

54. Kant, *Critique of Practical Reason*, 134, Ak. 5: 105.

55. Kant, *Critique of Practical Reason*, 134–35, Ak. 5: 106.

56. Kant, *Critique of Practical Reason*, 134, Ak. 5: 106.

57. See Chapter 2.

58. Henrich, *The Unity of Reason*, 110.

59. Henrich, *The Unity of Reason*, 111.

60. Kant, *Critique of Practical Reason*, 104, Ak. 5: 80.

61. This sense is in consonance with Kant's description, a few pages later, of the person who in giving priority to duty over his personal interest "does not have cause to be ashamed before himself and to dread the inner spectacle of self-examination . . . ." Kant, *Critique of Practical Reason*, 112–13, Ak. 5: 88.

62. Alenka Zupančič observes that Kant's term "respect" (*Achtung*) practically disappears after the second *Critique* and the *Religion*, and is often replaced by a word which was not even part of his vocabulary so far, "conscience" (*Gewissen*), which appears prominently in the *Metaphysics of Morals* (*Ethics of the Real*, 159 / *L'éthique du réel*, 76).

63. Kant, *Critique of Practical Reason*, 105–6, Ak. 5: 81–82.

64. Nancy, "Le Katègorein," 17 / "The *Kategorein*," 140–41.

65. Kant, *Critique of Practical Reason*, 48, Ak. 5: 33. This is the first time the word "autonomy" appears in the second *Critique*. To act ethically or according to the spirit of the law would be related, in other words, to remaining faithful to the law's unconditionality. Only thus can the subject be envisioned, from the perspective of the third antinomy, as functioning as unconditioned element of the causal chain, as I explained in Chapter 3.

66. In an essay titled "Kant's 'I' in 'I Ought To' and Freud's Superego," Béatrice Longuenesse argues that the moral law and the superego refer to the same thing. Her interesting analysis does not refer in particular to the chapter on "respect" in Kant's second *Critique*. Béatrice Longuenesse, "Kant's 'I' in 'I Ought To' and Freud's Superego," *Proceedings of the Aristotelian Society Supplementary* 86 (2012): 19–39.

67. See Rogozinski, *Le don de la Loi*, and Zupančič, *Ethics of the Real*, 140–69.

68. See, for example, Copjec, "Sex and the Euthanasia of Reason," 42.

69. Basterra, *Seductions of Fate*, especially 67–105.

70. Zupančič, *L'éthique du réel*, 75.

71. Kant, *Critique of Practical Reason*, 138, Ak. 5: 108.

72. In his introduction to the "System of Cosmological Ideas" at the beginning of the Antinomy chapter in the *Critique of Pure Reason*, Kant distinguishes between two ways of thinking of the unconditioned. "Either one thinks of it as consisting merely in the whole series, in which therefore all members would without exception be conditioned and only their whole would be absolutely unconditioned; and then the regression is called infinite. Or the absolutely unconditioned is only a part of the series, a part to which the remaining members of the series are subordinated but which itself is not subject to any other conditioned" (Kant, *Critique of Pure Reason*, 451, A 417/B 445). This second conception of the unconditioned (which is the one at play in the theses of the antinomic ideas), is the one I have referred to in my study of the third antinomy. Of the first type of unconditioned, the unconditioned totality of a series sought in the Dialectic of Practical Reason, Kant remarks: "The absolute whole of a series of conditions for a given conditioned is always unconditioned; for outside the series there are no further conditions in regard to which this whole could be continued. However, this absolute whole of such a series is only an idea—or, rather, a problematic concept whose possibility must be examined, viz., in reference to the way in which it may contain the unconditioned, which is the transcendental idea that is in fact at issue" (Kant, *Critique of Pure Reason*, 451–52, A 418/B 445n).

73. Zupančič, *L'éthique du réel*, 80.

74. See my reading of the third antinomy in Chapter 2.

75. Kant, *Critique of Practical Reason*, 140, Ak. 5: 109. Cf. Kant, *Grounding for the Metaphysics of Morals*, Ak. 4: 396, 399, 444–58.

76. Kant, *Critique of Practical Reason*, 145, Ak. 5: 114.

77. The thesis of the fourth antinomy reads: "There belongs to the world something that, either as its part or as its cause, is an absolutely necessary being" (Kant, *Critique of Pure Reason*, 476, A 552/B 480). The antithesis, in turn, contends: "There exists no absolutely necessary being at all, neither in the world nor outside the world, as its cause" (476, A 453/B 481). That the unconditioned introduced by the thesis of the fourth antinomy is outside the series is not evident from its formulation, which contemplates the possibility that the unconditioned may be a part of the world. The Comment on the Thesis, however, anticipates that "the pure cosmological proof can establish the existence of a necessary being only if it simultaneously leaves undecided whether this being is the world itself or a thing distinct from it" (Kant, *Critique of Pure Reason*, 482, A 456/B 484). Kant's solution (section 4, "Solution of the Cosmological Idea of Totality in the Dependence of Appearances as Regards Their Existence as Such"), finally, concludes, in effect, that "the necessary being would have to be thought as entirely outside the series of the world of sense." Kant, *Critique of Pure Reason*, 555, A 561/B 589.

78. Kant, *Critique of Pure Reason*, 554, A 561/B 580.

79. Kant, *Critique of Pure Reason*, 558, A 566/B 594n.

80. Kant, *Critique of Pure Reason*, 557–59, A 565–67/B 593–95.

81. In the case of the soul's infinite progress toward goodness, however, reason's presentations would be conceived in terms of progression rather than regression.

82. In his essay "Transcendence and Evil" (1978), Levinas, after praising Kant for having "the audacity to draw a more radical distinction between thinking and knowing" and for introducing the transcendental idea of freedom, criticizes him for reestablishing the relation to ontology with the postulates of the existence of God and the immortality of the soul. "A good will, utopian in some fashion, deaf to information, indifferent to the confirmations that could come to it from being . . . , proceeds from a freedom situated above being and prior to knowledge and ignorance. And yet, after an instant of separation, the relation with ontology is reestablished in the 'postulates of pure reason,' as though it were awaited in the midst of all these audacities." Levinas, "Transcendence and Evil," 123.

83. Kant, *Critique of Pure Reason*, 557–58, A 565/B 593.

84. Kant, *Critique of Practical Reason*, 133–34, Ak. 5: 105.

85. Zupančič interestingly explains this loss of Kant's conception of ethics by saying that when the difference between the letter and the spirit of the law collapses, when the subjective moment of being motivated solely by the law disappears, the law itself is subjectivized. See *L'éthique du réel*, 75.

86. Kant, *Critique of Practical Reason*, 134, Ak. 5: 105.

87. See Chapter 2.

88. Kant, *Critique of Practical Reason*, 111, Ak. 5: 86.

5. AUTONOMY, OR BEING INSPIRED

1. A former version of my reading of *Otherwise than Being* appeared in Gabriela Basterra, "Auto-Heteronomy, or Levinas' Philosophy of the Same," *Graduate Faculty Philosophy Journal* 31, no. 1 (2010): 109–32. I would like to thank Bettina Bergo and Ernesto Laclau for their generous reading of this essay and for their invaluable comments.

2. Levinas, *Autrement qu'être*, 221 / *Otherwise than Being*, 141 (translation modified).

3. Levinas, *Autrement qu'être*, 230 / *Otherwise than Being*, 147.

4. Levinas will evoke it as "this way for a command to sound in the mouth of the one that obeys." Levinas, *Autrement qu'être*, 230 / *Otherwise than Being*, 147.

5. Levinas, *Autrement qu'être*, 175 / *Otherwise than Being*, 111.

6. Levinas, *Autrement qu'être*, 232 / *Otherwise than Being*, 148.

7. Levinas, *Autrement qu'être*, 232 / *Otherwise than Being*, 148.

8. Levinas, *Autrement qu'être*, 175 / *Otherwise than Being*, 111.

9. It will be important to keep in mind that this relationship to the other is not dialectic; if it were, then the other would be reducible to an internalized source of

obligation, and thus ultimately engulfed in the oppositional logic that fuels self-consciousness.

10. Kant, "On the Incentives of Pure Practical Reason" (chapter 3 of the Analytic of Pure Practical Reason), *Critique of Practical Reason*, 94–114, Ak. 5: 72–89.

11. Levinas, "Humanism and An-archy," 133.

12. Levinas, *Autrement qu'être*, 22–23 / *Otherwise than Being*, 9 (translation modified).

13. Nancy, "Le Katègorein," 25–26 / "The *Kategorein*," 147 (translation modified).

14. "This book then does present itself as a defense of subjectivity," he writes in *Totality and Infinity*, 26.

15. See, for example, Emmanuel Levinas, "Meaning and Sense," trans. Alphonso Lingis, in *Basic Philosophical Writings*, ed. Robert Bernasconi, Simon Critchley, and Adriaan Peperzak (Bloomington: Indiana University Press, 1996), 62, and *Autrement qu'être*, 23, 25–26 / *Otherwise than Being*, 9, 11.

16. Levinas, *Totalité et infini*, 211 / *Totality and Infinity*, 194.

17. On the face in Levinas, see Hagi Kenaan's highly suggestive approach in "Facing Images," *Angelaki: Journal of the Theoretical Humanities* 16, no. 1 (2011): 143–59, and in *The Ethics of Visuality: Levinas and the Contemporary Gaze*, trans. Batya Stein (London: I. B. Tauris, 2013).

18. Jacques Derrida, "Violence and Metaphysics," in *Writing and Difference*, trans. Alan Bass (Chicago: University of Chicago Press, 1978), 109. See also Maurice Blanchot's responses to Levinas in "Knowledge of the Unknown," "Keeping to Words," and "The Relation of the Third Kind: Man without Horizon," originally published in 1961–1962, and collected in *The Infinite Conversation*, trans. Susan Hanson (Minneapolis: University of Minnesota Press, 1993).

19. Lyotard, "Levinas's Logic," 119–23.

20. Levinas, "Enigma and Phenomenon," in *Basic Philosophical Writings*, 70–73.

21. Levinas, *Autrement qu'être*, 175 / *Otherwise than Being*, 110.

22. On time in Levinas, see Joanna Hodge, "Ethics and Time: Levinas between Kant and Husserl," in *Diacritics* 32, no. 3/4 (2002): 107–34.

23. Levinas, *Autrement qu'être*, 23 / *Otherwise than Being*, 10.

24. For an excellent and thorough account of the evolution of Levinas's thinking from *Totality and Infinity* to *Otherwise than Being*, see Bettina Bergo, *Levinas between Ethics and Politics: For the Beauty that Adorns the Earth* (Pittsburgh, PA: Duquesne University Press, 2003).

25. See Lyotard's reflections on "the enunciative clause" in "Levinas's Logic," 119–23.

26. Levinas, *Autrement qu'être*, 20 / *Otherwise than Being*, 7. If skepticism has ability to return after all its " 'irrefutable' refutations," continues Levinas, it is because "a secret diachrony commands this ambiguous or enigmatic way of speaking, and because in general signification signifies beyond synchrony, beyond essence."

27. Levinas, *Autrement qu'être*, 20 / *Otherwise than Being*, 7.

28. "The infinite does not signal itself to a subjectivity, a unity already formed, by its order to turn toward the neighbor. Subjectivity in its *being* undoes *essence* by substituting itself for another. As one-for-another, it absorbs itself in signification, in saying or verb of the infinite. Signification precedes essence." Levinas, *Autrement qu'être*, 29 / *Otherwise than Being*, 13 (translation modified).

29. Levinas, *Autrement qu'être*, 24 / *Otherwise than Being*, 10. "Immemorial, unrepresentable, invisible, the past that bypasses the present, the pluperfect past, falls into a past that is a gratuitous lapse. It cannot be recuperated by reminiscence not because of its remoteness, but because of its incommensurability with the present." Levinas, *Autrement qu'être*, 25–26 / *Otherwise than Being*, 11.

30. Levinas, *Autrement qu'être*, 222 / *Otherwise than Being*, 141.

31. Levinas, *Autrement qu'être*, 24 / *Otherwise than Being*, 10.

32. Levinas, *Autrement qu'être*, 26 / *Otherwise than Being*, 11. It is not a matter of going from the present to the past, but rather of inhabiting temporalities other than the linear one of consciousness (with its operations of causation and teleology), such as that of the "always already" or of the future anterior in the mode of *perhaps* ("perhaps the subject will have been") that Levinas and Derrida try to inhabit. Levinas introduces the mode of *perhaps* as "a new modality" of "saying" in "Enigma and Phenomenon" (1965), 70–73. Derrida reflects on his own practice of this mode since the 1960s. See, for example, Jacques Derrida, *Politics of Friendship*, trans. George Collins (London: Verso, 1997).

33. See Gabriela Basterra, "Activité au-delà de toute autre activité," in *Emmanuel Levinas: Les territoires de la pensée*, eds. Danielle Cohen-Levinas and Bruno Clément, 323–38 (Paris: Presses Universitaires de France, 2007), and Gabriela Basterra, "Subjectivité inouïe," in *Quel sujet du politique? Rue Descartes 67*, Monographic Issue, (2010): 26–31.

34. See, for example, Levinas, *Autrement qu'être*, 28 / *Otherwise than Being*, 13.

35. Levinas, *Autrement qu'être*, 28 / *Otherwise than Being*, 13.

36. Levinas, *Autrement qu'être*, 28 / *Otherwise than Being*, 13.

37. Levinas, *Autrement qu'être*, 22–23 / *Otherwise than Being*, 9 (translation modified).

38. See especially his essays "Meaning and Sense" (1964) and "Enigma and Phenomenon" (1965). The trope of the trace is extensively developed by Derrida since his first incorporation of it in 1966. For a thorough study of the trace in Levinas, see Peter Zeillinger's essay "Phänomenologie des Nicht-Phänomenalen: Spur und Inversion des Seins bei Emmanuel Levinas," in *Phänomenologische Aufbrüche*, ed. Michael Blamauer, Wolfgang Fasching, and Matthias Flatscher (Frankfurt: Lang, 2005), 161–79.

39. Levinas, *Autrement qu'être*, 27 / *Otherwise than Being*, 12.

40. Emmanuel Levinas, "Meaning and Sense," 63 (translation modified) / "La trace de l'autre," in *En découvrant l'existence avec Husserl et Heidegger* (Paris: Vrin, 2001), 282.

41. Levinas, *Autrement qu'être*, 220 / *Otherwise than Being*, 140.

42. "This is what we are calling *obsession*, a relationship prior to the act, a relationship that is neither act or position, and that, as such, contrasts with the Fichtean thesis, which holds that all that is in consciousness is posited there by consciousness," writes Levinas in "Subjectivity as An-archy" (lecture delivered on February 10, 1976), in *God, Death and Time*, trans. Bettina Bergo, 172–75 (Stanford, CA: Stanford University Press, 2000), 173.

43. On Levinas's critique of representation, see his essays on Maurice Blanchot in *Proper Names*, trans. Michael Smith (Stanford, CA: Stanford University Press, 1997). See also Jill Robbins, *Altered Reading: Levinas and Literature* (Chicago: University of Chicago Press, 1999).

44. "My substitution for another is the trope of a sense that does not belong to the empirical order of psychological events." Levinas, *Autrement qu'être*, 200 / *Otherwise than Being*, 125.

45. Patricia Parker, "Metaphor and Catachresis," in *The Ends of Rhetoric*, ed. John Bender and David Wellbery (Stanford, CA: Stanford University Press, 1990), 60.

46. For significant instances of catachresis where the figural term originally refers to parts of the body, see Lisel Mueller's poem "Things," in *Alive Together: New and Selected Poems* (Baton Rouge: Louisiana State University Press, 1986).

47. As Parker outlines the history of the differentiation between the two tropes, she notes that "even in Quintilian . . . —the very source of the clear division between catachresis and metaphor—both are subsumed within the larger category of metaphorical transfer, the movement of a term from its original place to another place" (Parker, "Metaphor and Catachresis," 63). The implications of this for my analysis go in two directions: on the one hand, even with a trope which, like catachresis, signals an absence, one may run the risk of "filling" or "fixing" that absence. On the other, metaphor defies the simple definition of a figure standing for a real term. I am grateful to Bettina Bergo for her insights on this.

48. Levinas, *Autrement qu'être*, 221 / *Otherwise than Being*, 141.

49. In her essay, "Gai Savoir Sera: The Science of Love and the Insolence of Chance," Joan Copjec alludes to the trope "suppléance" that Lacan takes from eighteenth-century rhetoric and introduces at the beginning of Seminar XX. Joan Copjec, "Gai Savoir Sera: The Science of Love and the Insolence of Chance," in *Alain Badiou: Philosophy and its Conditions*, ed. Gabriel Riera (Albany: State University of New York Press, 2005), 123.

50. See Parker, "Metaphor and Catachresis," 60.

51. See the following studies of catachresis from rhetorical, psychoanalytical, and political perspectives: Parker, "Metaphor and Catachresis," 60–73; Copjec, "Gai Savoir Sera," 119–36; and Ernesto Laclau, *On Populist Reason* (London: Verso, 2005).

52. My thanks, again, for Bettina Bergo's insight.

53. Laclau, *On Populist Reason*, 71.

54. Levinas, *Autrement qu'être*, 145 / *Otherwise than Being*, 90.

55. Levinas, *Autrement qu'être*, 146 / *Otherwise than Being*, 91.

56. Levinas, *Autrement qu'être*, 145 / *Otherwise than Being*, 90.

57. Levinas, "Meaning and Sense," 63.

58. When Levinas refers to the "face" in *Otherwise than Being*, he considers the face to be a trace: "The order that orders me to the other does not show itself to me, save through the trace of its reclusion, as a face of a neighbor." Levinas, *Autrement qu'être*, 220 / *Otherwise than Being*, 140. On Levinas's face, Other-within-the-Same, and substitution, see Bettina Bergo's excellent essay "The Face in Levinas: Toward a Phenomenology of Substitution," *Angelaki* 16, no. 1 (2011): 17–39.

59. On this conception of alterity in Levinas, see Robert Bernasconi, "What Is the Question to Which 'Substitution' Is the Answer?," in *The Cambridge Companion to Emmanuel Levinas*, ed. Simon Critchley and Robert Bernasconi, 234–51, especially 249 (Cambridge: Cambridge University Press, 2002).

60. The exteriority of the other has become also inaccurate, unless autonomy requires an exteriorization of the other of thought, the conception of the embodiment of the other or of the intelligible in the world.

61. Levinas, *Autrement qu'être*, 234 / *Otherwise than Being*, 149 (translation modified).

62. Levinas, *Autrement qu'être*, 159 / *Otherwise than Being*, 101.

63. Levinas, "Subjectivity as An-archy," 173–74.

64. Levinas, *Autrement qu'être*, 159 / *Otherwise than Being*, 101 (translation modified).

65. Levinas, "Humanism and An-archy," 133.

66. Levinas, *Autrement qu'être*, 174 / *Otherwise than Being*, 110 (translation modified).

67. Levinas, *Autrement qu'être*, 22–23 / *Otherwise than Being*, 9.

68. Levinas, "Meaning and Sense," 63 (translation modified).

69. Levinas, *Autrement qu'être*, 226 / *Otherwise than Being*, 144.

70. Laclau, *On Populist Reason*, 111, and Copjec, "Gai Savoir Sera: The Science of Love." See also Joan Copjec, *Imagine There's No Woman: Ethics and Sublimation* (Cambridge, MA: MIT Press, 2003).

71. Levinas, *Autrement qu'être*, 175 / *Otherwise than Being*, 110.

72. Levinas, *Autrement qu'être*, 175 / *Otherwise than Being*, 110.

73. Levinas, *Autrement qu'être*, 172 / *Otherwise than Being*, 109.

74. Levinas, *Autrement qu'être*, 172 / *Otherwise than Being*, 109. More literally, "Recurrence which is 'incarnation.'"

75. Levinas, *Autrement qu'être*, 229 / *Otherwise than Being*, 146.

76. Levinas, *Autrement qu'être*, 175 / *Otherwise than Being*, 110. This taking in the other under one's skin no longer refers to an acting subject that represents or possesses the other, but rather to a passive self which is dispossessed of itself.

77. Levinas, *Autrement qu'être*, 175 / *Otherwise than Being*, 110.

78. Levinas, *Autrement qu'être*, 228 / *Otherwise than Being*, 146: "The subjectivity of the subject . . . is accused in uneasiness or the unconditionality of the accusative . . . . In the interval, it is *one* without attributes, and not even the unity of the one doubles it up as an essential attribute."

79. Levinas, *Autrement qu'être*, 229 / *Otherwise than Being*, 146.

80. Daniela Leder, "Skin in *Otherwise than Being*," unpublished essay, 2006.

81. Levinas, *Autrement qu'être*, 175 / *Otherwise than Being*, 110.

82. Levinas, *Autrement qu'être*, 229 / *Otherwise than Being*, 146.

83. Levinas, *Autrement qu'être*, 229 / *Otherwise than Being*, 146.

84. Levinas, *Autrement qu'être*, 229 / *Otherwise than Being*, 146.

85. Levinas, *Autrement qu'être*, 228–29 / *Otherwise than Being*, 145–46. Above I have been quoting from "Substitution," the core chapter (chapter 4) around which the rest of *Otherwise than Being* was generated. This chapter is the rewritten version of the 1968 essay "Substitution" (translated into English in *Basic Philosophical Papers*).

86. Levinas, *Autrement qu'être*, 234 / *Otherwise than Being*, 149.

87. Levinas, *Autrement qu'être*, 175 / *Otherwise than Being*, 110–11 (translation modified). The original paragraph reads: "Ou l'encombrement par soi et la souffrance de la constriction dans sa peau, mieux que des métaphores, suivent-ils le trope exact d'une altération de l'*essence* qui s'inverse—ou s'invertit—dans une récurrence où l'expulsion de soi hors soi est sa substitution à l'autre—ce qui signifierait proprement le Soi se vidant de lui-même?" Levinas, *Autrement qu'être*, 175.

88. Levinas, *Autrement qu'être*, 232 / *Otherwise than Being*, 148.

89. Levinas, *Autrement qu'être*, 175 / *Otherwise than Being*, 110.

90. The parallel operation in logic is that achieved by indefinite judgment, which as I indicated in Chapter 1 opens up the intelligible as an empty space beyond at the same time as it bounds the realm of what can be represented.

91. A (diachronic) relation of displacement or contiguity (from other to face to trace, other-within-the-same, tight skin, breathless breathing, hostage) that expresses the inhabitation of the self by the other becomes a catachrestic (synchronic) relation of substitution (the self substituting itself for the other).

92. Levinas, *Autrement qu'être*, 228 / *Otherwise than Being*, 146.

93. Levinas, *Autrement qu'être*, 175 / *Otherwise than Being*, 110–11 (translation modified).

94. Levinas, *Autrement qu'être*, 172 / *Otherwise than Being*, 109 (translation modified).

95. Levinas, *Autrement qu'être*, 232 / *Otherwise than Being*, 148.

96. Levinas, *Autrement qu'être*, 223–24 / *Otherwise than Being*, 143 (translation modified).

97. Levinas, *Autrement qu'être*, 239 / *Otherwise than Being*, 153. This "inversion of being" could also be understood in the sense of "inversion of ontology."

98. Levinas, *Autrement qu'être*, 223 / *Otherwise than Being*, 143 (translation modified).

99. As Laclau clarifies in his analysis of rhetoric in "Why Do Empty Signifiers Matter to Politics?," the notion of a signifier without a signified (a practical improbability that would only introduce noise in the symbolic system) belongs in differential logic, whereas an empty signifier does not express any preceding conceptual unity but rather gives a signification to what cannot be represented. See Ernesto Laclau, "Why Do Empty Signifiers Matter to Politics?," in *Emancipation(s)* (London: Verso, 1996), 37–46, and *On Populist Reason*, 101–17, especially 108.

100. In the closing paragraphs of *Otherwise than Being*, in one of his explicit acknowledgments of his debt to Husserl's phenomenology, Levinas emphasizes the incommensurability between the "unrecognized" origin of notions and the thematization that displaces them by locating every ontic "Said" in the diachronic horizon of its appearing that he names "Saying" (Levinas, *Autrement qu'être*, 280 / *Otherwise than Being*, 183). Beyond conceptual grasping "in which everything shows itself in a theme," the Said, he writes, "has to be reduced to its signification as *Saying*, beyond the simple correlation which is set up between the Saying and the Said" (*Autrement qu'être*, 280–81 / *Otherwise than Being*, 183). The relation between Saying—"antecedent to the verbal signs it conjugates, to the linguistic systems and the semantic shimmerings, a foreword preceding languages" (*Autrement qu'être*, 17 / *Otherwise than Being*, 5 [translation modified])—and Said may be considered to be both inspired in phenomenology (insofar as the Said is located in the horizon of its appearing) and in excess of it (since the pre-originary Saying lacks a place in representation). Hence the need to "venture . . . beyond phenomenology," as Levinas does here.

101. Levinas, *Autrement qu'être*, 281 / *Otherwise than Being*, 183. Levinas develops this notion in his 1960s essays on Husserlian time, "La trace de l'autre" (1963), "Intentionalité et sensation" (1965), and "Énigme et phénomène" (1965), collected in Levinas, *En découvrant l'existence avec Husserl et Heidegger*. They have been translated as "The Trace of the Other" (trans. Alphonso Lingis, in *Deconstruction in Context*, ed. Mark Taylor, 345–59 [Albany: State University of New York Press, 1988]), "Intentionality and Sensation" (trans. Richard A. Cohen and Michael B. Smith, in *Discovering Existence with Husserl*, ed. Richard A. Cohen and Michael B. Smith, 135–50 [Evanston, IL: Northwestern University Press, 1998]), and "Enigma and Phenom-

enon," in *Basic Philosophical Writings*. For an analysis of these essays, see John E. Drabinski, *Sensibility and Singularity: The Problem of Phenomenology in Levinas* (New York: SUNY Press, 2001), 129–66.

102. Levinas, "Meaning and Sense," 62.

103. Levinas, *Autrement qu'être*, 223 / *Otherwise than Being*, 143 (translation modified).

104. Levinas, *Autrement qu'être*, 224 / *Otherwise than Being*, 143 (translation modified).

105. Levinas, *Autrement qu'être*, 223 / *Otherwise than Being*, 143 (translation modified).

106. Levinas, *Autrement qu'être*, 223 / *Otherwise than Being*, 149.

107. Levinas, *Autrement qu'être*, 228 / *Otherwise than Being*, 145.

108. Levinas, *Autrement qu'être*, 232 / *Otherwise than Being*, 148–49 (translation modified). The French original reads:

> Inscription de l'ordre dans le pour-l'autre de l'obéissance: affection anarchique qui se glissa en moi 'comme un voleur,' à travers les filets tendus de la conscience, traumatisme qui m'a absolument surpris, l'ordre *n'a jamais été représenté*, car il ne s'est jamais présenté—pas même dans le passé venant en souvenir—au point que c'est moi qui dis seulement—et après coup—cette inouïe obligation. Ambivalence qui est l'exception et la subjectivité du sujet, son psychisme même, possibilité de l'inspiration: être auteur de ce qui m'avait été à mon insu insufflé—avoir reçu, on ne sait d'où, ce dont je suis l'auteur. Le dire inouï est énigmatiquement dans la réponse an-archique, dans ma responsabilité pour l'autre. La trace de l'infini est cette ambiguïté dans le sujet, tout à tour commencement et truchement, ambivalence diachronique que l'éthique rend possible. (Levinas, *Autrement qu'être*, 232)

One could argue that this whole paragraph has been written with Kant in mind. The first lines evoke Kantian notions such as "'transcendental foundation' of 'ethical experience'" and "ethics is the breakup of the originary unity of transcendental apperception" to underscore what ethics is not, alluding to the tradition that Levinas contests. (Kant is well aware, however, that a "transcendental foundation" may be a transcendental illusion.) The rest of Levinas's paragraph depicts ethics in a way that both draws inspiration from Kant and allows Kantian notions to appear in a new light that does them more justice than the post-Kantian tradition of autonomy does.

109. Levinas, *Autrement qu'être*, 232 / *Otherwise than Being*, 148.

110. Levinas, *Autrement qu'être*, 223 / *Otherwise than Being*, 143.

111. Levinas, *Autrement qu'être*, 170 / *Otherwise than Being*, 108.

112. Levinas, *Autrement qu'être*, 232 / *Otherwise than Being*, 148.

113. Levinas, *Autrement qu'être*, 229 / *Otherwise than Being*, 146 (translation modified).

114. Levinas, *Autrement qu'être*, 229 / *Otherwise than Being*, 146 (translation modified).

115. Levinas, *Autrement qu'être*, 229 / *Otherwise than Being*, 146.

116. This subject is not a person with an identity who consciously takes up the task of saying what another person cannot say, a historical subject who assumes the "representation" of another historical subject who cannot represent herself. Rather, it is a relationship between other and same, where what "same" is must still be qualified.

117. Levinas, *Autrement qu'être*, 230 / *Otherwise than Being*, 147 (translation modified).

118. Levinas, *Autrement qu'être*, 232 / *Otherwise than Being*, 148.

119. Levinas, *Autrement qu'être*, 226 / *Otherwise than Being*, 144.

120. Levinas, *Autrement qu'être*, 227 / *Otherwise than Being*, 145. Regarding this obligation that has not been chosen, Levinas also writes: "we discern in obsession a responsibility that rests on no free commitment, a responsibility whose entry into being could be effected only without any choice. To be without choice can seem to be violence only to an abusive or hasty and imprudent reflection, for it precedes the freedom non-freedom couple." Levinas, *Autrement qu'être*, 183 / *Otherwise than Being*, 116.

121. Levinas, *Autrement qu'être*, 201 / *Otherwise than Being*, 127.

122. See section titled "A Free Choice Not Made in Time" in Chapter 3.

123. Levinas, *Autrement qu'être*, 183 / *Otherwise than Being*, 116.

124. Levinas, *Autrement qu'être*, 229 / *Otherwise than Being*, 146.

125. Levinas, *Autrement qu'être*, 175 / *Otherwise than Being*, 110.

126. See my reading of the third antinomy in Chapter 2. This functioning of the unconditioned, however, presupposes an autonomous subjectivity that has freely chosen the law of freedom as its ultimate ground, for only thus, by embodying this relationship to freedom, may the subject be imagined to play the role of the unconditioned and insert freedom's effects in the world. Hence reason's need to envision the subject's adoption of its own disposition (*Gesinnung*) as a free act of the power of choice.

127. See Chapter 3.

128. Nancy, "Le Katègorein," 19 / "The *Kategorein*," 142. See Chapter 3.

129. Levinas, *Autrement qu'être*, 222 / *Otherwise than Being*, 141.

130. Levinas, *Autrement qu'être*, 227 / *Otherwise than Being*, 145. Levinas refers to this "unforeseeable response" as the "diachrony of creation." In creation, he writes, "what is called to being answers to a call that could not have reached it since, brought out of nothingness, it obeyed before hearing the order. Thus in creation *ex-nihilo*, if it is not a pure nonsense, a passivity that does not revert into an assumption is thought." Levinas, *Autrement qu'être*, 180 / *Otherwise than Being*, 113 (translation modified).

131. See section titled "Unconditionality and Address" in Chapter 3.

132. See sections titled "The Law's Letter" and "Alterity of the Law" in Chapter 3.

133. Levinas, *Autrement qu'être*, 200–1 / *Otherwise than Being*, 126 (translation modified).

134. Levinas, *Autrement qu'être*, 232 / *Otherwise than Being*, 148.

135. On Kant's and Levinas's different ways of understanding heteronomy, see Chalier, *What Ought I to Do?*, 60–84.

136. Levinas, *Autrement qu'être*, 232 / *Otherwise than Being*, 148.

137. It seems it is the "metaphor of the inscription of the law in consciousness" itself that effects the passage from what one could understand to be a "reverting of heteronomy into autonomy" into a "reconciliation" of autonomy and heteronomy in which none of the terms prevails, and which is, in fact, an interaction in the subject, the site of this relationship.

138. Levinas, *Autrement qu'être*, 232 / *Otherwise than Being*, 148.

139. Levinas, *Autrement qu'être*, 232 / *Otherwise than Being*, 148.

140. Levinas, *Autrement qu'être*, 232 / *Otherwise than Being*, 148.

141. Levinas, *Autrement qu'être*, 232 / *Otherwise than Being*, 148.

142. Levinas, *Autrement qu'être*, 230 / *Otherwise than Being*, 147.

143. Levinas, *Autrement qu'être*, 232 / *Otherwise than Being*, 148–49.

144. As I noted above, Kant did not produce a theory of self-consciousness. For my account of his understanding of the paradoxical relation between the "I" of transcendental apperception and inner sense, see Chapter 1.

145. Lacan also conceives of the subject as retroactive construction, and his readings of Kant are deeply illuminating. His goal, however, is not to account for ethical subjectivity, as is Levinas's goal.

146. See Basterra, "Tragic Autonomy Meets Ethical Heteronomy," in *Seductions of Fate*, 131–68.

147. "To be without a choice can seem to be violence only to an abusive or hasty and imprudent reflection, for it precedes the freedom non-freedom couple, but thereby sets up a vocation that goes beyond the limited and egoist fate of him who is only for-himself, and washes his hands of the faults and misfortunes that do not begin in his own freedom or in his present." Levinas, *Autrement qu'être*, 183–84 / *Otherwise than Being*, 116.

148. See Chapter 4.

149. See Basterra, *Seductions of Fate*, especially chapter 2.

150. See Chapter 3.

151. Kant, *Critique of Practical Reason*, 121–23, Ak. 5: 96–97.

152. Levinas, *Autrement qu'être*, 170 / *Otherwise than Being*, 107.

153. Levinas, *Autrement qu'être*, 221 / *Otherwise than Being*, 141.

154. Emmanuel Levinas, "Philosophy and the Idea of Infinity," in *Collected Philosophical Papers*, trans. Alphonso Lingis (Pittsburgh, PA: Duquesne University Press, 1998), 49.

155. Levinas, *Autrement qu'être*, 228 / *Otherwise than Being*, 145.

156. In Levinas's words, this interval is the "undoing of the substantial nucleus of the ego that is formed in the same, a fission of the mysterious nucleus of inwardness of the subject by this assignation to respond, . . . alteration without alienation or election." Levinas, *Autrement qu'être*, 221–22 / *Otherwise than Being*, 141.

157. On the entry of the third, see Peter Zeillinger, "Radical Passivity as the (Only) Basis for Effective Ethical Action: Reading the 'Passage to the Third' in *Otherwise than Being*," in *Radical Passivity: Rethinking Ethical Agency in Levinas*, ed. Benda Hofmeyr, 95–108 (London: Springer, 2009).

158. Levinas, *Totality and Infinity*, 213.

159. Levinas, *Autrement qu'être*, 247 / *Otherwise than Being*, 159.

160. Levinas, *Autrement qu'être*, 250 / *Otherwise than Being*, 160–61.

161. Levinas, *Autrement qu'être*, 245 / *Otherwise than Being*, 157.

162. Levinas, *Autrement qu'être*, 245 / *Otherwise than Being*, 157.

163. Levinas, *Autrement qu'être*, 245 / *Otherwise than Being*, 157.

164. Would it be accurate to say that the third is the other in plural? As Alenka Zupančič remarks in a different context, referring to Lacan, we "should note that the Lacanian thesis that 'there is no Other (of the) Other' aims not at the exclusion of the third, but, on the contrary, at its inclusion. The Other (of the Other) is included in the Other—and this is precisely what makes the Other Other, not just a duplication or repetition [or complement] of the One." Alenka Zupančič, *The Shortest Shadow: Nietzsche's Philosophy of the Two* (Cambridge, MA: MIT Press, 2003), 137–38. Though "the Other" to which Lacan and Levinas refer is not the same other, the structure is clarifying: precisely because the other is plural (in number), it is not the complement of the same.

165. Levinas, *Autrement qu'être*, 245 / *Otherwise than Being*, 157.

166. "We will of course have to show that the necessity of thinking is inscribed in the sense of transcendence. Cf. *infra*. 156ff." Levinas, *Autrement qu'être*, 21n1 / *Otherwise than Being*, 8n6.

167. Basterra, "Subjectivity at the Limit."

168. Levinas describes this enigma as a "claim laid on the same by the other in the core of the same . . . , beyond the logic of same and other, of their insurmountable adversity." Levinas, *Autrement qu'être*, 221 / *Otherwise than Being*, 141.

169. "Substitution is not an act." Levinas, *Autrement qu'être*, 185 / *Otherwise than Being*, 117.

170. Illuminating approaches to the relation between ethics and politics in Levinas may be found in Jacques Derrida, *Adieu to Emmanuel Levinas*, trans. Pascale-Anne Brault and Michael Naas (Stanford, CA: Stanford University Press, 1999), Bettina Bergo, *Levinas Between Ethics and Politics*, and Howard Caygill, *Levinas and the Political* (London: Routledge, 2002).

171. Levinas, *Autrement qu'être*, 245 / *Otherwise than Being*, 157 (translation modified).

172. Levinas, *Autrement qu'être*, 245 / *Otherwise than Being*, 157.

173. Levinas, *Autrement qu'être*, 245 / *Otherwise than Being*, 157.

The third party . . . is of itself the limit of responsibility and the birth of the question: What do I have to do with justice? A question of consciousness. Justice is necessary, that is, comparison, coexistence, contemporaneousness, assembling, order, thematization, the visibility of faces, and thus intentionality and the intellect, and in intentionality and the intellect, the intelligibility of a system, and thence also a copresence on an equal footing as before a court of justice. *Essence* as synchrony: *togetherness-in-a-place.* Proximity takes on a new meaning in the space of contiguity. . . . Thus one would understand, in proximity, in the saying without problems, in responsibility, the reason for the intelligibility of a system. (Levinas, *Autrement qu'être*, 245–46 / *Otherwise than Being*, 157 [translation modified])

174. Levinas, *Autrement qu'être*, 183 / *Otherwise than Being*, 116 (translation modified). "The self," continues Levinas, "is *Sub-jectum*; it is under the weight of the universe, responsible for everything. The unity of the universe is not what my gaze embraces in its unity of apperception, but what is incumbent on me from all sides, regards me in the two senses of the term, accuses me, is my affair. In this sense, the idea that I am sought out in intersidereal spaces is not science-fiction, but expresses my passivity as a Self." Levinas, *Autrement qu'être*, 183 / *Otherwise than Being*, 116 (translation modified).

175. Levinas, *Autrement qu'être*, 205 / *Otherwise than Being*, 129. An earlier formulation can be found in Levinas, "Humanism and An-archy," 138. For an excellent interpretation of this passage that insightfully emphasizes the proximity between Kant and Levinas, see Atterton, "From Transcendental Freedom to the Other," 346–47. My own approach has deep affinity with Atterton's in this respect.

176. Levinas's entire passage reads:

If one had the right to retain one trait from a philosophical system and neglect all the details of its architecture (even though there are no details in architecture, according to Valéry's profound dictum, which is eminently valid for philosophical construction, where details alone prevent collapse [*où le détail seul empêche les porte-à-faux*]), we would think here of Kantism, which finds a sense [*un sens*] to the human without measuring it by ontology and outside of the question "What is there here . . . ?" that one would like to take to be preliminary, outside the immortality and death ontologies stumble upon. The fact that immortality and theology would be unable to determine the categorical imperative signifies the novelty of the Copernican

revolution: sense [*le sens*] that is not measured in terms of being or not being, with being determining itself, on the contrary, on the basis of sense [*le
sens qui ne se mesure pas par l'être ou le ne pas être, l'être se déterminant, au
contraire, à partir du sens*]. (Levinas, *Autrement qu'être*, 205 / *Otherwise
than Being*, 129 [translation modified])

A few pages earlier in "Substitution," Levinas formulates a similar thought,
though this time he does not attribute it explicitly to Kant: "From the Good to me,
there is assignation: a relation that 'survives' the 'death of God.' The death of God
perhaps signifies only the possibility to reduce every value arousing an impulse to
an impulse arousing a value." Levinas, *Autrement qu'être*, 196 / *Otherwise than Being*, 123.

177. Levinas, *Autrement qu'être*, 234 / *Otherwise than Being*, 149.

178. In terms of the signification *Otherwise than Being* performs, subjectivity surpasses the realm of differential representation in which it belongs and thus embodies the meeting of metonymic and metaphorical relations, the fleeting and recurrent
anchoring of the diachronic by the synchronic.

179. Levinas, *Autrement qu'être*, 174 / *Otherwise than Being*, 110 (translation
modified).

180. It would be accurate to understand Kant's practical subject also in this sense,
as a subjectivity that, animated by the causality of freedom, is the addressee of the
unconditioned law and a "beginning by itself."

181. We should keep in mind, once again, that the "unconditionality [*l'incondition*]
of the subject . . . does not have the status of a principle" (Levinas, *Autrement qu'être*,
183 / *Otherwise than Being*, 116) and that "substitution is not an act" (Levinas, *Autrement qu'être*, 185 / *Otherwise than Being*, 117).

182. Levinas, *Autrement qu'être*, 188n / *Otherwise than Being*, 119n22.

183. Levinas, *Autrement qu'être*, 188n / *Otherwise than Being*, 119n22.

184. Levinas, *Autrement qu'être*, 183 / *Otherwise than Being*, 116.

185. Levinas, *Autrement qu'être*, 246 / *Otherwise than Being*, 158.

BIBLIOGRAPHY

Atterton, Peter. "From Transcendental Freedom to the Other: Levinas and Kant." In *In Proximity: Kant and the Eighteenth Century*, edited by Melvyn New, Richard Bernasconi, and Richard A. Cohen, 327–53. Lubbock: Texas Tech University Press, 2001.

Basterra, Gabriela. "Activité au-delà de toute autre activité." In *Emmanuel Levinas: Les territoires de la pensée*, edited by Danielle Cohen-Levinas and Bruno Clément, 323–38. Paris: Presses Universitaires de France, 2007.

———. "Auto-Heteronomy or, Levinas's Philosophy of the Same." *Graduate Faculty Philosophy Journal* 31, no. 1 (2010): 109–32.

———. *Seductions of Fate: Tragic Subjectivity, Ethics, Politics.* New York: Palgrave Macmillan, 2004.

———. "Subjectivité inouïe." *Quel sujet du politique? Rue Descartes* 67, Monographic Issue (2010): 26–31.

———. "Subjectivity at the Limit: Velázquez, Kant, Levinas." *Diacritics* 40, no. 4 (2012): 46–70.

Bergo, Bettina. "The Face in Levinas." *Angelaki: Journal of the Theoretical Humanities* 16, no. 1 (2011): 17–39.

———. *Levinas Between Ethics and Politics: For the Beauty that Adorns the Earth.* Pittsburgh, PA: Duquesne University Press, 2003.

———. "What Is Levinas Doing? Phenomenology and the Rhetoric of an Ethical Un-Conscious." *Philosophy and Rhetoric* 38, no. 2 (2005): 122–44.

Bernasconi, Robert. "What Is the Question to Which 'Substitution' Is the Answer?" In *The Cambridge Companion to Emmanuel Levinas*, ed. Simon Critchley and Robert Bernasconi, 234–51. Cambridge: Cambridge University Press, 2002.

Bernstein, Richard J. *Radical Evil: A Philosophical Interrogation.* Cambridge: Polity Press, 2002.

Blanchot, Maurice. *The Infinite Conversation.* Translated by Susan Hanson. Minneapolis: University of Minnesota Press, 1993.

Butler, Judith, Ernesto Laclau, and Slavoj Žižek. *Contingency, Hegemony, Universality: Contemporary Dialogues on the Left*. London: Verso, 2000.

Caygill, Howard. *Levinas and the Political*. London: Routledge: 2002.

Chalier, Catherine. *What Ought I to Do? Morality in Kant and Levinas*. Translated by Jane Marie Todd. Ithaca, NY: Cornell University Press, 2002.

Chrétien, Jean-Louis. *The Unforgettable and the Unhoped For*. Translated by Jeffrey Bloechl. New York: Fordham University Press, 2002.

Copjec, Joan. "Gai Savoir Sera: The Science of Love and the Insolence of Chance." In *Alain Badiou: Philosophy and its Conditions*, edited by Gabriel Riera, 119–36. Albany: State University of New York Press, 2005.

———. *Imagine There's No Woman: Ethics and Sublimation*. Cambridge, MA: MIT University Press, 2003.

———. "Sex and the Euthanasia of Reason." *Supposing the Subject*, edited by Joan Copjec, 16–44. London: Verso, 1994.

Custer, Olivia. *L'exemple de Kant*. Leuven, Belgium: Peeters, 2012.

Cutrofello, Andrew. *Continental Philosophy: A Contemporary Introduction*. London: Routledge, 2005.

David-Ménard, Monique. *La folie dans la raison pure: Kant lecteur de Swedenborg*. Paris: Vrin, 1990.

Davies, Paul. "Sincerity and the End of Theodicy: Three Remarks on Levinas and Kant." In *The Cambridge Companion to Emmanuel Levinas*, edited by Simon Critchley and Robert Bernasconi, 161–87. Cambridge: Cambridge University Press, 2002.

Deleuze, Gilles. *Difference and Repetition*. Translated by Paul Patton. New York: Columbia University Press, 1994.

———. *Kant's Critical Philosophy: The Doctrine of the Faculties*. Translated by Hugh Tomlinson and Barbara Habberjam. London: Athlone, 1984.

Derrida, Jacques. *Adieu to Emmanuel Levinas*. Translated by Pascale-Anne Brault and Michael Naas. Stanford, CA: Stanford University Press, 1999.

———. *Politics of Friendship*. Translated by George Collins. London: Verso, 1997.

———. "Violence and Metaphysics." In *Writing and Difference*, 79–153. Translated by Alan Bass. Chicago: The University of Chicago Press, 1978.

Drabinski, John E. *Sensibility and Singularity: The Problem of Phenomenology in Levinas*. New York: State University of New York Press, 2001.

Feron, Etienne. "Intérêt et désintéressement de la raison: Levinas et Kant." In *Levinas en contrastes*, edited by Michel Dupuis, 83–105. Brussels, Belgium: De Boeck-Wesmael, 1994.

Guyer, Paul. *Kant's System of Nature and Freedom: Selected Essays*. Oxford: Oxford University Press, 2005.

Henrich, Dieter. *Between Kant and Hegel: Lectures on German Idealism*. Edited by David S. Pacini. Cambridge, MA: Harvard University Press, 2003.

———. *The Unity of Reason: Essays on Kant's Philosophy.* Edited by Richard Velkley. Translated by Jeffrey Edwards, Louis Hunt, Manfred Kuehn, and Guenter Zoeller. Cambridge, MA: Harvard University Press, 1994.

Henry, Michel. *The Essence of Manifestation.* Translated by Girard Etzkorn. The Hague: Martinus Nijhoff, 1973.

Hodge, Joanna. "Ethics and Time: Levinas between Kant and Husserl." *Diacritics* 32, no. 3/4 (2002): 107–34.

Kant, Immanuel. *Anthropology from a Pragmatic Point of View.* Edited and translated by Robert B. Louden. Cambridge: Cambridge University Press, 2006.

———. *Critique of Judgment.* Translated by Werner S. Pluhar. Cambridge: Cambridge University Press, 1997.

———. *Critique of Practical Reason.* Translated by Werner S. Pluhar. Indianapolis, IN: Hackett, 2002.

———. *Critique of Pure Reason.* Translated by Werner S. Pluhar. Indianapolis, IN: Hackett, 1996.

———. *Grounding for the Metaphysics of Morals with On a Supposed Right to Lie because of Philanthropic Concerns.* 3rd ed. Translated by James W. Ellington. Indianapolis, IN: Hackett, 1993.

———. *Logic.* Translated by John Richardson. London: Printed in Stationers' Court for W. Simpkin and R. Marchall, 1819.

———. *The Metaphysics of Morals.* In *Ethical Philosophy.* Translated by James W. Ellington. Indianapolis, IN: Hackett, 1983.

———. *Opus Postumum.* Edited by Eckart Förster and Michael Rosen. Translated by Eckart Förster. Cambridge: Cambridge University Press, 1993.

———. *Religion within the Bounds of Bare Reason.* Translated by Werner S. Pluhar. Indianapolis, IN: Hackett, 2009.

Kenaan, Hagi. *The Ethics of Visuality: Levinas and the Contemporary Gaze.* Translated by Batya Stein. London: I. B. Tauris, 2013.

———. "Facing Images." *Angelaki: Journal of the Theoretical Humanities* 16, no. 1 (2011): 143–59.

Laclau, Ernesto. *On Populist Reason.* London: Verso, 2005.

———. "Why Do Empty Signifiers Matter to Politics?" In *Emancipation(s).* London: Verso, 1996.

Leder, Daniela. "Skin in *Otherwise than Being.*" Unpublished essay, 2006.

Levinas, Emmanuel. *Autrement qu'être ou au-delà de l'essence.* Paris: Le Livre de Poche, 2004.

———. *En découvrant l'existence avec Husserl et Heidegger.* 3rd ed. Paris: Vrin, 2001.

———. "Enigma and Phenomenon." Translated by Alphonso Lingis. *Basic Philosophical Writings,* edited by Robert Bernasconi, Simon Critchley, and Adriaan Peperzak, 65–78. Bloomington: Indiana University Press, 1996.

———. *God, Death, and Time*. Translated by Bettina Bergo. Stanford, CA: Stanford University Press, 2000.

———. "Humanism and An-archy" (1968). Translated by Alphonso Lingis. In *Collected Philosophical Papers*, 127–39. Pittsburgh, PA: Duquesne University Press, 1998.

———. "Intentionality and Sensation." Translated by Richard A. Cohen and Michael B. Smith. In *Discovering Existence with Husserl*, edited by Richard A. Cohen and Michael B. Smith, 135–50. Evanston, IL: Northwestern University Press, 1998.

———. "Is Ontology Fundamental?" In *Basic Philosophical Writings*, edited by Robert Bernasconi, Simon Critchley, and Adriaan Peperzak, 1–10. Bloomington: Indiana University Press, 1996.

———. "Kant and the Transcendental Ideal." In *God, Death, and Time*. Translated by Bettina Bergo, 153–56. Stanford, CA: Stanford University Press, 2000.

———. "Meaning and Sense." In *Basic Philosophical Writings*, edited by Robert Bernasconi, Simon Critchley, and Adriaan Peperzak, 33–64. Bloomington: Indiana University Press, 1996.

———. *Of God Who Comes to Mind*. Translated by Bettina Bergo. Stanford, CA: Stanford University Press, 1998.

———. *Otherwise than Being, or Beyond Essence*. Translated by Alphonso Lingis. Pittsburgh, PA: Duquesne University Press, 1998.

———. "Philosophy and the Idea of Infinity." In *Collected Philosophical Papers*, 47–59. Translated by Alphonso Lingis. Pittsburgh, PA: Duquesne University Press, 1998.

———. "The Primacy of Pure Practical Reason." Translated by Blake Billings. *Man and World* 27 (1994): 445–53.

———. *Proper Names*. Translated by Michael Smith. Stanford, CA: Stanford University Press, 1997.

———. "The Question of Subjectivity." In *God, Death, and Time*. Translated by Bettina Bergo, 149–52. Stanford, CA: Stanford University Press, 2000.

———. "The Radical Question: Kant against Heidegger." In *God, Death, and Time*. Translated by Bettina Bergo, 56–61. Stanford, CA: Stanford University Press, 2000.

———. "Subjectivity as An-archy." In *God, Death, and Time*. Translated by Bettina Bergo, 172–75. Stanford, CA: Stanford University Press, 2000.

———. *Totalité et infini: essai sur l'extériorité*. Paris: Livre de Poche, 1990.

———. *Totality and Infinity: An Essay on Exteriority*. Translated by Alphonso Lingis. Pittsburgh, PA: Duquesne University Press, 1969.

———. "The Trace of the Other." Translated by Alphonso Lingis. In *Deconstruction in Context*, edited by Mark Taylor, 345–59. Albany: State University of New York Press, 1988.

———. "Transcendence and Evil." In *Of God Who Comes to Mind*. Translated by Bettina Bergo, 122–34. Stanford, CA: Stanford University Press, 1998.

Llewelyn, John. *The HypoCritical Imagination: Between Kant and Levinas*. New York: Routledge, 2000.

Longuenesse, Béatrice. *Kant on the Human Standpoint*. Cambridge: Cambridge University Press, 2005.

———. "Kant's 'I' in 'I Ought To' and Freud's Superego." *Proceedings of the Aristotelian Society Supplementary* 86 (2012): 19–39.

Lyotard, Jean-François. "Levinas's Logic." In *Face to Face with Levinas*, edited by Richard A. Cohen, 117–58. Translated by Ian McLeod. Albany: State University of New York Press, 1986.

Mueller, Lisel. *Alive Together: New and Selected Poems*. Baton Rouge: Louisiana State University Press, 1986.

Nancy, Jean-Luc. "Le Katègorein de l'excès." In *L'imperatif catégorique*, 5–32. Paris: Flammarion, 1983.

———. "The *Kategorein* of Excess." In *A Finite Thinking*. Edited by Simon Sparks, 133–51. Translated by James Gilbert-Walsh and Simon Sparks. Stanford, CA: Stanford University Press, 2003.

Parker, Patricia. "Metaphor and Catachresis." In *The Ends of Rhetoric*, edited by John Bender and David Wellbery, 60–73. Stanford, CA: Stanford University Press, 1990.

Pippin, Robert B. *The Persistence of Subjectivity: On the Kantian Aftermath*. Cambridge: Cambridge University Press, 2005.

Robbins, Jill. *Altered Reading: Levinas and Literature*. Chicago: University of Chicago Press, 1999.

Rogozinski, Jacob. *Le don de la Loi: Kant et l'énigme de l'éthique*. Paris: Presses Universitaires de France, 1999.

Shell, Susan Meld. *Kant and the Limits of Autonomy*. Cambridge, MA: Harvard University Press, 2009.

Shepherdson, Charles. *Lacan and the Limits of Language*. New York: Fordham University Press, 2008.

Silber, John R. "Ethical Significance in Kant's *Religion*." In Immanuel Kant, *Religion within the Limits of Reason Alone*, lxxix-cxlii. Translated by T. M. Greene and H. H. Hudson. New York: Harper Torchbooks, 1960.

Surber, Jere Paul. "Kant, Levinas, and the Thought of the 'Other.'" *Philosophy Today* 38, no. 3 (1994): 294–316.

Velkley, Richard L. "Introduction: Unity of Reason as Aporetic Ideal." In *The Unity of Reason: Essays on Kant's Philosophy*, by Dieter Henrich, 1–15. Edited by Richard L. Velkley. Cambridge, MA: Harvard University Press, 1994.

Zeillinger, Peter. "Phänomenologie des Nicht-Phänomenalen. Spur und Inversion des Seins bei Emmanuel Levinas." In *Phänomenologische Aufbrüche*, edited by

Michael Blamauer, Wolfgang Fasching, and Matthias Flatsche, 161–79. Frankfurt: Lang, 2005.

———. "Radical Passivity as the (Only) Basis for Effective Ethical Action. Reading the 'Passage to the Third' in *Otherwise than Being*." In *Radical Passivity: Rethinking Ethical Agency in Levinas*, ed. Benda Hofmeyr, 95–108. Dordrecht, Netherlands: Springer, 2009.

Žižek, Slavoj. "Is There a Cause of the Subject?" In *Supposing the Subject*, edited by Joan Copjec, 84–105. London: Verso, 1994.

———. *Tarrying with the Negative: Kant, Hegel, and the Critique of Ideology*. Durham, NC: Duke University Press, 1993.

Zupančič, Alenka. *Ethics of the Real: Kant, Lacan*. New York: Verso, 2000.

———. *L'éthique du réel: Kant avec Lacan*. Caen, France: Nous, 2009.

———. *The Shortest Shadow: Nietzsche's Philosophy of the Two*. Cambridge, MA: MIT Press, 2003.

INDEX

spirit of the law, 9–10, 75, 76–77
subject/subjectivity: as the being
    practical of pure reason, 2;
    concept of, 3
  in Kant: affect of the law, 11–15;
    anchoring of signification, 18–19,
    133–34; causality of freedom and,
    8–11, 66–68, 88–90, 126–27; as the
    cause, 60–63; coexistence of
    freedom and nature in, 56–59;
    coherence of causality and
    signification in, 133; election by
    subjection, 125–26; free
    disposition to choose moral law,
    85–90, 93, 119, 125–26; freedom
    and, 2–3, 65, 66–68; moral law
    and, 10–11, 15, 16, 91–98, 126;
    notion of respect and, 11, 15,
    91–98; practical reason and, 57–58,
    59, 112; as relationship, 63–65;
    threatening law and, 12–13, 101–4,
    129–30. *See also* unconditioned
    subjectivity
  in Levinas: anchoring of
    signification, 18–19, 133–34; bearing
    witness by its own voice, 124;
    embodiment of the relationship
    between two incommensurate
    realms, 125–26; enigma of
    sameness and, 130; ethical
    subjectivity and, 15–19, 133–34;
    inspiration and, 127–28; Kant's
    conception of unconditioned
    law and, 112; Kant's moral law
    and, 98; Levinas's notion of,
    111–16; obsession and, 118–19;
    reconciliation of autonomy and
    heteronomy, 115–16, 127–28, 131, 132,
    134; as a relationship between self
    and other, 123–24; as a retroactive
    construction, 128–29; as a sign of

signification, 122–24; skin trope,
    119–22; as substitution for the other,
    121–25, 130–31, 133–34; the third party
    and, 18, 131–34; trace of the event of
    other, 116–19; unconditioned affect
    and, 125
substitution: catachresis as, 118; ethical
    subjectivity and, 16; Levinas's
    notion of, 117
substitution for the other: Levinas's
    notion of subjectivity and, 121–25,
    130–31, 133–34
successive regression, 28–30, 31–33
superego, 104, 168n66
synchrony, 121–22
synthesis: of the imagination and
    understanding, 20–23

temporal origin, 164n104
thesis/antithesis: first antinomy, 25–28;
    fourth antinomy, 169n77
thinking "I," 17
third antinomy: causality as a dynamic
    system, 48–49, 63; freedom and
    causality, 47–48, 49, 50, 55–57, 63;
    negation of freedom in the
    antithesis of, 63–65; the subject
    becomes the cause, 60–63;
    subjectivity as relationship, 63–65;
    synthesis of causal linkage, 52–53;
    the unconditioned, 53, 54–56, 61–62,
    63–65, 108, 150n10, 156n86;
    unconditioned cause, 14, 17, 49–50,
    108; unconditioned subjectivity,
    6–8, 48, 50–51
third party, 18, 131–34, 180n164
threatening law, 12–13, 101–4, 109–10,
    129–30
time and space: first antinomy, 25–28;
    as the formal condition of all
    series, 60–61

totality: reason and the problem of, 23–24; rules of reason and, 30–31; unconditioned, 104–9

Totality and Infinity (Levinas), 113–14, 118

trace: of the event of other, 116–19; face and, 174n58

"Transcendence and Evil" (Levinas), 170n82

transcendental: senses of, 148n120

transcendental apperception, 22

Transcendental Dialectic, 24–25

transcendental ideas, 23, 24, 30

transcendent other, 106–9

trauma, 119

unconditioned: causal series and, 53, 61–62, 63–64; dilemma of existence and, 29; in the dynamical antinomy, 51–55; ethical subjectivity and, 15–19, 133–34; fourth antinomy, 53–54, 151n25; freedom and, 151–52n30; Kant's concept of, 169n72; reason and, 24; solution to the mathematical antinomy, 5; third antinomy, 53, 54–56, 61–62, 63–65, 108, 150n10, 156n86; of the whole of a series, 63–64

unconditioned affect: Levinas's notion of subjectivity and, 125

unconditioned cause: causality and, 49–50, 53–55, 58; concept of, 49–50; fourth antinomy, 14–15; freedom

and, 6–7; third antinomy and, 14, 17, 49–50, 108

unconditioned law: Levinas's notion of subjectivity and, 112

unconditioned subjectivity: boundaries and, 51; causality and, 50–51; coherence of causality and signification in, 133; concept and function of, 48, 50–51; embodiment of the relationship between two incommensurate realms, 125–26; freedom and, 6–8, 51, 59; Kant's concept of, 6–8; third antinomy, 6–8, 48, 50–51

unconditioned totality, 104–9

understanding: imagination and, 20–23

universalization, 79, 127

"Violence and Metaphysics" (Derrida), 113

Widerstreit, 38

will: free disposition to choose the moral law, 85–90, 93, 119, 125–26; heteronomy and, 9; impact of the moral law on, 92–94; Kant's concept of, 85, 163n95; letter of the law and, 9, 77, 78–79; moral law and, 9–10, 74, 77; practical freedom and, 70–72; practical reason and, 74

Wolff, Christian von, 39

Žižek, Slavoj, 154–55n72

Zupančič, Alenka, 13, 105, 180n164

Kevin Attell, *Giorgio Agamben: Beyond the Threshold of Deconstruction.*

J. Hillis Miller, *Communities in Fiction.*

Remo Bodei, *The Life of Things, the Love of Things.* Translated by Murtha Baca.

Gabriela Basterra, *The Subject of Freedom: Kant, Levinas.*

Roberto Esposito, *Categories of the Impolitical.* Translated by Connal Parsley.